Russia and China Strategic Partnership and Diplomatic Grief for India

Russia and China Strategic Partnership and Diplomatic Grief for India

Dr. Sanjay Singh
Ashutosh Kumar

PRASHANT PUBLISHING HOUSE
DELHI-110094

Published by :
Prashant Publishing House
C-34, 28 Foota Road, Gali-3,
West Karwal Nagar, Delhi-110094
Phone : 011-22963970, Mob. : 9810396373
e-mail.: prashantpublishinghouse@gmail.com

Russia and China Strategic Partnership and Diplomatic Grief for India

First Published 2018

ISBN 978-81-938012-6-0

PRINTED IN INDIA
Published by Mr. R.K. Jha M/s Prashant Publishing House and Published at H.S. Offset House Press, Delhi.

Contents

Preface

China's and Russia's strategies for international expansion, in each of their respective areas of policy specialization, are not necessarily mutually exclusive. Arguably, both countries' intensified involvement on the world stage is not only complementary but to a growing extent directly and indirectly supportive of each other's increasingly commonly-defined interests. The growing international significance of China and Russia's key political and economic partnership must be considered a major factor in global policymaking going forward.

The rise of a more politically and militarily assertive Russia and an economically and institutionally ascendant China may be characterized as the two principal forces challenging the United States in global policymaking.

Historically, Indo-Russian relations have been far stronger than Sino-Russian and Sino-India relations. Today, while relations between China and Russia are improving, Russia and India have drifted apart, and ties between China and India have also weakened. Meanwhile, China is suspicious of Indo-Russia relations, India is anxious about close Russia-China relations, and China and Russia are also concerned about the recent uptick in Indo-US relations.

For India, the critical question is whether Russia will stand by India in any dispute with China. Moscow's stand during last year's Doklam crisis did not inspire much confidence in New Delhi. On the other hand, New Delhi understands that it cannot afford to drive Moscow into Beijing's hands. Any strategic partnership between Russia and China does not augur well for India. Whether India can do much about this is unclear, but New Delhi is definitely trying.

But this is not an alliance in the making. Alliances are passé and only a few continue gingerly from the Cold War era. We live in a world today driven by "strategic partnerships". States find themselves in an interdependent system where the traditional power politics of yesteryear doesn't quite fit. After all, every major relationship characterised by strategic tension such as U.S.-China, Japan-China, India-China is simultaneously one of economic gain. The U.S. and China are each other's chief trading partners, while China ranks at the top for Japan and India. Besides, India might confront China at Doklam but it also wants Chinese investment.

This is a reference book. All the matter is just compiled and edited in nature, taken from the various sources which are in public domain.

Strategic Partnership represents a new mode of state-to-state alignment. Yet our understanding of this phenomenon is obscured by a lack of definitional precision, resulting in a frequent misapplication of the term. This book seeks to rectify this shortcoming and apply some conceptual rigor to the analysis of strategic partnerships in international relations. This is achieved through the employment of a model drawn from the field of organization studies. The model is designed to assist us in better grasping the purpose, properties, and behaviour of strategic partnerships.

—Editor

1

Introduction

STRATEGIC PARTNERSHIPS

But this is not an alliance in the making. Alliances are passé and only a few continue gingerly from the Cold War era. We live in a world today driven by "strategic partnerships". States find themselves in an interdependent system where the traditional power politics of yesteryear doesn't quite fit. After all, every major relationship characterised by strategic tension such as U.S.-China, Japan-China, India-China is simultaneously one of economic gain. The U.S. and China are each other's chief trading partners, while China ranks at the top for Japan and India. Besides, India might confront China at Doklam but it also wants Chinese investment.

Strategic partnerships carry certain characteristic features falling short of alliances. First, unlike alliances, they do not demand commitments to a partner's disputes with other countries. New Delhi does not take a strong position on Japan's territorial disputes with China and Russia. Likewise, Tokyo does not openly side with India in its quarrels with China and Pakistan. For instance, Japan's reaction to the Doklam stand-off, though critical of China implicitly, did not go beyond saying that "all parties involved should not resort to unilateral attempts to change the status quo by force." India's reaction to the verdict of the arbitral tribunal on the South China Sea last year, urging "all parties to show utmost respect for the UNCLOS", reflected a similar dispensation despite Japan's push for a stronger statement. There was also no explicit mention of the South China Sea in the latest joint statement.

Strategic partnership means, first, that both retain the flexibility to continue political engagement and economic cooperation with their common adversary. Second, they avoid "entrapment", or being dragged into a partner's disputes and potentially into conflict, which happened in the First World War. Third, regular high-level political and military interactions facilitate a collaborative approach to strategic policies over a range of economic and military activities. India and Japan, for instance, are not only moving forward on economic and defence cooperation but are also cooperating on other important issues such as civil nuclear energy and Security Council reform.

Given that resort to war is undesirable owing to economic interdependence as well as the presence of nuclear weapons, the aim of major strategic partnerships is to strengthen defences against marginal conflict, convey a determination to stand up to a strategic adversary and, overall, generate a persuasive environment that discourages potential intimidation. Occasionally, as between India and China, a "strategic partnership" is a way of opening a channel of communication and minimal cooperation intended to stabilise and develop the potential for a détente and conceivably something warmer. In this particular case, not much has been accomplished thus far, but it remains a low-cost option for expanding cooperation in the event the political fundamentals of the relationship show an upward swing.

Looking ahead

India's two main strategic partnerships, with the U.S. and Japan, are dovetailing nicely. For New Delhi, the U.S. will remain its chief backer both to enhance India's conventional defence capabilities and to draw political support in global political institutions, for example in components of the nuclear non-proliferation regime. Japan, in the meantime, is becoming its primary collaborator in developing its economic sinews and for building a geostrategic network that offers Indian Ocean states an alternative to dependence on China. Together, the emerging structure of triangular cooperation should give Beijing pause to think.

RUSSIA'S NEW GAME PLAN - ANALYSIS

On September 9, geopolitics unexpectedly hit the news headlines when Russian Deputy Foreign Minister Sergei Ryabkov made an important statement about the ongoing talks between Moscow and Islamabad on the delivery of Russian multirole Mi-35M attack helicopters and the latest Su-35 fighter jets. Ryabkov said Pakistan is Russia's "closest partner" and the ties between the two countries are evolving beyond the military sphere to include other sectors such as energy. At the same time, he also suggested that this will not have a negative impact on relations between Moscow and New Delhi.

Coming from a top Russian official, these statements cannot be considered as a mere kite flying stunt by the Russian media. Such a tectonic strategic shift may not have come as a pleasant news to Indian ears, but before we react to this startling change in the Russian position, it is important to first understand the deeper and nuanced aspects of Russia's motives.

Interestingly, within days of Ryabkov's statement, a prominent Russian political analyst *Andrew Korybko* provocatively detailed why Pakistan is gaining pivotal importance in the Russian geo-strategic calculus. The article, titled "*Pakistan is the "Zipper" of Pan-Eurasian Integration*", appeared on 15 September on the website of the Russian government funded think-tank – Russian Institute for Strategic Studies (RISS) established by the President of the Russian Federation. The RISS puts up policy papers to the President's office, the Federation Council, the State Duma and the Security Council as well as to Government offices, ministries and departments. (*The RISS has closely interacted with IDSA in the past and the two institutions have signed a MoU for joint research. However, the Russian think-tank has not shown much interest for cooperation with IDSA in the past few years*).

As a keen watcher of Eurasian affairs, I thought it is important to share the significant points articulated by *Andrew Korybko in his rather* astounding article so that the Indian strategic community can understand the new thinking among informed Russian circles.

In Part I of his article, *Korybko* deals with the 'zipper' concept of how Pakistan can draw together four of Eurasia's most prominent economic entities, and examines the key imperatives for Russia to build a strong Strategic Partnership with Pakistan. In Part II, he does crystal gazing on the most probable ways in which the US can attempt to offset everything or derail Pakistan's future destiny of joining the Eurasian integration process.

Korbyko's article begins by saying that contrary to popular myth about Pakistan as a "backward land of terrorism and poverty" that carries little actual weight, the West purposefully neglects the country's rising geopolitical importance in Eurasia and its potential to connect the massive economies of the Eurasian Union, Iran, SAARC, and China to create an integrated pan-Eurasian economic zone.

The article then elaborates why Russia recognises Pakistan's prime geopolitical potential and how it is manoeuvring to speed up the development of full-spectrum relations with this "South Asian gatekeeper." It says that Russia's overarching goal is to provide a "non-provocative balancing component to bolster Pakistan's regional political position and assist with its peaceful integration into the multi-polar Eurasian framework being constructed by the Sino-Russian Strategic Partnership."

Interestingly, it draws attention to China's grand vision of building a trans-Pakistani trade corridor under the China-Pakistan Economic Corridor (CPEC), which could be a catalyst for connecting the four economic blocs together. This includes linking of the Russian-led Eurasian Economic Union (EEU) with SAARC intersecting at the Xinjiang-Pakistan junction to be developed under the CPEC.

From the Russian perspective, the article suggests, the CPEC not only represents a "geopolitical pivot for China, but also a geo-economic one", for "it'll position the country within easy access to the Mideast oil fields". This is the only way China will be able to quell the "externally orchestrated destabilization that it's lately found itself experiencing in Xinjiang."

It stresses the importance of the Iran-Pakistan-China pipeline project (a part of the CPEC) becoming a reality and suggests that "should Xinjiang succeed in becoming a significant Eurasian trading hub in connecting China, Eurasian Union, SAARC, and Iran, then it would catapult in geo-economic significance to become an ultra-strategic Heartland region."

On the prospect of India joining the Eurasian system, Korbyko's article says that the touchy issue of India's claim over "Pakistan-administered Kashmir" could come in the way. However, "if Indian companies employ this route, the economic allure might be too tempting to resist." Further, if Indo-Pak differences could be relaxed (perhaps within the SCO framework), then "the organization would finally be able to cash in on its economic capability and fully integrate with itself and the rest of Eurasia."

Importantly, the article discloses how Russia's strategic ties with Pakistan are moving towards very "exciting future possibilities" despite Russia being "India's closest friend". It notes that the emerging trend might appear somewhat "perplexing" but it isn't all that "unexpected." Because, the end of the Cold War and the subsequent emergence of South Asian "nuclear bipolarity" have reduced the intensity of Indo-Russian strategic ties as well as America's dealings with Pakistan. These shifts in focus (India's westward and Pakistan's eastward) do not, however, suggest that either India or Pakistan has completely deserted its erstwhile partner; only that they are seeking adjustments to protect their national interest in the changed context. But at the same time, these shifts in focus have not yet altered the Indo-Pak standoff. In this context, the article notes, both India and Pakistan seem to be willing to give multilateralism under Eurasia a chance, as evident from their entry into the SCO.

More interestingly, the author points to the Kremlin's calculation of its ability to intermediate between Beijing and New Delhi in the event of a major India-China crisis. But he also says that Russia does not enjoy the same leverage to do so in an India-Pakistan conflict situation. As a result, in the latter situation, Moscow would prefer to "push the US into the mix – giving it plenty of opportunity to divide and conquer according to the present geopolitical circumstances." Korybko then goes to point out that "if Russia were to compensate for its diplomatic 'blind spot' with Pakistan and reinvigorate the bilateral relationship with Islamabad, then it could mirror the role that it plays between India and China in also helping to balance the tension between India and Pakistan." This strategy, the article argues, would eventually "push the US out of the playing field, though India will still retain its current level of ties with the US but not for the purpose counterbalancing Pakistan." It suggests that both India and Pakistan would then rather rely on their same "trusted partner Russia", which for its part will be able to mediate between the two (like it does with India and China).

The article admits to the trust deficit between India and Pakistan as the weakest link in the 'zipper' vision, though the vision could still succeed without the SAARC component because the "EEU would gain by India's physical incorporation into the unified Eurasian infrastructural framework." Korybko also points to Russian diplomatic and strategic competence being capable of minimizing Indo-Pak discord and exploring the economic benefit of their peaceful collaboration.

The Russian analyst then explains how Russia made the first strategic move in this regard in June 2014 by offering to sell attack helicopters to Pakistan for the latter's drug-combating efforts.

Though the "paradigm shift" was attributed by many to Russia's concerns over post-2014 NATO withdrawal from Afghanistan, the main idea was to initiate the process of depolarisation in India-Pakistan tensions and to make the multipolar concept more cohesive as a result. The article says that Russia's next move would be to help Pakistan with technical expertise for building a portion of the Iran-Pakistan-China gas pipeline in the near future.

According to the write up, Pakistan's own excitement has increased after sensing the enormous economic opportunities that will unfold after CPEC completion. Pakistanis could see the "writing on the wall" and even contemplate sealing a free trade agreement with the Eurasian Union. This signifies how seriously Russia takes its evolving partnership with Pakistan. The article underlines how the relationship is also gaining a soft power touch, with both sides preparing for their first-ever cultural exchange year. In a symbolic significance of what is likely to come, the article says that "Pakistan's national military band performed at the Moscow International Music Festival."

The article notes that "there should thus be no doubt at this point about the commitment of both sides for deepening the relationship as the ongoing interactions between the two are beyond passing convergence of business interests." It further says that "Both sides understand the larger significance of what they're doing", which is to work for the "shared vision of an integrated and multi-polar Eurasia."

However, on the down side and for the Eurasian enterprise to succeed, the author anticipates that CPEC and the 'zipper' plan could face a major blow either due to instability within Pakistan or India's possible refusal to participate in it.

Interestingly, the article notes that any possibility of all-round Russia-Pakistan engagement could speed up Indo-US proximity which, in turn, will lead to provocation by the "US and its information proxies". Things could also be exacerbated by an exaggerated "Indian threat assessment of Russia's activities." Any Indian paranoia over Russia's 'sliding away' to join the China-Pakistan 'axis' would consequently negate the main reasons behind the Russian-Pakistan strategic partnership, which is to "place Moscow in a position to intermediate between New Delhi and Islamabad and keep regional relations stable enough so as to jump start the envisioned multilateral economic partnership."

The author, however, argues that Russia's Pakistan gambit might fail most likely because of the United States playing dirty. In such a scenario, Russia would be worse off and risk losing a major strategic partner in India. Pakistan, on the other hand, will "never see its relation with Russia as equal level to one it has with China."

The article cautions that Russia needs to proceed delicately taking into consideration how the Indian establishment views Russia's evolving ties with Pakistan. It does not discount the ability of the US to split Russia and India through Pakistan, like it did with Russia and the European Union through Ukraine (although for different reasons).

The author fears the possibility of the US creating a rift through "information warfare" especially when Indo-US defence ties are deepening. He notes that this could have in a way "possibly played a part in influencing Moscow's decision to resume arms exports to Pakistan." The article draws attention to the saliency of "underreported military development" that makes the US more integral to India's national security, and this it says coincides with New Delhi's strategic overlap with the US in containing China. "The longer this progresses, the further the US will embed itself into India's deep state apparatus, with all of the unfortunate foreign policy consequences for the multi-polar world" the article notes.

The writer then dwells on the personal rapport shared between Modi and Obama and other aspects of the Indo-US friendship which, he thinks, could be an "exaggerated charade for political purposes, there's nothing tangible to indicate that this is the case" and by itself doesn't pose any worries for Russia." But what really worries Russia is the possibility of Obama leveraging his friendship with Modi to "enact certain policy shifts", such as "his encouragement to India's Act East policy for unstated reason that can aggravate relations with China." According to Korybko, Russian interests would be most endangered by the "US winning over India into viewing the Russian-Pakistan strategic partnership as a threat" and suggests that Putin should "continually reinforce his relationship with Modi so that the latter is insusceptible to being tricked by Obama into doubting the Russian President's intentions."(It is pertinent to note here that in his congratulatory message to Prime Minister Modi on his 65th birthday, issued by the Kremlin on September 17, President Putin praised how the Prime Minister rightly enjoys high international authority both in his homeland and abroad as a proficient politician and statesman. The message says "we highly appreciate your efforts to strengthen the special and privileged strategic partnership between our countries, develop Russian-Indian interaction in solving topical issues of the regional and global agenda.")

Further, the article points to the likelihood of American involvement in creating instability in Baluchistan. Baluch separatism driven by American interests is not just for destabilising Gwadar (the source of CPEC) or for the political fragmentation of Pakistan but to create a new geopolitical space to be carved out of the Iranian province of Sistan and Baluchistan as well. Such a Baluch proxy, it says, could provide the US with a greater degree of influence over both Iran and India in controlling trans-regional transport connectivity. Of course, the author cites the Pentagon's foremost author Lieutenant-Colonel Ralph Peters' infamous map *Blood Borders: How a Better Middle East Would Look*, which specifically earmarks a "Free Baluchistan" carved out of Iranian and Pakistani territory.

Korybko then moves beyond the Baluch separatist scenario to highlight the presence of militant Islamic radicalism in FATA – the most important destabilising factor in Pakistan. To add to that he draws attention to the rise of ISIL and its "expansive neo-Caliphate ideology" in Afghanistan's three provinces of Farah (west), Helmand (south), and Nangarhar (east). The ISIL, he says, could use Nangarhar province as a staging ground for pushing deeper into Pakistan by eliminating the Durand Line and "annex" the 'state of Hind' (Pakistan,

India, Bangladesh, and Myanmar). Further, Korybko also says that if more "Taliban fighters defect to the up-and-coming group" a scenario of a birth of a "transnational 'mini-Caliphate' between Nangarhar and parts of FATA would evoke the shades of ISIL's prior successes along the Syrian-Iraqi border." Not just that, the article vividly points to how ISIL is also moving in the northern direction, citing the defection in May of Colonel Gulmurod Khalimov, the head of Tajikistan's Internal Special Forces, to ISIL. It hints at the possibility of ISIL gaining invaluable intelligence and employing Khalimov's knowledge in infiltrating into the most 'ideal' location in Gorno-Badakhstan region. If this occurs concurrently, the article suggests, the "US then would be keen, among other things, to take revenge for Kyrgyzstan denouncing its cooperation agreement with the US." Therefore, the article does not rule out the possibility of a quadrilateral South-Central Asian Caliphate emerging in "heavily fortified Pamir and Hindu Kush mountain ranges, with Pakistan being the southern peg of this vile construction."

The article paints another disruptive scenario of how the US could derail Pakistan's geo-economic destiny by engineering a possible "Colour Revolution against Prime Minister Sharif or any of his successors", although it also says that the violent protests last year did not pan out as a doom and gloom scenario for Pakistan. Korybko does not foretell the exact contours of the follow-up disruptive attempt, but says that with the "improved political technology available" it might likely embrace "anti-corruption" slogans led by an amorphous and superficially apolitical "civil society" in Pakistan. Such a structural innovation, the article suggests, would "allow the coup's leaders to readjust their social infrastructure (leadership, members, slogans, etc.) on the fly a lot more efficiently than if they followed the comparatively rigid practices of their predecessors in organizing the event around clearly defined political parties led by a few well-known (and easily compromised) individuals."

This scenario to be deployed in Pakistan would be "Colour Revolution 1.5". The article notes that this will be halfway between the comparatively 'docile' 2003 Colour Revolution 1.0

in Georgia and the "out-of-control Hybrid War mayhem of Colour Revolution 2.0 in EuroMaidan." Colour Revolution 1.5 in Pakistan could go either way, "towards 1.0 if it sputters out like in Armenia or towards 2.0 if it dangerously intensifies like it did in Syria." The article says that 1.5 could become a dangerous innovation to "regime change strategy" and that the US would be committed to apply it first with smaller targets before being "perfected and repackaged to Pakistan."

The article argues that Moscow has rightly taken the "bold step in reaching out to Islamabad and soliciting a strategic partnership" and the quick pace of the partnership taking a revolutionary shape is a "natural fit for both partners." But this trend, according to the article, has incited the US' "geopolitical jealousy", which is keen to call upon a "mixed bag of secessionist, terrorist, and Colour Revolution destabilizations to offset Pakistan's catalytic role in bringing Eurasia together." The author then calls upon Russia, China, and Iran to defeat the threat so that Pakistan can become Eurasia's economic 'zipper' and linking these (and perhaps even SAARC's) economies together in an emboldened multi-polar future.

The article concludes by saying that the EU is mistakenly staying out (due to US pressure) of this trans-Eurasian integration process, which is becoming the primary theme of the 21st century. But "the rest of the main continental economic powers – the Eurasian Union, Iran, SAARC, and China – stand poised for closer integration with one another owing to the infrastructural overlap that Pakistan's geostrategic location provides."

The central theme of Korbyko's article is to highlight the pivotal importance of Pakistan and the Russian eagerness to build a foundation of political trust with the Pakistani leadership so as to better assist in the management of Pakistani-Indian tensions.

To be sure, Pakistan can certainly help Russia shift its focus away from its current difficulties but Moscow should be doubly careful whether Pakistan will not become a staging ground to break up Russia further. The Americans have already tested the Pakistani betrayal, and China too sooner or later will become another victim of Pakistani treachery.

CHINA AND RUSSIA: THE WORLD'S NEW SUPERPOWER AXIS

Leaders of the Brics countries (Brazil, India, China and South Africa) will meet Putin in Ufa on Wednesday, then make way for the Asian powers grouped in the Shanghai Cooperation Organisation. Russia and China are the common denominators, as in so much geopolitics these days. The UN security council, Apec, the G20 - Russia and China are the ever-presents, a powerful pairing whose interests coincide more often than not. Moscow and Beijing have lots in common apart from a 2,500-mile border, economies dominated by state-run firms and oligarchies that can enrich themselves as long as they play by the prevailing political mood of the day. Officially, Putin is dismissive about suggestions of a new eastern alliance. "We are not creating a military alliance with China," he said last month. "We are not creating a bloc-based approach, we are trying to create a global approach."

And yet both countries share a desire to limit American power; they enjoy a burgeoning trade relationship in which, in essence, hydrocarbons are swapped for cheap consumer goods; and they have a mutual interest in promoting an alternative model to western diplomacy. Trade has increased sixfold over the past decade. Last year they trumpeted the biggest gas deal in history. The summer will be bookended by two striking events: Russian and Chinese warships puttering about together in the eastern Mediterranean in May, gaming war; and Russian and Chinese presidents standing shoulder to shoulder in Beijing for the 70th anniversary of the end of the second world war in September.

Geopolitics

For China, one of the main attractions of closer relations with Russia is the potential for challenging Washington's still dominant global position. "In China, where until recently the official line was 'non-alignment', some prominent scholars have started to make unambiguous calls for a comprehensive strategic alliance with Russia," Alexander Korolev, at the National University of Singapore's centre on Asia and globalisation, argued recently. "[They are] arguing on the pages of the CCP [Communist party] central party school's internal publications that 'China-Russia strategic relations are the most substantive ones' and elsewhere that 'China will be unable to shift the world from unipolarity to bipolarity unless it forms a formal alliance with Russia.'"

But often cooperation and tension are two sides of the same coin. Take Central Asia. China's president, Xi Jinping, has set his sights on a "new silk road", using China's billions to help neighbours and regional allies to develop, indirectly supporting growth at home and the expansion of Chinese soft power.

However, this is also Russia's traditional sphere of influence and any Chinese presence that goes beyond commercial dealings is likely to raise hackles in Moscow.

"It's totally possible for China to develop its relations with central Asian countries without challenging Russia," said Liu Jun, a Russian studies expert at East China Normal University. "It's true that Russia would be concerned if China's influence in Central Asia grew too much, but the concerns are not mainstream in the bilateral relations – there are more benefits in cooperation than otherwise."

Russia shares the strategic goal of challenging US hegemony in favour of a more multipolar world, and the two powers often find themselves on the same side in the UN security council, where they wield vetoes as permanent members.

No deal on regulating Iran's nuclear programme can be made without Russia and China, which have staunchly backed its atomic expansion in the past, and the two countries' support is largely the reason Bashar al-Assad has been able to hold on to power in Syria. Recently, Russia has been making political and economic overtures to North Korea, which relies on food, arms and energy from its key ally, China, to survive.

As they support the idea of a multipolar world against American dominance, Moscow and Beijing will also tacitly back each others' attempts to defend their own spheres of influence, said Dmitry Trenin, director of the Carnegie Moscow Centre. In the past two years, Russia has annexed Crimea and backed a separatist campaign to frustrate Ukraine's turn to the west, and China has been disputing islands with western allies in the South China Sea.

"China admits de facto that Russia has interests in eastern Europe, Russia admits that China has interests around the perimeter of its borders, and even though neither will actively help its partner in Ukraine or the South China Sea, both will observe an advantageous neutrality," Trenin said. "There won't be criticism of each other in the areas of their core interests."

Leadership

Government enthusiasm for warmer ties with Russia is summed up by a recent video from the state-controlled Xinhua news agency entitled What Do Chinese People Think About Russia?"

It features Chinese children describing Russia as "even bigger than China", an old man praising Russia's strength, demands for more investment, gas sales, a high-speed train, and plenty of airtime given to adulation of the Russian president.

Putin has long been popular in China, where he is seen as a strong leader who has bolstered national pride, and is not a little admired for his topless photo shoots. "Putin you're a handsome man," says one middle-aged woman on being asked what message she would like to send to Moscow.

There is also an overt comparison to Xi, who has fostered a personality cult of bold leadership that has echoes of the Russian leader's (though with less bare flesh). "Putin is the same as our 'Papa Xi'," says one young man, using a government endorsed affectionate term for the president.

For their part, Russians are more ambivalent about Xi, who has a far lower profile in Russia than does his counterpart in China.

Trade

China's interest in Russian exports has until now been largely focused on natural resources and military hardware. Beyond that they do not make natural partners. Russia can offer little by way of famous brands or innovation in consumer technology to tempt ordinary Chinese customers.

"It's a good thing that there is political will behind the business cooperation. Without it, a lot of things won't happen," Liu said. "Most big projects are backed by the governments and the volume of trade along the border is quite small."

The imbalance of the relationship can be seen in the breakdown of their bilateral trade, worth around $100bn a year. China is Russia's second largest trading partner after the EU, while Russia only just scraped into a list of China's top 10 trading partners, accounting for barely 3% of the country's total trade volume.

Moscow is also hoping Beijing will help with finance for businesses, after western funds dried up last year. Some Chinese firms have seen the Russian economic wobble as an opportunity to make capital investments in the country.

Energy

China and Russia should make natural partners in energy deals, but in reality they have struggled to turn past agreements into real supply deals; pipelines announced last decade have still not been built because of disagreements over pricing and other conditions. Earlier this year, Russia overtook Saudi Arabia as the largest supplier of oil to China for the first time, with Russian exports to China more than doubling since 2010. But Beijing is accustomed to shopping around for energy and driving a very cheap bargain with its suppliers, while Russia is used to controlling prices for European customers with few other options. The expansion of shale gas production may have weakened Russia's hand by improving global supply, but China is also increasingly concerned about climate change and needs to wean itself off the dirty coal that still provides well over half its energy.

Since Russia has rarely agreed to sell stakes in strategic land-based deposits to western companies, Putin's offer of a stake in state oil champion Rosneft's biggest production asset, the Vankor oilfields, to China in September underlined the new direction the country's energy policy is taking.

The offer was made at a ceremony to start construction of Russia's $55bn Power of Siberia pipeline, a breakthrough project that is planned to deliver an annual 38bn cubic metres of gas to eastern China over the next 30 years. In November, the two countries also signed a framework agreement for an Altai gas pipeline to potentially supply 30bn cubic metres of gas to western China each year for 30 years.

But neither pipeline deal appears to have been completely finalised, and economic sanctions and a weak rouble will probably make financing the huge projects difficult for Russia's Gazprom.

"It seems like at every meeting there's some sort of document signed and hailed as another big agreement ... but Gazprom will need to develop large fields and construct the pipelines," said Grigory Birg, an analyst at Investcafe. "I think in the current environment securing the finances is the major holdup, and we don't have any indication as to the economics of the project." Although Birg estimated the rate of return on the Power of Siberia investment to be a modest 9% to 10% when the deal was signed, the profitability is likely to be even less if global oil prices remain weak. Beijing will, by all appearances, be able to drive an even harder bargain for the gas price under the proposed Altai pipeline to western China, a region that has less demand than the industrialised east of the country and already receives cheap gas from nearby Turkmenistan.

Nonetheless, analysts expect energy cooperation to continue to grow as Russia seeks alternatives to the politically thorny European market, and China addresses growing demand and problems with pollution and blackouts. Last year, China replaced Germany as Russia's biggest buyer of crude oil. "China is the major alternative market and is easily accessible for Russia given the [location of energy] reserves and the geopolitical partnership, so it's an obvious fit," Birg said. "But the timing at which it is happening is not in favour of Russia."

Currency

Both Russia and China have an interest in loosening the US dollar's dominance in global trade as the world's reserve currency. Russia now accepts yuan for oil payments (something that other oil exporters, such as Saudi Arabia, don't do).

Following the imposition of sanctions, Russian companies and banks – traditionally reliant on dollar-denominated syndicated loans – started to look to China for a financial escape route. The rouble-yuan currency pair reached records in trading volumes last summer.

Russian companies are not new to the renminbi market, nor to the issuing of "dim sum bonds" – bonds denominated in Chinese yuan and largely issued by entities based in China or Hong Kong. In the past these options represented a cheaper source of funding. Now they're a necessity. However, yields on Russian corporate bonds denominated in yuan have increased as the list of sanctions started mounting up.

Military

Russian arms sales to China have been estimated at $1bn a year, the Russians were previously hesitant to give advanced weaponry to the Soviet Union's one-time military rival. But the recent announcement by Russia's state arms exporter of a deal to supply China with its S-400 surface-to-air missile systems has taken their relationship to a new level at a time when Beijing is seeking new air and naval defence technologies.

The higher-level arms sales have been accompanied by greater military cooperation, which was on display in May with the war games in the Mediterranean Sea. Such exercises in what has traditionally been a "Nato pond" are designed to expand the Chinese navy's reach while showing the United States that Russia is a potentially important military partner, according to Trenin.

Following the Ukraine crisis, which soured relations with the west, he said the main considerations behind Russia's "entente" with China were political. "Now Russia has an important stimulus to grow relations with China, because relations with the west are troubled, and China is the only large player in the world that can be considered as economic, political and to a certain extent military ally," Trenin said.

China and Russia have repeatedly stated that they will become partners, not allies. Both sides, meanwhile, are concerned that the unrest in Pakistan and Afghanistan could spill over into their territory, or serve as incubators for militants who may one day return home.

But none of that means that either side has forgotten past disputes or present differences. Russia is nervous about China sapping its revenue by reverse engineering the equipment it buys, and is also monitoring Beijing closely for any attempts to project military power into central Asia.

"China and Russia's strategic partnership is a result of the times, but it is totally different from a military alliance such as the one between the US and Japan," the Global Times, a Chinese nationalist tabloid, said in a recent editorial.

"China and Russia have repeatedly stated that they will become partners, not allies. They do mean that. China also cares about relations with western countries. Russia does not want to see relations with the west become a deadlock."

Cyber security

Both Russia and China share a concern over the US domination of the internet. In January, Russia, China and a number of central Asian dictatorships jointly submitted a new proposal for an international code of conduct on information security to the UN general assembly.

In a clause clearly aimed at the US, the document calls for countries "not to use information and communications technologies and ... networks to interfere in the internal affairs of other states or with the aim of undermining their political, economic and social stability". At a recent internet security forum in Moscow, officials from both countries called for a new approach to online security.

"It's great they [the US] invented the iPhone but when you open your iPhone and see the camera you have to guess whether it's photographing you at that moment or not," said Konstantin Malofeyev, a controversial businessman known for his backing for the Russian Orthodox church and the pro-Russian separatist movement in east Ukraine. "Russia went into space first and Antarctic first but we don't control those things, they are controlled by international charters. Why should the US control the internet?"

Chinese official Chen Xiaohua said: "We should join hands to build cyberspace order. Various countries share a consistent vision of enhancing the governance of cyberspace ... following the principles of mutual trust and mutual respect." In the meantime, Beijing and Moscow signed a landmark cyber-security deal recently that could bolster defence against external attack as well as allowing them to share technology for domestic control.

The two countries have poured resources into managing the internet, aiming to curb its potential as a platform for dissent. Beijing's "great firewall" is a powerful and sophisticated filter of the online world, but is still porous enough that most people inside China do not need to bother trying to evade it.

Both countries also field armies of both hackers and paid pro-government commenters, known in China as the "50 cent" group, because of how much they are paid for each post. However, experts say their focus on internal controls may have come at the expense of security.

"Prioritising political information control over technical cyber defence also damages China's own cybersecurity," Jon Lindsay of Harvard University's Belfer centre for science and international affairs said in a recent briefing. "Lax law enforcement and poor cyber defences leave the country vulnerable to both cyber criminals and foreign spies."

Business mood

Among some business people, there is a fear that the enforced turn to the east will mean Russia selling out from a position of weakness.

"The downturn in relations with the west is bad for Russia and bad for the west; the only beneficiary is China," one top Russian businessman said. "The number of Chinese delegations coming to Russia has gone up tenfold, and the Chinese will only enter the market when they see the conditions are very beneficial to them."

Russian media have been told to play up links with China and other non-western countries, and companies have felt pressure from the government to look eastwards even if it makes little business sense. But what initially seemed pointless may be starting to bear some fruit.

"It started as theatre, but now there are some companies out there really getting stuff done," said Tom Blackwell, CEO of EM, a consultancy firm that has worked with a number of major Russian companies on exploring the Chinese market. "Chinese investment funds have very little experience or knowledge about Russia and it's a hard sell. But the strategy seems to be to do the big state deals first and assume smaller ones will follow. Slowly, real things are happening."

Russia's federal migration service is especially wary of an influx of Chinese migrants across the Russia-China border. It has stated that Chinese could become the largest ethnic group in Russia's far east by the 2020s or 2030s; last summer a border official said that 1.5 million Chinese illegally entered the region from January 2013 to June 2014.

RUSSIA'S DEFENCE PACT WITH PAK SHOWS MODI GOVT'S DIPLOMACY FAILURE

This would go down as one of the worst strategic and diplomatic failures of India in recent times. Russia has stepped up its rapprochement with India's arch-rival Pakistan just as India is getting closer to the United States.

The unthinkable happened on 20 November when Russia-- India's tried and trusted friend, ally and strategic partner – signed a never-before defence cooperation agreement with Pakistan. The defence pact scripts a new history as Russia agreed to cooperate with Pakistan in combating terrorism and offered advanced counter-terrorism training to Pakistan.

The landmark Russia-Pakistan defence pact was inked during Russian Defence Minister Sergei Shoigu's visit to Pakistan, the first visit by a Russian Defence Minister to Pakistan in 45 years. The last visit to Pakistan was made by Soviet Union's defence minister Andrey Grechko.

The Russian move comes just about three weeks before Russian President Vladimir Putin visits India for an annual summit between India and Russia, an exercise going on since 2000.

Russia was the first country with which India has an institutionalized mechanism of holding annual summits, signifying the extremely close political relations between the two sides. The first such Indo-Russian annual summit was held in 2000.

Till date only Japan has been added to this extremely select list of countries with which India has been having an institutionalized mechanism of holding annual summits. This explains the importance of Indo-Russian bilateral relations.

The increasing bonhomie between Russia and Pakistan marks a stunning change in the rapidly changing and evolving international statecraft. It lives up to the old adage: There are no permanent friends or permanent enemies in politics; there are only permanent interests.

The Russians had already warned of decaying ties with India way back in June when they lifted their embargo on arms supplies to Pakistan and began negotiations for sale of combat helicopters to Pakistan. Despite India's strong protests the Russians are moving ahead with the proposed chopper sales to Pakistan and at least 20 attack helicopters are all set to be sold by the Russians to the Pakistanis.

Moscow has rubbed it further for the Indians and declared its intentions by sending its defence minister to Pakistan and by inking a defence cooperation agreement with Pakistan.

Russians have been miffed with New Delhi for several years. It started in 2012 when Russia lost contract for several big-ticket Indian defence deals and the situation exacerbated in 2013. By 2014 the Americans had usurped the number one position as India's top arms exporter – a position that the Russians had traditionally enjoyed for decades.

Now let's go back to the point made upfront: how the growing Russia-Pakistan synergy is a failure of Indian diplomacy in recent years.

The failure started with the previous UPA government. The failure of the present government led by Prime Minister Narendra Modi is that it has failed to stem the rot for the past six months it has been in office.

While Russian deputy Prime Minister Dmitry Rogozin has traveled to India since the Modi government took over, no senior political functionary of the Modi government has visited Russia.

However, all is still not lost. Signing of a defence pact between Russia and Pakistan does not mean that Russia has signed on the death warrants of Indo-Russian strategic partnership.

Similarly, Russia may have lost out on Indian arms deals worth several billion dollars, it cannot compensate for it by selling a few combat helicopters to Pakistan for a few scores of million dollars.

True, it is Russia's way of warning India against New Delhi's dalliance with the Americans. But the Russians also have genuine strategic interests in stepping up their bilateral cooperation with Pakistan, particularly in the sphere of security.

Russia had to open out to Pakistan in view of the upcoming thinning of American and NATO troops in Afghanistan. A lawless Afghanistan falling back into the clutches of Taliban is as hair-raising a nightmare for the Russian security managers as it is for the Indians. Pakistan is a crucial and unique stakeholder for Russia in this context.

The Indians will have to be genuinely concerned about the impact of the Russia-Pakistan defence agreement only if the Russians end up with harming Indian interests. But this is highly improbable. Russians are no fools. They won't sacrifice a carefully-nurtured relationship with a major power like India for the sake of improving relations with a country like Pakistan.

India has erred big time in allowing its relations with Russia to sour to this extent that Russia has inked a defence pact with Pakistan. The talk of Russia selling combat helicopters to Pakistan was a mere talk. But signing of a defence pact between Russia and Pakistan is a serious business which is not conducive either to India's national interests or to Indo-Russian friendship.

PM Modi will have to intervene in a big way to save the floundering Indo-Russian friendship. The problem needs to be fixed as early as possible. Modi's upcoming summit with Putin in New Delhi offers this opportunity.

SCO AND STRATEGIC PARTNERSHIP BETWEEN CHINA AND RUSSIA

China and Russia share similar positions and close views on important international issues. The strategic partnership between China and Russia is based on high-level political trust, on the common interests of the two countries. All kinds of relations between countries are influenced from the outside, and relations between China and Russia are not an exception. But thanks to close ties and high-level confidence between the two countries the strategic partnership between China and Russia is already developing to a certain extent according to its internal logic.

Absent external pressure, relations between China and Russia would have advanced anyway. Maybe they would have evolved in other directions. Of course, in current conditions, relations between China and Russia are more important for the recovery and balance in international relations, which are undergoing radical changes.

The projects of Belt and Road and the EAEU were underway before Donald Trump came to power. The two projects envisage the development of infrastructure for the sake of progress and prosperity of the peoples of the concerned countries, and are not directed at sowing violent conflicts between peoples and disorder in the world. It is necessary to judge not by words, but by deeds. The implementation of the Belt and Road and the EAEU benefits economic cooperation between the participating countries in accordance with accepted international rules and promotes understanding between peoples. After its membership expansion, the SCO acquired even more opportunities to implement economic cooperation in the Eurasian region, including cooperation within the framework of the Belt and Road and the EAEU projects.

THE RUSSIA-INDIA PARTNERSHIP

South Asia as a Place for Primakov Intelligence

India's position on Russian foreign policy sounds different from China's. India is far from Russia and has no shared border. Russia and India are rarely antagonistic toward each other, and are able to cooperate when there is a strong need to do so. In this sense, India seems to offer a perfect opportunity for Russia's "balance" foreign policy. Reviewing post-Cold War Russian foreign policy toward India, close attention should be paid to the two Soviet periods of "balance" policy before and after the Russo-Chinese military conflict of 1969.

The first period began with India achieving independence from British rule in 1946. Combatting US influence was Russia's top priority at the time. Russia never supported India unilaterally and balanced its position between India and Pakistan to maintain its interests against the US. In the 1950s when Pakistan joined the SEATO and the Baghdad Pact under the auspices of the US, The Soviet Union sought to weaken US influence in South Asia. Nikita Khrushchev supported India's position on Kashmir (that it belonged to India), which brought India closer to the Soviet Union, and then proposed to offer Pakistan economic aid and atomic technology for peaceful use in order to make a rapprochement with Pakistan. In the 1960s, the Soviet Union revised its complete support for India on the Kashmir issue (Russia now believing that it should be negotiated between the parties concerned, while still backing India's position) and signed a barter trade agreement with Pakistan. In 1965, Pakistan's president visited Moscow and Premier Aleksei Kosygin, as a show of goodwill, organized the "Tashkent meeting" to mediate between the belligerents India and Pakistan. China's active influence was growing in the region. China's geopolitical position toward South Asia is different from Russia's. China has a shared border with Afghanistan, Pakistan and India. China and India had serious disputes over the border and the status of Tibet. In the mid-1950s, China and India sought a policy of "good neighborliness" over the border to achieve a "balance" against the US, but it did not last long. War erupted on the border. The Soviet Union did not fully side with China, and this later proved to be one of the reasons that Soviet-Chinese relations deteriorated. Why did the Soviet Union not fully support China? It is true that the Soviet Union was tired of Chinese aggression against the US, exemplified by Mao Tsedong's assertion about a possible nuclear war against the US. The underlying reason was that South Asia was, for the Soviet Union, a space for "balancing" vis-à-vis the US. The Soviet Union seemed not to realize that Sino-Indian border antagonism could exceed the centripetal force between India and China against the US. The dissymmetry of India's positioning between Russia and China should have been considered.

After the border clash between the Soviet Union and China in 1969, the meaning of a South Asian space for the Soviet Union shifted to another dimension of the "balance" policy: "deterrence of a neighbouring power." The Soviet Union was inclined to rely on India to deter China, while China and Pakistan strengthened the axis in reaction. After the Soviet invasion of Afghanistan in 1979, the US strongly assisted Pakistan while India went out of its way not to criticize Soviet action. In South Asia, Soviet-Indian relations functioned as a balance against the China-Pakistan axis backed by the US. South Asia was the perfect place to test Primakov's maxim.

Back from Inertia to Balance

In the late Gorbachev era, Perestroika foreign policy, which assigned higher priority to the US, Europe and China, did not pay much attention to India. However, Mikhail Gorbachev visited India twice in 1986 and 1988 and played up their "traditional friendship" to others. In particular, the former was famous for the "Delhi Declaration." However, the declaration, entitled "For Principles of Non-Nuclear and Non-Violence in the World," obviously followed a Gorbachev initiative on the "disarmament of nuclear weapons" and a "new world order" on the basis of the "New Thinking." The declaration was provocative to the US and was closely related to the unsuccessful Reykjavik summit with US President Ronald Regan in October 1986. On the other hand, India had concerns over Gorbachev's Vladivostok speech in which he urged Russia to "reconcile" with China and put forth his idea of building a comprehensive security regime in Asia.

At the time, the Soviet priority in Asia was with China and the war in Afghanistan. After 1989, when Gorbachev withdrew the Soviet army from Afghanistan and paid a historic visit to Beijing, India was low on the Soviet Union's foreign policy priority list. In this context, its relations with Pakistan had a chance of improving, but Pakistan overestimated the "Delhi Declaration" as a sign of close partnership between the Soviet Union and India. Foreign Minister Eduard Shevardnadze's visit to Islamabad did little to improve Soviet-Pakistan relations. Gorbachev next turned his attention to improving its ties with Japan. India officially kept its position as best partner in South Asia for the Soviet Union, but economic relations were downsized. In fact, bilateral trade had waned to somewhere between the $3 billion and $4 billion level, similar to its bilateral trade with China, but below that with Japan. Soviet-India relations were nominal at best and a de facto vacuum at worst. Neither the Soviet Union nor India showed much interest in improving their relations.

Following the birth of the new Russia, the early foreign policy of Russia was more pro-Western than Gorbachev's, but it did not necessarily ignore its Asian "far neighbours": Gennady Burbulis visited in May and Ruslan Khasbulatov visited in August 1992. At the end of 1992, Foreign Minister Kozyrev, departing from Russia's pro-Western policy, naturally reminded his fellow Russians of India's importance. He tried to redefine Russo-Indian relations in the post-Cold War period. President Yeltsin visited Delhi and signed a friendship and cooperation treaty, as well as certain agreements such as rescheduling of Indian debt and military cooperation, including rocket technology transfer.

It is, however, apparent that the new treaty was a step back from the previous one: the new treaty omitted the word "peace" and the clause "mutual consultant in crisis." Military cooperation was also suspended. President Yeltsin suspended the transfer of technology to India, accepting US concerns regarding the situation.

Their economic relations faltered as well: less than one billion dollars from 1992 to 1994, and not exceeding more than $2 billion since 1995. In contrast, India's new open economic policy was given a warm welcome by the US, and India enjoyed a sort of honeymoon with the US because of the keen attention paid to Asia by the Clinton administration, which came to a halt following the exposure of India's nuclear capabilities in May 1998. Russo-Indian relations are the only variable subordinate to US-Indian relations or to US-Russian relations. The better the latter becomes, the worse the former becomes, and vice versa.

Following the deterioration of US-Russian relations in 1994, Russia began to urgently retreat from the prolonged inertia of Russo-Indian relations. Russia did not hesitate to sell its most sophisticated weapons to India; big deals concerning the sale of MIG–29, Su30–MKI, S–300 and submarines were quickly and satisfactory arranged. Energy cooperation including the construction of an atomic station and space exploitation facility was advanced.

India's traditional dependence on Soviet weapons in the Cold War and Indian tactics of maintaining its distance from the US caused India to move toward accepting a Russian proposal. After the US imposed an economic embargo on India after India's nuclear experiment in 1998, Russia only verbally criticized India and did not participate in the embargo. With Russia seeming to be a good "card" for Indian interests, Primakov visited Delhi and disclosed the idea of a "strategic triangle." India considered its relations with the US extremely important and vital to its interests, and much to Russia's dismay, maintained a cool attitude toward Russia.

Here, it is important to note the new dynamics of Russo-Indian relations that emerged in the mid-1990s. An independent Central Asia became a contributing factor to the dynamics in their relations.

Although India and Russia have no shared border, the area between the two countries had begun to transform, which had an effect on Russo-Indian relations. Since the early 1990s, India has been concerned about the stability of Central Asia because of the ruling Taliban regime in Afghanistan and the civil war in Tajikistan that had the potential to adversely affect the Kashmir issue. The disputed region of Kashmir controlled by Pakistan shares a border with both China and Afghanistan. Border politics in this context are analysed with the presence of Pakistan in the region.

Pakistan in Border Politics

While the differences between the Russian approach to India and the Indian approach to Russia were apparent, Pakistan kept a close eye on Russia. To insure its own security against India, Pakistan sought to "balance" the great powers in the region.

Undoubtedly, the major actors are the US, China and Russia. Although the US has been Pakistan's most important partner, US support of Pakistan has been contingent on Pakistan's ability to contain or conduct war against such "big enemies" as the Soviet Union in the Cold War era or the Taliban and al Qaeda in the "post-9/11" era. US concerns about Pakistan's Islamic statehood and political instability, e.g., repeated military coups, also need to be factored in. In contrast to the political regime of Pakistan, which leaves little to be desired or emulated, the US admires Indian democracy. The better US-Indian relations, the worse US-Pakistan relations.

Concerning the Soviet Union, Pak-Soviet relations were relatively good in the 1960s, but after Russo-Chinese military conflicts and the third Pak-Indian war, they deteriorated (although it should be noted that Premier Zulfikar Ali Bhutto did visit Moscow in 1974, so relations were not completely frozen). The decisive halt to relations happened after the Soviet invasion of Afghanistan in 1979. Pakistan was now a de facto "enemy" of the Soviet Union.

After the Soviet withdrawal from Afghanistan, the Soviet-Chinese reconciliation changed the basis of Soviet-Pak relations. But Gorbachev's "indifference" (particularly on Pakistan) to South Asia and the collapse of the Soviet Union lessened the chances of drastic improvement.

CHINA'S PERSPECTIVE ON ITS STRATEGIC PARTNERSHIP WITH RUSSIA

China has used the deterioration of Russia's relations with the EU and U.S. to strengthen its position within a strategic partnership with the Russian Federation. The PRC's goals are to counterbalance the U.S., secure its own economic interests in the post-Soviet area, increase border security and obtain Russian support for Chinese international initiatives. In exchange, China supports Russia by abstaining from open criticism on its annexation of Crimea and by importing raw materials. The partnership brings more benefits to China, which is positive for the EU. The PRC, unlike Russia, is concerned about destabilisation of NATO's Eastern Flank and favours European integration.

China responded positively to Russia's Far East policy after the latter's deterioration of relations with the EU and U.S. in 2014. China has cautiously made Russia economically dependent on it, for example, by importing gas and investing in Central Asian states. Through these instruments, China tries to stabilise the situation in states located in Russia's traditional sphere of interest in exchange for its support of Chinese international initiatives and security along its western borders.

Since Chairman Xi Jinping rose to power, and specifically since 2014, there has been a visible intensification of bilateral contact, confirmed in 2014 by the establishment of a new intergovernmental committee at the vice premier level. On the Chinese side, it is chaired by Zhang Gaoli, a member of the Chinese Communist Party's (CPC) Politburo Standing Committee and Xi's trusted associate. The Chinese leader, as well as Russian President Vladimir Putin, exercise strong leadership of their countries, which eased the establishment of personal relations between them. After his ascension to chairman of the CPC in May 2013, Xi choose Russia for his first foreign trip. Both leaders meet every few months—15 times since 2014. Under previous chairman Hu Jintao, high-level meetings between China and Russia took place less often.

Common Interests?

From a political perspective, China considers it essential to build a multipolar global order as a tool of U.S. containment. That is the vision behind new regulations and ventures for which China seeks Russian support, such as the Asian Infrastructure Investment Bank and "Belt and Road" initiative (BRI). China counts on Russia's assistance on these and emphasises the complementarity between Russia's Eurasian Economic Union and China's BRI. At first, Russia viewed the Chinese concept with distrust. Today, though, after its pro-China pivot, Russia is presented as China's most important partner, for example, during the Belt and Road Forum in Beijing in May. China is also trying to push other common initiatives, such as Internet legal regulations. In 2015, the PRC, together with Russia, Kazakhstan, Tajikistan and Uzbekistan, submitted to the UN General Assembly a revised draft of a 2011 resolution on the International Code of Information Security.

Both China and Russia accuse the U.S. of inspiring the Arab Spring and Ukraine crisis. The PRC also cooperates with Russia on UN Security Council votes, for example, vetoing draft resolutions on Syria six times. Western support for the overthrow of the Libyan regime in 2011 is another binding factor. China has taken an ambivalent stance on Russia's annexation of Crimea and its actions in eastern Ukraine, hoping for a similar Russian position on Chinese territorial disputes.

Economically, the Russian pivot to Asia enabled China to strengthen its presence in Central Asia, which is especially important from the BRI perspective. China makes use of Russia's low capability to generate capital and actively invests in states in the region by providing them a measure of economic stability. China has expressed interest in buying shares of Russian companies and energy projects located on Russian territory. Until 2014, such actions were blocked by Russian authorities afraid of Chinese domination. In 2015, the Silk Road Fund acquired 9.9% of the Yamal LNG project. Chinese enterprises already have around 30% of the shares of that project and construction works are financed by Chinese state-owned banks. The cooperation between Russia's Rosneft and the China National Petroleum Company is also growing. The PRC's collaboration with Russia is also helpful in internationalisation of the yuan and the establishment of non-Western credit card payment systems and separate rating agencies.

China also finds cooperation with the Russian Federation important in the context of security of its western border and internal stability. The PRC is guarding against terrorism, particularly by radicals amongst the Uyghur ethnic minority living in Xinjiang province and across the border in Kazakhstan. The danger of terrorism is intended to be counterbalanced by the capabilities of the Shanghai Cooperation Organisation as well as Russia's military presence in Central Asia. The Russian Federation has finally consented to sell China modern military equipment, including 24 Su-35 fighters and four S-400 surface-to-air missile systems, which will probably be deployed to the South China Sea region. China also uses Russia's objection to the U.S. THADD anti-missile system being deployed in South Korea as international confirmation of its own objections.

WHAT'S NEXT FOR THE INDIA-RUSSIA STRATEGIC PARTNERSHIP?

When Indian Prime Minister Narendra Modi and Russian President Vladimir Putin had an "informal" meeting in Sochi in late May, the two leaders discussed a number of bilateral issues such as military and defense cooperation and international issues relevant to both India and Russia. The meeting once again put the attention on the strategic partnership between New Delhi and Moscow, which continues to be significant, but also faces a number of challenges.

Many of the areas of convergence were unsurprisingly on display during the meeting at Sochi. In terms of outlook, the two leaders endorsed and emphasized the importance of their Special and Privileged Strategic Partnership for global peace and stability and the role of the two in shaping "an open and equitable world order." Both Modi and Putin underlined the need to develop "a multipolar world order" while increasing consultations and coordination including on the Indo-Pacific, even though the two sides differ in their characterization. Foreign Minister Lavrov, while speaking to the media on the informal summit, talked about it as the Asia-Pacific region, a formulation preferred by China, whereas the Indian Ministry of External Affairs referred to it as the Indo-Pacific region. Putin and Modi also reiterated the importance of continuing their work together in platforms such as the United Nations,

Shanghai Cooperation Organization (SCO), Brazil, Russia, India, China, South Africa (BRICS), and G-20.

Issue-wise, cooperation in the energy and economic sectors dominated the two leaders' discussions. The progress seen in the bilateral trade – about 20 percent in 2017 and about 40 percent in the first few months of 2018 – was highlighted by both sides. In an effort to keep up the momentum, the NITI AAYOG and the Russian Ministry of Economic Development will be engaged in an annual strategic economic dialogue.

More fundamentally, while the two leaders highlighted the tried and tested nature of their partnership, in truth India-Russia ties have been lately going through a rough patch. For more than a decade now, the bilateral relationship has been characterized by increasing strains.

Several factors have contributed to it. For one, in the wake of the Ukraine crisis in 2013, it is clear that Russia wanted China's support because China's opinion carries greater weight globally than India's. This is evident in the continued strategic outreach efforts made by Russia towards China, further reflected in a number of strategic agreements between Moscow and Beijing. The manner in which Putin in 2013 rapidly wrapped up an agreement on natural gas sale to China for 30 years – negotiations that had been dragging on for a decade – was a reflection of Moscow's eagerness to work with China. This was over and above the earlier deals in 2009 and 2013 for the sale of oil on a long-term basis.

But far more consequential is the Russian sale of weapons systems to China that have direct security implications for India. Moscow's sale of Su-30 30MKK/MK2 fighters and especially the Su-35 are likely to have an immediate and tangible impact on the Sino-Indian military balance and India's security. Then there is the sale of S-400 long-range anti-aircraft missiles, which China is reportedly already deploying, though it seems like India may get the same system too.

Second, India's efforts at diversifying its defense procurement and thus bringing in other partners such as the

United States, Israel, and France has also impacted the relations. In the absence of a strong bilateral economic and trade relationship, India-Russia relations must have a robust defense ties and any downgrading of those ties could have adverse impact on the overall state of India-Russia ties. Till a few years ago, India's largest defense trade partner was Russia, but Israel and the United States have overtaken Russia in the last few years.

Even so, India's defense inventory continues to be dominated by Soviet/Russian systems, to the tune of close to 70 percent. Also, when it comes to certain critical platforms such as nuclear submarines, Russia's importance cannot be understated. Therefore, as India engages in the process of diversifying its defense trade partners, perception management and explaining the rationale and imperative to Russia will go a long way in assuaging Moscow's concerns about India's leanings.

Third and possibly the most significant has been India's growing proximity to the United States. Driven by fear of China, India has grown strategically closer to Washington in recent years, though lately New Delhi's foreign policy leaning may appear a lot more confused. Prime Minister Modi's Shangri-La Dialogue speech earlier this month in Singapore was a good reflection of this.

These three developments have dampened bilateral relations between India and Russia. For India, the critical question is whether Russia will stand by India in any dispute with China. Moscow's stand during last year's Doklam crisis did not inspire much confidence in New Delhi. On the other hand, New Delhi understands that it cannot afford to drive Moscow into Beijing's hands. Any strategic partnership between Russia and China does not augur well for India. Whether India can do much about this is unclear, but New Delhi is definitely trying.

2

Behind China and Russia's 'Special Relationship'

The rise of a more politically and militarily assertive Russia and an economically and institutionally ascendant China may be characterized as the two principal forces challenging the United States in global policymaking.

China's and Russia's strategies for international expansion, in each of their respective areas of policy specialization, are not necessarily mutually exclusive. Arguably, both countries' intensified involvement on the world stage is not only complementary but to a growing extent directly and indirectly supportive of each other's increasingly commonly-defined interests.

The growing international significance of China and Russia's key political and economic partnership must be considered a major factor in global policymaking going forward.

CHINA-RUSSIA RELATIONS BEFORE 2014

China and Russia have largely formulated their economic and political relations based on an evolving series of strategic partnerships. While there is no "model" strategic partnership, in the sense that the terms are negotiated individually with a partner state, both countries have incorporated certain core principles into each partnership.

Following two partnership agreements in 1994 and 1996 and a Treaty of Friendship and Cooperation in 2001, the 2012 comprehensive strategic partnership of cooperation (the 2012 Strategic Partnership), underlined the principles of mutual benefit, mutual trust, and equality in addition to setting specific economic targets in China-Russia bilateral relations.

Notably, although the 2012 Strategic Partnership, signed by President Hu Jintao, China's president at the time, and Russian President Vladimir Putin, was intended to provide the basis for implementation of relations over a ten-year period, it was prematurely superseded by the 2014 agreement calling for a new stage in the comprehensive strategic partnership of cooperation, the 2014 Strategic Partnership.

In this case, China's President Xi Jinping, was the co-signatory. The involvement of Xi, who came to power in 2013, a year after Putin's re-election as Russian president, has become a key driver in the intensification of bilateral relations.

AFTER THE UKRAINE CRISIS

The 2014 Strategic Partnership, ratified shortly after Russia's annexation of Crimea, amid the launch of U.S. and EU sanctions against Russia, is widely regarded as the most enhanced in terms of depth and breadth of economic, political, and security relations of any one of China's or Russia's network of strategic partnerships.

Some of the much-publicized and high-profile deals emerging from the 2014 Strategic Partnership included a 40-year gas supply agreement between Gazprom and China National Petroleum Corporation (CNPC). The landmark gas supply deal, including plans to build the "Power of Siberia" gas pipeline, was indirectly referred to in the 2014 Strategic Partnership as a measure aiming to "strengthen the Sino-Russian energy partnership."

A further deal with Russia's largest oil company, state-owned Rosneft, involving financing deals with CNPC to supply oil worth up to $500 billion from Russia's largest oil field, was also established shortly after, prospectively enabling Russia to surpass Saudi Arabia as China's main supplier of oil.

Also in 2014, the People's Bank of China (PBOC) and the Central Bank of Russia signed an arrangement for a currency swap worth 150 billion yuan and 815 billion rubles ($24 billion at the time). The first such Chinese currency swap to be announced for any country outside of Asia, the deal was meant to facilitate settlement in national currencies and boost bilateral trade.

Since 2014, and particularly in 2015, Russia has become one of the five largest recipients of Chinese outbound direct investment in relation to the Chinese government's Belt and Road Initiative (BRI) connecting Asia with Europe. Meanwhile, China was Russia's largest bilateral trade partner, in 2015; in spite of declining overall bilateral trade in U.S. dollar terms (mainly due to sharp declines in the ruble as well as the yuan), relative to 2014, trade flows continued to expand in terms of volume.

In this context, it was significant that Russia's exports of mechanical and technical products to China rose by about 45 percent over the course of 2015 possibly signifying an important trend in the diversification and competitiveness of Russia's non-energy sector in terms of bilateral trade prospects with China.

Importantly, the economic relationship between China and Russia has been driven by a variety of bilateral intergovernmental commissions, including 26 subcommissions. According to Putin, in spite of often slow progress in reaching agreements, both sides invariably maintain a common goal of cooperation to eventually find a solution on a wide range of complex issues.

INTEGRATING OF HIGH-LEVEL POLITICAL INTERESTS

Since the 2014 Strategic Partnership, amid a strengthening of personal ties in the Putin-Xi relationship, there has been an extensive broadening of bilateral relations beyond merely focusing on economic interests. This has centered on mutual support concerning each country's "core interests," including "strengthening close coordination in foreign policy." They have also jointly advocated for reform of the international financial and economic architecture to accord with the rapidly-changing global real economy.

The relationship between China and Russia has, therefore, evolved into intensified cooperation in political areas in the last couple of years. Chief among those developments was the announcement on May 8, 2015 in Moscow, on the occasion of the annual parade commemorating the end of World War II, of the planned integration of the Chinese-led BRI with Russia's Eurasian Economic Union (EEU).

The BRI comprises the Silk Road Economic Belt and the 21st Century Maritime Silk Road, with the objective of developing a trade and infrastructure network connecting Asia with Europe and Africa along the ancient Silk Road routes. The EEU groups Armenia, Belarus, Kazakhstan, Kyrgyzstan, and Russia in an inward-focused trading network.

Beijing's policy of integrating the BRI, its flagship international development program, with Moscow's EEU stood in sharp contrast to the European Union's Eastern Partnership program with former Soviet states. The latter program required these countries to sign up to EU economic and political associations and to relinquish their trade agreements and political affiliations with Russia.

Further evidence of the growing high-level political relations between China and Russia was manifested in the international financial markets under the co-arrangement of up to 6 billion yuan in "Baikalbonds" (a yuan-denominated Russian government bond issued in Russia). The co-arrangers were China's ICBC and state-owned Gazprombank — Russia's third-largest bank, which has been under U.S. sanctions since July 2014. This issuance of offshore yuan foreign sovereign bonds was the largest ever undertaken, exceeding the U.K. government's earlier 3 billion yuan sovereign bond issue.

Both Putin and Xi reiterated the significance of their growing bilateral political relations at the BRICS development summit in Goa, India, in October 2015, where they noted that China and Russia should strengthen coordination and cooperation within global and regional multilateral institutions.

INTENSIFICATION OF BILATERAL COOPERATION IN MULTILATERAL INSTITUTIONS

At the Hangzhou G20 Summit, held in September 2016, the China-Russia dialogue was accorded a high-level agenda by both leaders. The dialogue focused, especially, on principles such as the "rule of law" in promoting tax and legal concepts for enhancing investments, investment protection, privatization, and the provision of state guarantees on finance for projects. There was also dialogue on how to bridge each side's differing interpretations of legislative concepts, such as public-private partnerships and concession agreements.

At the level of the Shanghai Cooperation Organization (SCO), Putin and Xi's proposals for integrating China's BRI with the Russian-led EEU played a key role in significantly elevating the status of the SCO. Although the SCO is a separate institution to the BRI and EEU, it is increasingly viewed by governments across the world as an organization reflecting the political and economic ascendancy of the Eurasian region. Partly, as a result, India and Pakistan, currently holding SCO observer status, have submitted applications for full membership, anticipated to become effective by early 2017. Moreover, an increasing number of other countries from around the world have also requested to join the organization.

At the recent November 2016 summit of SCO prime ministers, in Bishkek, Kyrgyzstan, China's Prime Minister Li Keqiang proposed a free trade area among SCO members. The proposal was supported by Putin, who stated that the long-term economic interests of China and Russia should outweigh national protectionist sentiments to protect local producers.

The Russia-India-China (RIC) trilateral grouping is considered by its participants as an important arrangement in securing political stability, both globally and in the region. India and Russia's relations have remained strong for several decades, with Russia being India's largest defense and nuclear energy partner. However, while China's and Russia's relations have clearly improved in the last few years, the China-India relationship has somewhat lagged the development of the other two legs of the triangle. Consequently, Russia has played a role in bringing both sides closer together through its interactions in the RIC grouping.

At the Asia-Pacific Economic Cooperation (APEC) forum held recently on November 2016, in Peru, Putin and Xi further reiterated their close cooperation and ongoing communication on policy matters with an international dimension. They agreed to promote the APEC bloc by fostering regional and economic growth strategies. This included their support for an Asia-Pacific free trade area for all 21 member states. Their joint support for regional free trade came on the heels of U.S. President-elect Donald Trump seeming to back away from the Trans-Pacific Partnership free trade agreement – an exclusive U.S.-led trade bloc including 12 states on both sides of the Pacific Ocean.

At the summit, Putin and Xi also affirmed their common interest in upholding security and stability in Central and Northeast Asia, as well as regions neighboring their countries' borders.

INTENSIFYING CULTURAL EXCHANGES

An important element of China-Russia relations, beyond the political and economic dimensions, has been the countries' promotion of sociocultural integration at various levels of society. In this regard, toward the end of the APEC summit, Putin and Xi stated their interest in holding a 2017 China-Russia Media Exchange Year, wherein the media has become the most direct channel for communication between the two sides. Additionally, the two leaders stated their support for other cultural and people-to-people exchanges in the coming year.

The important role which the media increasingly plays in cultural matters was highlighted by recent headline reports about the gift of Russian ice cream by Putin to Xi, who declared it to be his favorite Russian dessert. The purpose of the media coverage was not only to portray an ever-closer personal relationship between the two leaders, but also to convey the idea of a growing friendship, built on a greater understanding of mutual cultural awareness, between Chinese and Russian peoples. Consequently, Xi's interest in Russian ice cream has reportedly spawned a craze of interest for the dessert across China.

In early 2016, Putin and Xi urged that both countries' legislative bodies enhance exchanges and mutual learning so as to further elevate China-Russia ties. Accordingly, Russia's Federation Council and Russia's State Duma, the upper and lower houses of the Russian parliament, respectively, and China's National People's Congress agreed to strengthen their cooperation on legislative initiatives and supervision to enhance coordination on regional, municipal and industrial development policies and plans.

JOINT MILITARY AND SECURITY COOPERATION

A major feature of China's and Russia's defense and geostrategic interests has been rising levels of official support for each other's security, increasingly pitched as common defense concerns. The most prominent recent affirmation of this position came in the form of China's and Russia's stated opposition to the deployment of the U.S. Terminal High Altitude Air Defense (THAAD) missile defense system in South Korea, a decision made in mid-2016. Both governments have warned that THAAD risks igniting an arms race in the Asia-Pacific that could potentially destabilize the region.

In this vein, China and Russia have been accelerating their joint military drills including holding their first joint naval drills conducted in the South China Sea this year. According to senior officers at China's Central Military Commission and

Russia's Defense Ministry, since both sides are faced with a more complex international security environment, closer mutual cooperation has been widely considered a necessity.

The Russian government has also voiced its support for the Chinese government's position in the South China Sea, backing Beijing's call opposing interference by powers outside the region. In turn, China has increasingly provided verbal support intimating its sympathy with Russia's annexation of Crimea (mainly attributing the move to Crimea's historical links as part of Russia), in addition to backing Russia's intervention in Syria, while calling for a political settlement to the war.

LONGER TERM HEADWINDS

Possibly the most serious undermining of the China-Russia relationship could come from its very success. As both countries integrate more quickly and as migration flows expand, there is likely to be mounting concern in Russia of a "Chinese takeover" of the sparsely-populated Russian Far East and other regions of Siberia.

Should this pose China's and Russia's greatest challenge going forward – in light of the popularity of Russia's opposition nationalist party in the Far East and Siberian regions during the 2016 Duma elections – then both sides will need to need to consider jointly upgrading the regulation and monitoring of migration flows. Detailed satellite mapping of the two countries' common border, in addition to having resolved all outstanding border disputes in 2005, should facilitate the necessary cooperation in managing migration across Russia's politically-sensitive regions.

CONCLUSION

Driven by strengthening personal ties between Putin and Xi, the breadth and depth of China-Russia relations have spilled over into multiple spheres of governmental and institutional policymaking. This has included both countries' central governments, as well as regional and municipal governments, in addition to the increasing role played by state and private companies and various sectors of civil society.

As a result, the speed and scale of the relationship may be more aptly described as "revolutionary" rather than evolutionary. Clearly, external factors such as the Ukraine crisis were pivotal in turning the Russian leadership away from its post-Soviet relations with western Europe. The degree to which the Russian public were going to back their government's shift from West to East, however, was more questionable. Nevertheless, Chinese and Russian state-led activism in supporting this process has, thus far, brought some degree of success.

3

Russia-China Strategic Partnership: On the Road to United Eurasia

Deals, of course, matter; in Beijing, China and Russia advanced 58 projects worth $50 billion. These include a $6.2 billion loan from Beijing to build the 770 km-long high-speed railway between Moscow and Kazan and $12 billion in loans to build an LNG plant in the Russian Arctic.

Russian Railways, Russian investment company Sinara Group, China Railway, and Chinese CRRC will also invest in a plant in Russia to build 100 high-speed trains, designed for the Moscow-Kazan high-speed railway. The railway inevitably will be connected to the future, $100 billion, high-speed expansion of the Trans-Siberian between Moscow and Beijing.

It goes without saying, this is all part of an essential node of the New Silk Roads. And as if this was not enough, in a further, graphic instance of geoeconomic interpolation, Russia and China's central banks are setting up a yuan clearing mechanism in Russia.

THE INTER-CONNECTIVITY BONANZA

Putin and Xi met for the 15th time just after Xi concluded a three-nation Eurasia tour – Serbia, Poland and Uzbekistan – where, alongside Foreign Minister Wang Yi, he explicitly laid down the bridge between the New Silk Roads, or One Belt, One Road (OBOR), as they are officially referred to in China, and the development of the Shanghai Cooperation Organization (SCO).

Not by accident China has now also struck a « comprehensive strategic partnership » with Serbia, Poland and Uzbekistan – on the way to weaving a broad « China-Europe strategic partnership » in parallel to the development of the SCO.

This already translates into projects such as the Hungary-Serbia railway; the Pupin Bridge on the Danube River in Belgrade; the expansion and upgrading of a power plant in Kostolac; what Beijing calls the China-Europe freight train service (from eastern China to Duisburg in Germany and also Madrid); the Kamchiq Tunnel in Uzbekistan; and last but not least the massive China-Central Asia natural gas pipeline system.

No wonder Xi keeps stressing the « inter-connectivity » theme over and over gain, as economic corridors are being built at breakneck speed, and the China Railway Express all the way to Europe – although not yet on high-speed rail – is already a go.

So there was plenty to talk about at the 16th SCO Council in Tashkent. Plus, the acceleration of full membership to both India and Pakistan; next year will be Iran's turn.

What this translates to in practice is the amalgamation of the New Silk Roads/OBOR; the Eurasia Economic Union, EEU (as Putin stressed in the St. Petersburg forum); the SCO; financing mechanisms such as the Asia Infrastructure Investment Bank (AIIB); and the overarching Russia-China strategic partnership.

No wonder a certain Sultan Erdogan was watching all this in Ankara with trepidation, and decided to make a move. Erdogan's attempt at a rapprochement with Russia involves not being hopelessly sidelined in this OBOR/EEU/SCO amalgamation. Turkey cannot afford to be alienated from Russia; the Turkish Stream gas pipeline will be essential to consolidate

Ankara's position as a key energy crossroads towards Europe. At the same time, Ankara must imperatively position itself as a key hub in OBOR.

With India and Pakistan, and later Iran, as full members, the SCO will be able, in the medium term, not only to interface with OBOR on all sides (via the China-Pakistan Economic Corridor, CPEC, and also the Indian investment in the Iranian port of Chabahar); but also to be the key player in brokering a solution to the Afghan drama, something that the Americans and NATO would never be able to accomplish. Russia and China have always insisted that Afghanistan needs an Asian solution.

Lean, clean and green

Almost simultaneously to the Putin-Xi meeting in Beijing, and also not by accident, the AIIB turbo-charged its operations. The AIIB started doing business only six months ago, with 57 founding member countries and $100 billion in committed capital. It's scheduled to invest $1.2 billion in 2016. Once again with trademark understatement, Chinese Finance Minister Lou Jiwei said, « the AIIB needs to establish its comparative advantage », profiting from « lessons of developing countries' years of development. »

The board approved its first four deals, worth $509 million, with three projects co-financed with the World Bank, the Asian Development Bank (ADB), the United Kingdom Department for International Development and the European Bank for Reconstruction and Development. They refer to a slum renovation in Indonesia and highways in Pakistan and Tajikistan. A power grid upgrade in Bangladesh will be solely AIIB financed.

And this is just the beginning. The head of AIIB may be Chinese, Jin Linqun (he has promised a « lean, clean and green » AIIB), but one of the five vice presidents is British, Daniel Alexander. Beijing holds 30% of the initial capital but has only 26% of voting power. India holds 7.5% and Russia 5.9%, followed by Germany and South Korea. This is a real multipolar project.

Almost simultaneously to the AIIB in action, Russia and China's foreign ministers signed a declaration supporting the role of international law, stressing sovereign equality of states; non-interference into internal affairs; and peaceful resolution of disputes. Considering the recent historical record, not exactly The Empire of Chaos's cup of tea.

Commenting on Brexit, Boris Titov, the Kremlin's small business ombudsman, ventured, « it's not long until a united Eurasia – about 10 years. » Considering the slowly but surely interpenetration of OBOR, EEU, SCO, AIIB, the NDB and the solid Russia-China partnership inside the G20, that's more than feasible.

In Beijing, Putin and Xi did discuss their common position in the upcoming G20, only three months away in China; that's where the real action is, not the G7. Compare it also with NATO's upcoming warmongering summit in Warsaw; that's what the West has to « offer » the global South.

In a nutshell; the option to a united Eurasia is chaos. And there's no question the Empire of Chaos will stop trying to sow chaos. Expect Beijing ordering 1,000 heavy transport aircraft from Russia and Russian ships possibly spotted sooner or later in the South China Sea to add to those perennial howls of anger in the neocon/neoliberalcon galaxy.

EVOLUTION OF RUSSIAN-CHINESE STRATEGIC RELATIONS

Towards a bilateral partnership

The first years of transition in Russia were dominated by radical economic reforms and desire to integrate rapidly the occidental community. However, this period soon left the place for a more auto-centric approach, which meant a retreat of radical economic reforms and a more equilibrated foreign policy between its Western and Eastern axis. Since the normalization of Soviet-Chinese relations announced by M. Gorbachev in 1989, the Presidents B. Yeltsin and Jiang Zemin announced for the first time "constructive partnership" in 1994, and "strategic partnership" in 1996. Strategic relations between Russia and China should be seen as a part of the triangle including both countries and the US. Promoting a multipolar world and the desire to counteract the dominance of the US in the post-cold war world are among the common objectives of Moscow and Beijing.

Another element is the refusal of interference in internal affairs, notably for the human rights and local separatism issues. So, Russian policy towards China (and *vice versa*) is inversely correlated with the policy towards the US. Consequently, the political or strategic factors play a dominant role in the conception of Russian policy in Asian-Pacific region.

The Russian-Chinese Treaty of Good-neighbourliness, Friendship and Cooperation between Russia and China was signed in 2001. It partially repeats the Sino-soviet treaty expired in 1980, precisely, concerning the respect of territorial integrity and sovereignty, Russian engagement for the "one-China" policy (non-recognition of Taiwan independence), and expansion of links in numerous domains (of which the military one).

Further, two articles of the new treaty indicate the military alliance, even if the parties deny this fact and the Treaty doesn't contain a clause of mutual defence. Finally, the treaty mentions actual problems related to countries economic inequality issues revealed especially at the regional level. So, Russia and China should renounce any form of pressure and facilitate cooperation in frontier regions (art.14), and cooperate to combat illegal immigration (art.20).

The bilateral Treaty (2001) consolidated the basis for Russian-Chinese political partnership. However, in spite of the proclaimed strategic partnership, Russian and Chinese interests diverge on several aspects of regional policy in Central Asia.

Convergence and divergence of interests at the regional level

In Central Asia, China and Russia interact in the framework of the Shanghai Cooperation Organisation (SCO). The SCO was formally created in 2001 by Russia, China, Kazakhstan, Kyrgyzstan, Tajikistan and Uzbekistan. In reality, the SCO is the continuation of the Shanghai Forum, created in 1996 by the above-mentioned countries except Uzbekistan aiming to stabilize the post-soviet Central Asia.

The main goals were the demarcation and protection of the common border and also, for China, solution of ethnic minority problems in the frontier zone. So, regional security is the first objective of the SCO.

However, one can note that Shanghai Forum was founded in 1996, a period of tensions in both Russian-American and Chinese-American relations. Later, the regional preoccupation of the SCO will not exclude the orchestrated action of the organization against the US. Moreover, the acceptance of Mongolia, Pakistan, India and Iran as observers reinforces the international role of the SCO.

At the same time, the SCO reveals the conflict of interests between Russia and China as both countries are searching to increase their presence in Central Asia. On the one hand, China demonstrates a growing interest towards this zone which was submitted to its influence in the past. The SCO is the only structure at China's disposal to promote its interests in the region, rich in hydrocarbons. In this way, China and Russia become rivals for access to oil and gas reserves of Central Asia.

On the other hand, the SCO is one of several organizations serving to promote Russian interests in the region. Russia is present through the CIS and panoply of sub-regional blocs and treaties concluded between different CIS states. In this context, the activation of the Eurasian Economic Community (EurAsEC, regrouping Russia, Belarus, Kazakhstan, Kyrgyzstan, Tajikistan and, since 2006, Uzbekistan) can be viewed as an attempt to oppose the growing influence of China in Central Asia (Facon (2006)). The reinforcement of EurAsEC arrives when China stresses the importance of economic issues within the SCO. More precisely, the Framework Agreement to enhance economic cooperation (signed in September 2003; and also the action plan approved in September, 2004) fixes the main orientations for 2020 aiming to establish a SCO free-trade zone.

However, the economic mission of the SCO remains weakly defined, while the non-coordinated accession of its members to the WTO puts into question its emergence as a trading bloc.

Moreover, the growing competition of Chinese goods in such a case could have negative effects on Russian producers. The latter puts a strong limit for the development of regional trade integration within the SCO. In this context, the Russian Ministry of Economic development and trade officials propose to limit the scope of economic partnership within the SCO. Russian economic interests should be promoted through the EurAsEC while the SCO should be limited to security issues only.

Nevertheless, in spite of numerous discrepancies, the global framework of Russian-Chinese relations creates a favourable context for the development of economic cooperation and the creation of costly energy exports infrastructures.

RUSSO-CHINESE RELATIONS ELEVATED

Despite the declaration and reputation of the "strategic partnership" between Russia and China established in 1996, relations developed at snail's pace. The promise to boost trade ties between the two countries to the $20 billion level by 2000 was not realized. Border negotiations were deadlocked over a couple of remaining disputed points: Heixiazi Island near Khaborovsk and Abagaitui Island on the Argun River.

The 1991 agreement, excluding the two points above, was juristically reconfirmed in 1999. In September 1999, when Russian sinologists began to emphasize a would-be "strategic triangle" between Russia, China and India during a symposium session held at the Institute of the Far East in Moscow, a correspondent from a Chinese newspaper did not take their reports very seriously, and a Russian diplomat criticized the idea for its impracticality. A prestigious Chinese academic journal on Russia mentioned that Russo-Chinese relations are on a second axis that is easily influenced by Russo-US and Sino-

US relations. The better the latter becomes, the worse the former becomes, and vice versa.

Just after his inauguration, Russian President Vladimir Putin was eager to visit to Europe in early 2000. He welcomed US President Bill Clinton in Moscow in early June, while waiting until July to visit Beijing. The joint statement published there on missile defence unveiled a different approach between Russia and China. China was afraid that the new Russian president was overly pro-western at China's expense. Even when President Putin paid his first visit to India in October 2000, a high-ranking Chinese correspondent suggested in an internal report that this trip may have been held to counter China as a part of Russia's "balance" foreign policy.

Emerging problems in relations were, however, worked out through bilateral cooperation, particularly over the border region, which kicked off during the later years of the Yeltsin period. Successful enforcement of the 1991 agreement, strict management of Chinese migration, joint control of the border regime and other border cooperation had a positive effect in stabilizing the border region. It was undoubtedly shown that border cooperation had moved forward, regardless of any divergence of opinion or disputes between governments. Then, Putin urged the conclusion of a "neighbourly friendship and cooperation" treaty, which Jiang Zemin had proposed to Yeltsin earlier, in order to solidify the basis of Russo-Chinese relations. On the eve of signing of the treaty in July 2001, it was reported that Putin, wanting to bring the border dispute to an end, repeatedly argued for a compromise on the remaining border disputes, although it was unrealized.

After both of them successfully completed the treaty and played up the "partnership," new challenges emerged in the aftermath of "9/11." Russia and China immediately responded to US President George W. Bush's call for a "united front" against "international terrorism." If the Chinese view on the Sino-Russian axis mentioned above were true, Russo-Chinese relations had again hit another stumbling block.

In fact, bilateral relations were neither disturbed nor worsened. In addition to border stability and cooperation, economic relations gradually developed: $8 billion in 2000, $17.7 billion in 2001, and $11.0 billion in 2002. Russian arms sales to China were also progressive, with the sale of A–50 AWACS going through in November 2000, while deals over an upgraded SU–27K jetfighter and six submarines were finalized (the total amount is said to have been around $1.5 billion). It went beyond the estimated arms sales of $1 billion, at that time. Since 2000, energy issues have been at the top of their agenda. China's urgent demand for oil and gas made possible the close cooperation over the construction of a pipeline through Siberia and the Far East. The move was put forward during a Mikhail Kasiianov-Zhu Rongji meeting in September 2001. The Russo-Chinese treaty provided the full basis for further cooperation, and was not influenced by outside factors.

President Putin, just after his meeting with Jiang Zemin in June 2002, praised Russo-Chinese relations: "The recent improvement in Russo-US relations never ignores Russo-Chinese relations, and the latter reaches a higher level than the former because of the existence of the friendship treaty." Nevertheless, problems soon emerged between Russia and China: China's unfriendly attitude toward Russia's entry into the WTO (China countering it with a demand that Russia lift its "barrier" policy against "Chinese migration" as a condition for Chinese support), problems over Russia's "dumping" of Russian exports, such as steel and chemical fertilizer, and Khabarovsk's severe reaction and propaganda over the Heixiazi Island issue. By the end of 2002, Putin was describing Russo-Chinese relations as "friendly but businesslike."

Breakthrough: The New "Partnership"

In March 2003, Hu Jingtao was selected as the new president of China. For his first trip abroad, he chose Russia. To say that Russia and China were somewhat irritated by Bush's unilateral approach would be an understatement; the presence of the US army in Central Asia for an undetermined period of time, and the US invasion and its subsequent occupation of Iraq being the most obvious irritants.

Nevertheless, Russia and China did not closely coordinate against the US-UK "collation" on Iraq. Russia leaned upon a French initiative to soften the UN resolution on sanctions against Iraq. China cautiously watched the process but did not make its position clear at first.

For the most part, rapid economic interactions between the two countries started in 2003. In 2003, the trade volume hit $15.6 billion (up $4.6 billion from 2002) which, if the negative effects of the SARS epidemic on the economy in May of that year are considered, is a tremendous achievement. It reached $21.2 billion in 2004 and $25.2 billion in 2005. Meanwhile, some twenty-four SU–30 jetfighters (at a cost of almost $1 billion) were sold in 2003, while the total amount of arms sales reached $2 billion. Defence Minister Sergei Ivanov visited Beijing and concluded the sale of six S–300 missiles. Nevertheless, when economic issues were internationalized, the Russo-Chinese "partnership" remained "businesslike." Problems related to the proposed Siberian pipeline illustrate the realities of Russo-Chinese relations. Despite repeated Chinese calls for a route to go through China, Russia did not finalize it, and in September 2003 put its final decision on hold. Instead, Russia emphasized the importance of a direct route to the Pacific Ocean.

A drastic push for better "relations" was brought about by the border arrangement. In October 2004, Russian President Putin and Chinese President Hu Jintao declared that Russia and China had successfully resolved the remaining border dispute by cutting each disputed island, Heixiazi and Abagaitui Islands, in half. The two presidents were proud of the results and declared it a "win-win" compromise. They also strongly suggested that it could potentially be applied as a model to other border disputes around the globe. 21 The present condition of Russo-Chinese relations would not have been possible without defusing and resolving the border issue first, with little chance of bilateral cooperation in the vital areas of energy and arm sales. Who would have imagined an oil and gas pipeline crossing over the Amur River or a joint military exercise prior to the border dispute being resolved? With regional stability enhanced, mutual trust between the two countries has grown. As shown in this article, basic challenges to Russo-Chinese relations originated mostly from border disputes. The better the situation of the border, the better the relations. Lessons gained from Russo-Chinese relations suggest that they have not been a secondary axis, and have been affected little by the US. It is a considerably independent variable, basically controlled by bilateral factors, and has been particularly modified by border politics in the aftermath of the Cold War.

THE SINO-SOVIET RAPPROCHEMENT IN THE CONTEXT OF STRATEGIC TRIANGLE

It is rarely disputed that enmity and mistrust toward the Soviet Union brought China and the United States together in the 1970s. American diplomacy, actuated in accordance with Henry Kissinger's realist ideals, sought to play the "China" card in its fight against the Kremlin. The China factor in U.S. foreign policy thus played an important role in calculations about how to manage the United States' adversary relationship with the Soviet Union (Talbott, 1981: 82). China, for its part, was seeking to pursue normalization with the United States in order to counterweight the Soviet Union.

Galenovich (2001) noted that China's posture vis-à-vis the Kremlin in the 1970s was openly aggressive. Beijing called for creating a joint front against the USSR, ceased to recognise the 1950 treaty of Friendship, Solidarity, and Mutual Assistance, and repeatedly demanded the Soviet Union withdraw its forces from Mongolia, halt assistance to Vietnam, and reduce the troop presence along the Sino-Soviet border (Galenovich, 2001: 1). Beginning in 1979, the first talks between China and the Soviet Union were terminated when the Soviet Union conducted the invasion of Afghanistan (Hyland, 1981: 138).

In the early 1980s, a shift in the power balance occurred. The Soviet Union's deteriorating relations with the United

States, troubled economy, and declining defence capabilities made the Kremlin seek ways of invigorating its relationship with China. At that juncture, the Chinese leadership was discontented with U.S. foreign policy toward the Taiwan issue (i.e. increased contacts and arms sales), U.S. criticism of the human rights situation in China, and Washington's unwillingness to provide industrial technology so coveted by Beijing. The above-mentioned factors played a key role in bringing China and the Soviet Union together after 1985 when the Sino-Soviet rapprochement commenced.

In March 1982, the then Soviet leader, Leonid Brezhnev, in his Tashkent speech opined upon China as a "socialist state" and strongly criticized the U.S. "two China" policy, thus sending a signal to Beijing that Moscow was ready for renewing a dialogue (Wishnick, 2001a: 75). In response to Brezhnev's appeal, the Chinese leadership subsequently announced its determination to conduct "independent foreign policy" aimed at improving relations with both the Soviet Union and the United States without attaching itself to any big power (Goldstein, 1990: 122). As a consequence, the Soviet Union and the People's Republic of China began a round of talks devoted to the normalization of Sino-Soviet relations and resolution of border disputes.

The results of negotiations, albeit not as fruitful as parties had envisioned, had a significant impact on the increased levels of trade between the two nations. The volume of trade, for instance, skyrocketed from $300 million in 1982 to $1.2 billion in 1984 (Voskressenskii, 1999: 244).

However, three crucial challenges, the so-called "three obstacles," which had been thwarting rapprochement between Moscow and Beijing since the beginning of the 1980s, remained. Beijing still expressed its dissatisfaction with the deployment of Soviet troops along the Sino-Soviet border, the Soviet Union's support for Vietnam's occupation of Cambodia, and the Soviet invasion of Afghanistan in 1979. The Soviet leaders Andropov and Chernenko fell short of achieving any substantial progress on these issues largely due to the short tenure of their offices. It was Mikhail Gorbachev who gave impetus to the normalization of Sino-Soviet relations after ascending to the Communist Party's leadership in 1985.

The Soviet response to addressing the "three obstacles" in Sino-Soviet relations was reflected in Mikhail Gorbachev's speech in Vladivostok on July 28, 1986. In his speech, the new Soviet leader signalled his willingness to resolve the main points of contention between Moscow and Beijing. Gorbachev announced his decision to reduce the number of troops along the Sino-Soviet border and withdraw a considerable part of the Soviet contingent from Mongolia and Afghanistan by the end of the year. The Soviet leader, however, stopped short of giving concessions on the Soviet support of Vietnam's occupation of Cambodia. Only two years later when the Soviet Union began withdrawing forces from Afghanistan, Moscow suggested Hanoi should follow suit (Su, 1989: 115), and in December of that year Vietnam withdrew its troops from Cambodia. Thus, by the end of 1980s China and the Soviet Union made significant progress in overcoming the impasse in the relationship and were gradually moving toward full normalization.

Nevertheless, the two countries had different motives underlying their pursuit of better relations. While China was seeking to establish a peaceful milieu within the strategic triangle in order to focus on its economic development, the Soviet Union sought to restore the ideological nexus between the two communist countries (Voskessenskii, 1999: 247) with an intent to avert a possibility of a two-front conflict, and boost the Soviet economy. During Gorbachev's first visit to China in 1989 for the Sino-Soviet summit in Beijing, Chinese and Soviet leaders reached a mutual understanding on how to improve the Sino-Soviet relations.

Accordingly, Mikhail Gorbachev and Deng Xiaoping agreed that the new relationship would be based on the principles of peaceful coexistence and mutual respect, would not be aimed against any third country, and the ideological factor would not play any role in the normalization of Sino-Soviet relations. The aforementioned goals were reflected in the joint Sino-Soviet communiqué of 1989. According to the document, the Soviet Union and People's Republic of China agreed to develop their relations on the basis of the five principles of peaceful coexistence, including respect for international norms such as sovereignty, noninterference, and peaceful resolution of disputes (Wishnick, 2001a: 105). Further, any attempt or action by any country to impose its own will on others and seek "hegemony in any form" would be discarded by Moscow and Beijing.

The end of Sino-American confrontation following the decay of the Soviet Union removed the main rationale behind U.S.-Chinese cooperation, and the image of an opening China was replaced overnight by an image of a defiant China ruled by dictators (Zhu, 2006: 90). A month after the Sino-Soviet summit, the Chinese leadership witnessed a hitherto unseen degree of public discontent. The Tiananmen crackdown sparked harsh criticism from the United States which imposed sanctions against China. The Soviet Union, on the contrary, issued a response stating that the events in China were an internal affair, and suggested political dialogue as a means to resolve social problems. Besides, it was not in Gorbachev's interests to undermine the overwhelming progress in Sino-Soviet relations achieved during the previous four years of his tenure. Socio-economic problems in the Soviet Union (mass protests in Tbilisi, Georgia and other Soviet republics) also made Gorbachev refrain from open criticism of China's violent quelling of the protests in Beijing.

In the final analysis, the events in China made the Soviet leadership consider the consequences of liberalization that had been gaining momentum since the beginning of *perestroika*, while a fragile rapprochement between the two countries after two decades of confrontation dissuaded Gorbachev from taking a more assertive stance towards Beijing.

The Soviet Union soon became embroiled in painful process of disintegration, and Sino-Soviet relations were no longer atop the Kremlin's agenda. The Soviet Union and the communist bloc in Eastern Europe subsequently began to unravel.

In sum, the Sino-Soviet rapprochement in the second half of the 1980s was caused by important power shifts within the strategic triangle between the USA, USSR, and PRC. The United States under the Reagan administration was determined to economically exhaust the Soviet Union, thus eliminating it as a major geopolitical threat, while engaging China in order to maintain a strategic advantage in containing the USSR. In light of the worsening economy and political stagnation, the Soviet Union began to reverse its course toward China in the early 1980s for economic, political, and security reasons (Tucker, 1995-96: 518). China, for its part, was also looking forward to resolving disputes with the USSR because of the security threat emanating from the troop presence along the Sino-Soviet border and around China (i.e. Vietnam and Afghanistan). Although the "three obstacles" constantly stymied negotiations between the Soviet Union and China under Brezhnev, Andropov, and Chernenko, Sino-Soviet relations began to mend after Mikhail Gorbachev's ascension to power, and by the end of the 1980s most disputes were resolved.

The normalization of Sino-Soviet relations did not have a long-lasting impact, however, for the Soviet Union and China failed to achieve substantial progress in their economic cooperation. Because Sino-Soviet trade was markedly lower than trade between China and the United States, China considered U.S.-Chinese relations more important. The volume of Sino-Soviet trade amounted to $2 billion by 1985, whereas Sino-U.S. trade had already reached $6 billion by 1984 (Mills, 1986: 543). Thus, although the strategic triangle by and large lost its military component after the end of the Cold War, its political and economic implications remained important well into the following decades.

DISRUPTION OF THE POWER BALANCE: SINO-RUSSIAN RELATIONS IN THE 1990S-2000S

The looming collapse of the Soviet Union was greeted with alarm in Beijing. The Chinese leadership grew increasingly cautious of the political transformation in the Soviet Union, and reacted with criticism to the plans of restoring capitalism in the former communist country. Moreover, China was openly supportive of the putschists (the KGB generals), who attempted to preserve at least the core of the Soviet Union by carrying out a coup in August 1991. After Boris Yeltsin quelled the *putsch*, Beijing accused Russia's new leader of dismantling the socialist system, damaging nascent Sino-Russian relations (Wishnick, 2001a: 122). Yet, in spite of mounting ideological differences between China and the Soviet Union, relations between countries were expanding in 1990 and 1991.

During the Chinese Prime Minister Li Peng's visit to Moscow in April 1990, the Soviet Union and China signed a number of agreements on mutual cooperation in the spheres of border security, economics, science and technology, and peaceful use and research of space (Xia, 1997: 24). The most important among them was the agreement on guiding principles of mutual and balanced force reductions and confidence-building measures along the Sino-Soviet border. According to this agreement, China and the Soviet Union expressed their commitment to reduce their troop presence to the lowest level in the area of the Sino-Soviet border, which would pave the way for good neighbourly relations based upon mutual security (Yuan, 1998: 8). Further, during Jiang Zemin's visit to Moscow in May 1991, Moscow and Beijing made significant progress on border issues. Mikhail Gorbachev and Jiang Zemin signed an agreement on the "Eastern Section of the Sino-Soviet Border," which settled 98 per cent of the 7,400 km border stretching from Russia's Vladivostok to Eastern Tajikistan in the Central Asia (Moltz, 1995: 516). Under this agreement, China also received once fought for Zhenbao (Damansky) Island and was allowed free navigation on the Amur River. However, further progress on border-related issues was disrupted by the dissolution of the Soviet Union following the signing of the Belavezha accords in December 1991.

The new leadership of Russia became more focused on forging closer ties with the West, and with the United States in particular, rather than with authoritarian China or the former

Soviet Republics, which Russia nevertheless considered its exclusive sphere of interests. Russian foreign policy thus prioritised Moscow's adherence to democratic values, pluralist institutions, and respect for human rights. This Western-centrism in Russian foreign policy making pioneered by Minister of Foreign Affairs Andrei Kozyrev in the first part of the 1990s could be defined as quixotic, for it expected Russia to be accepted as an equal by Western countries (despite its lack of geopolitical power) and deemed emphasis on relations with China tantamount to the rejection of Western values and identities (Lo, 2002: 23). Although Wilson (2004: 192) argued that Russia's new political elite was largely uninformed and uninterested in China, the new leadership nonetheless deemed Sino-Russian relations necessary and, therefore, did not fully discard them.

By the end of 1992, the Kremlin's pro-Western sentiment gradually began to subside in light of growing U.S. influence in global affairs, especially during the Gulf War in Iraq, and internal opposition to the Kremlin's pro-Western foreign policy. In response to the above-mentioned concerns, during his first visit to China in December 1992, President Boris Yeltsin proclaimed that Russia was seeking balanced relations in both Europe and Asia, admitted common interests between Moscow and Beijing, and also noted that the Taiwan issue was primarily China's internal affair (Rozman, 1998: 400). For its part, China sought to establish better relations with Russia due to the growing diplomatic isolation and sanctions levied against Beijing in the aftermath of the Tiananmen upheaval. Furthermore, China considered the Sino-Russian relationship a counterweight to American influence and a partnership, which would subsequently give way to a multipolar world (Wishnick, 2001b: 800). Thus, the desire to shape a new international order based on multipolarity as opposed to U.S. hegemonism resonated with Beijing and Moscow alike. In his 1994 article in *Foreign Affairs*, Russian Foreign Minister Andrei Kozyrev accordingly maintained: "The international order in the 21st century will not be a *Pax Americana* or any other version of unipolar or bipolar dominance. The United States does not have the capability to rule alone ... the nature of modern international problems calls for solutions on a multilateral basis" (Kozyrev, 1994).

During Jiang Zemin's visit to Moscow in September 1994, Russia and China signed a joint communiqué, which defined the Sino-Russian relationship as a new "constructive partnership" based on the principles of peaceful coexistence, equality, good-neighborliness, friendship, mutually beneficial cooperation, and nonalignment. Further, the 1994 communiqué reaffirmed the parties' commitment to the United Nations as a mechanism for creating a multipolar world order; their mutual respect for each other as major powers; their intolerance for expansionism; and ultimately, their opposition to hegemony, power politics, and the establishment of antagonistic political, military, and economic blocs (Wilson, 2004: 147). This joint declaration reflected Moscow and Beijing's shared concerns over the expansion of the North Atlantic Treaty Organization (NATO) eastwards in particular, and the U.S. role as a global hegemon in general. During the summit in 1994, the two presidents also signed an agreement on the demarcation of the Western part of the Sino-Russian border and expressed their willingness to increase interregional economic cooperation. In June 1995, China's Premier Li Peng attended the second Sino-Russian summit in Moscow, where the Chinese Prime Minister and his Russian counterpart Viktor Chernomyrdin confirmed their mutual support, commitment to maintaining regional stability and cooperating in global affairs. This meeting coincided with deterioration of Russia and China's relations with the United States caused by Taiwanese President Lee Tenghui's visit to the United States and Western criticism of the military intervention in Chechnya (Wishnick, 2001a: 128).

Thus, once again, a power shift in the strategic triangle caused by the U.S. aggressive foreign policy brought China and Russia together in the second half of the 1990s. This period saw a dramatic change in Russian foreign policy and Sino-Russian relations alike. In January 1996, Evgenii Primakov was appointed as Russia's new Minister of Foreign Affairs. This decision was widely perceived as a reorientation of Russian foreign policy toward the East, and namely China and India (Pant, 2004: 21). Unlike his pro-Western predecessor Kozyrev, Yevgenii Primakov, a geopolitically savvy adherent of orientalism and Eurasianism, held that Russia must reassert its interests in Asia and in the Middle East and focus more on developing multilateral cooperation with the former Soviet Republics (Wishnick, 2001a: 800). Like Chinese leaders, Yevgenii Primakov was a staunch advocate for a multipolar world, in which, according to his vision, no country would play a dominant role. The second half of the decade was marked by Russia's reassessment of its geopolitical role in the world, which policymakers in the Kremlin started to associate more with the East rather than West after Moscow's failed rapprochement with the United States.

In April 1996, Russian president Boris Yeltsin and his Chinese counterpart, Jiang Zemin, signed a joint communiqué, which proclaimed a "strategic partnership" between Russia and China and marked a new stage of partnership between Moscow and Beijing directed towards strategic cooperation in the 21st century. The two presidents reiterated their determination to seek a multipolar world and stressed that the new partnership would not be aimed at any third country. Nonetheless, given U.S. assertive policy toward the Taiwan issue and NATO expansion, Moscow and Beijing considered this "strategic relationship" an effective mechanism to counter U.S. power in the world. Furthermore, during the summit, Chinese and Russian leaders announced an ultimate goal of increasing trade toward $20 billion by the end of the century and identified energy, nuclear power, and large-scale construction as priorities for both sides (Garnett, 2001: 46). Besides, in April 1996, China, Russia, Kazakhstan, Kyrgyzstan, and Tajikistan signed the Shanghai agreement, which addressed such issues as confidence-building measures along the shared borders between states, and exchange of information on military exercises. A year later, significant progress was made on the reduction of troops along China's border with the former Soviet countries after the signing of a five-party agreement in April 1997.

During the 1997 Sino-Russian summit in Moscow, Boris Yeltsin and Jiang Zemin again emphasized their shared goal of establishing a multipolar world in a "Joint Declaration on a Multipolar World and the Formation of a New International Order" (Buszynski, 2010: 266). However, rhetoric aside, as China's prospects for cooperation with the United States increased, Beijing's reasons for strengthening relations with Moscow reached their limit (Rozman, 1998: 404). Moreover, economic relations between China and Russia, lagged far behind political achievements. Despite pledges to achieve the level of $20 billion in bilateral trade, both countries fell significantly short of attaining this objective (level of $20 billion was surpassed only in 2004). Accordingly, in 1997, only 5 per cent of Russia's exports flowed to China, and only 2.5 per cent of Chinese exports went to Russia. The prospects of joint Sino-Russian energy projects were overshadowed by the economic crisis in Russia as late of 1998. By the end of the 1990s, bilateral trade between Russia and China was in a steady decline.

STRATEGIC PARTNERSHIP BETWEEN CHINA AND RUSSIA

The friendship between Russian President Vladimir Putin and Chinese President Xi Jinping is turning back in the centre of global powerful relations. Russia and China have strengthened their cooperation and proved their partnership has been getting stronger during this year.

China's shift in strategic focus from the Soviet Union to the United States seems to be the most important geopolitical realignment of the last several years. In addition, Beijing is now proud of having great relations not only with Washington, but also better relations with Moscow than does Washington. The relationship between China and Russia is seen as a mutual and beneficial partnership. Moscow claims that this is the greatest Russian foreign policy achievement during the post-Soviet period.

In May 2016, Boris Titov, co-chairman of the Russian-Chinese Friendship committee and Russia's ombudsman for entrepreneurs' rights commented on the conference titled 'Russia and China: Taking on New Quality of Bilateral Relations', "together we can become a centre that can influence global processes." The sanctions, which have been a major issue in the European-Russian relations, do not pose a great challenge for the cooperation between China and Russia. According to Titov, they do not affect mutual projects where businesses of middle or small size play a role. China creates huge markets and opportunities for the Russian products.

"Politics always contradicts economic interests, business is far away from politics, we need honest and direct relations," the co-chairman stated, drawing the attention to the main obstacles of closer cooperation which comes with excessive bureaucracy and adherence to official rules and formalities of both countries. However, considering China's extent of living experience under sanctions, Russia and China "will be able to go through this period significantly better together."

During Putin's visit to Beijing in June 2016, which was his fourth visit to China since 2013, both countries highlighted the importance of their bilateral relationship. "President Putin and I have unanimously decided that the more complicated the international situation, the more determined we should be, guided by the spirit of strategic cooperation and the idea of eternal friendship," Xi said in a press statement following their talks. "Russia and China stick to points of view which are very close to each other or are almost the same in the international arena," Putin added.

After successful joint naval exercises in the South China Sea in September, the 21st (2016) regular meeting of the Russian and Chinese heads of government, which was held in November 2016, came with the usual agreements and memorandums in St. Petersburg. The major topic of discussion was trade, in particular free trade, the World Trade Organization (WTO), and protectionism. Dimitry Medvedev, Russian's prime minister disagreed with the statement as if the WTO should be destroyed and replaced with something else. He encouraged Chinese premier Li Keqiang to develop integration projects between China and Russia without the other countries of the WTO. Following a new way of a 'Chinese-Russian path', Russia and China would develop their relation in creating bilateral economic projects and integration strategies. Russia has aspirations to increase trade turnover with China to $200 Billion in the next three to seven years, by 2020 as a target.

That said, the two countries have made no small show of trying to expand ties. Nevertheless experts argue that the relationship between China and Russia is imbalanced and fraught: the two countries hold significant cultural prejudices about each other and have different interests that are probable to diverge even more in the next years. Moreover, the Chinese-Russian relationship is an inherently restricted partnership conditioned on its power to rise both parties' interests.

"The reality is that Russian and Chinese relations are probably the best [they've been] in modern history... They're both opposed to a world dominated by a source of power that isn't one of them," said Roy J. Stapleton, founding director of the Kissinger Institute for Chinese-U.S. Studies, and a former U.S. ambassador of Singapore, China and Indonesia. "They both feel threatened by U.S. unilateralism." Stapleton raises the issue of the complicated and winding diplomatic relationships between the U.S., Russia and China. The three countries together represent the largest geographic area. They constitute the most economically powerful and militarily significant states. Furthermore, they hold a quarter of the world's population and an account for 41 percent of its gross domestic product. If all three can agree with one another they could vastly benefit. However, 'two is company and three is a crowd'. Bearing in mind the close proximity of China and Russia, rumours suggest that a two-vs.-one scenario is arising.

At one time, the Soviet Union and China were close to starting a war against each other. Nowadays Russia and China tighten their strategic relations and are seen as building the world's second and third biggest military powers. History seem to suggest that enemies can become friends but as the old saying goes, "keep your friends close and your enemies even closer". Both China and Russia realize the importance of partnership with each other, while remaining suspicious and cautious.

What if Russia's relations with the United States are about to change? What happens if Vladimir Putin and Donald Trump, the currently elected president of the United States of America, follow the rapprochement as both parties claim they want? What if America limits Putin's powerful position in Europe? All those issues have an impact on the strategic partnership to China as well. When talking about the meaningfulness of the renewed strong partnership between China and Russia, we cannot extract one alliance out of the global context but need to see the international cooperation as a whole.

Events from the history between those two countries can serve as a reminder that there is no escaping the fundamental tension between Russia and China when it comes to the need for economic ties with rising powers and developing their world position as leaders. This should be considered in analysing the questions in order to project what the future of China-Russia relations could mean for the regional politics of Asia in an emerging multipolar order.

THE SINO-RUSSIAN RELATIONSHIP IN THE 21ST CENTURY

Since the end of the Cold War, Russia and China have been the only permanent U.N. Security Council members, whose political systems are undemocratic (Grant, 2012: 16). This is one of the main reasons why China and Russia cooperate on a wide range of international issues in an effort to counterbalance the United States and other Western countries. However, there is one important difference in these countries' statuses in global affairs. China's increasing role in world politics is widely associated with its extraordinary economic growth, whereas Russia's assertive posture in the international arena stems from Moscow's nostalgia of its former superpower status and relatively high energy prices, which allowed the Kremlin to salvage its faltering economy after 2000 (Larson and Shevchenko, 2010: 64). Thus, internal weaknesses and fears of U.S. power make Russia and China hold similar positions on many global issues. Moscow and Beijing remain strongly committed to the principle of noninterference in internal affairs of sovereign states mainly due to domestic problems and regional separatism. Further, both countries maintain relations with the pariah states, including North Korea, Iran, Cuba, Myanmar, and Syria, and object to Western sanctions against these regimes. For instance, in 2005, China and Russia blocked U.S. sanctions against Myanmar the Security Council, labeling such efforts as "meddling in internal affairs." The same held true for China and Russia's position on sanctions against Burma (2007), Sri Lanka (2009), Zimbabwe (2008), and, most lately, Syria (2012). With regard to regional affairs, Russia and China cooperate on trade and security issues within the Shanghai Cooperation Organization, but the latter is far from being considered a substantive body, in part, due to disputes between Moscow and Beijing over leadership in the organization (Scheineson, 2009).

The economic partnership between Moscow and Beijing remains the weakest aspect of bilateral relations. Although the volume of bilateral trade has been growing steadily throughout the previous decade reaching $60 billion in 2010, it is still far below its potential. One of the reasons underlying slow progress in establishing closer economic ties between Russia and China is the difference in patterns of economic growth. Accordingly, the strengthening of Russian national currency and a rise in international energy and raw material prices fuelled Russia's economic growth in the 2000s. These developments had a positive impact on Sino-Russian economic relations (Moshes and Nojonen, 2011: 43). However, bilateral trade during 1996-2010 was marked by the decrease in Russia's exports of machinery and transport equipment from 17.7 per cent to 1.3 per cent, whereas exports of raw materials to China increased from 7.1 per cent to 20.6 per cent. By contrast, China's exports of machinery and transport equipment increased from 5.7 per cent in 1996 to 35.4 per cent in 2010, while manufactured goods started to constitute 18.6 per cent of China's exports to Russia as opposed to 7 per cent in 1996. Despite the fact that Sino-Russian trade has been growing remarkably in the last decade (Itoh and Kuchins, 2011), the above-mentioned economic disparity in trade capacities raises grave anxieties that Russia is gradually becoming a "junior partner" in Sino-Russian economic relations, or a natural resource appendage (*pridatok*) to China (Kutchins, 2010: 33). Russia's exports of energy resources to China are likely to either remain on the same level or may even increase in light of Russia's inability to reform its economic structure and China's growing demand for natural resources.

Conclusions

The strategic triangle among the United States, China, and the Soviet union has undergone a host of vicissitudes throughout the last four decades of the Cold War, culminating in a unipolar world order based on U.S. dominance in international relations. The collapse of the power balance within the triangular system in 1991 had a consequential impact on Sino-Russian relations and U.S.-Chinese relations alike. As regards the U.S.-Russian relationship in the new millennium, both powers attempted to forge closer ties with China, albeit not simultaneously, when relations between Washington in Moscow deteriorated. By the end of the 1990s China and Russia began to express their dissatisfaction with U.S. unilateralism, and such a stance was reflected in the countries' shared vision of a multipolar world and the concept of the "strategic relationship directed towards the 21st century." Despite grandiose proclamations of the "strategic partnership," shared vision of a multipolar world, and increased diplomatic cooperation, Sino-Russian relations are utterly lacking in substance. Much like during the Cold War, the relationship between Moscow and Beijing is based upon counterbalancing the United States in global politics, for cleavages within the strategic triangle among the three powers have generally led to the reorientation of China and Russia's foreign policies in the 1990s and late 2000s.

In so far as economic relations between Moscow and Beijing are concerned, notwithstanding increased economic interaction, neither country truly regards another as a strategic partner. Russia still considers its relations with the European Union indispensable, while the United States remains priority for China (Kotkin, 2009). This configuration is unlikely to change in the future: besides military hardware and natural resources, there is little Russia can offer to its "strategic partner." Likewise, most joint projects between Russia and China are aimed at enhancing energy cooperation through building oil and gas pipelines in Central Asia. Given the resource-oriented model of Russia's economy, Moscow will likely remain China's resource and weapons supplier for decades to come. China, for its part, has been using its "strategic" alliance with Russia as "strategic" leverage vis-à-vis Washington. Diplomatic cooperation with Moscow has helped China promote the idea of multipolarity as it relates to Beijing's national interests. It can be assumed that China's relationship with Russia will become irrelevant as soon as China becomes an independent power in global affairs.

This, in all likelihood, will mark the end of the "strategic" partnership between the two powers, paving the way for U.S.-China rivalry.

4

China-Russia-India Security Cooperation and Geopolitical Signalling

The China-Russia relationship has global significance. Particularly when united, these two countries could pose a severe challenge to the US and to the broader liberal international order, a sentiment that was clearly articulated in President Donald Trump's National Security Strategy published in December 2017. The two countries have increased and enhanced their political and security cooperation in recent years. The cooperation takes multiple forms from high-level attendance at each other's military parades to coordinated foreign policy actions, joint military exercises and even joint development of military equipment. How should we interpret these recent trends? How does this cooperation benefit China, which is a much bigger player economically than Russia and rapidly developing its indigenous defence industry? In an attempt to address these questions, this Briefing Paper duly looks at the Chinese motivations for enhanced collaboration with Russia in the political and security spheres.

CHINA-RUSSIA STRATEGIC PARTNERSHIP AND POLITICAL COOPERATION

After the dissolution of the Soviet Union, China's relations with its neighbour improved considerably. In January 2017

China defined Russia as a "priority in diplomacy" in its White Paper titled China's Policies on Asia-Pacific Security Cooperation. In December 2017 Chinese Ambassador to Russia, Li Hui, stated that "The comprehensive strategic partnership of coordination between China and Russia occupies a special position in the major-country diplomacy with Chinese characteristics and is an important manifestation of practicing Xi Jinping Thought on Socialism with Chinese Characteristics for a New Era." These recent developments are remarkable considering the history of the Sino-Soviet split and the fact that the two countries formed their "strategic partnership of coordination" in 1996, only five years after China established diplomatic relations with the Russian Federation. The war in Kosovo accelerated the process of forming closer bilateral ties. Both countries opposed NATO operations in Kosovo as constituting interference in a sovereign state's internal affairs. In China, public opinion turned strongly against the US after NATO's bombing of the Chinese embassy in Belgrade in which three Chinese citizens were killed.

While China has so-called strategic partnerships with multiple countries, the term "coordination" is reserved for describing the China-Russia strategic partnership. At the institutional level, the mechanisms in China's strategic relationship with Russia are the most comprehensive and effective. The presidents, premiers and heads of the National People's Congress and the Duma meet annually. In addition, the two countries have different institutionalized settings for various key sectors, such as the Energy Negotiators' Meeting and China-Russia Strategic Security Consultation. China and Russia are also founding members of the Shanghai Cooperation Organization (SCO), which was established in 2001 and accepted its first new members in June 2017 when India and Pakistan joined the SCO. Particularly where new members are concerned, the SCO lacks cohesion and its regional importance has decreased.

Politically, China and Russia have a common interest in promoting a multipolar world and non-interference in states' internal affairs. The principle of non-interference is mentioned in their 1997 joint communiqué entitled The Russian-Chinese Joint Declaration on a Multipolar World and the Establishment of a New International Order. In the UN context this preference is manifested in voting behaviour on issues involving military intervention and other forms of interference in states' internal affairs. Both China and Russia were against placing the human rights situation in North Korea on the UN Security Council's agenda, for example. Between 2001 and 2012, China and Russia intensified their political cooperation in the UN Security Council and started to show elements of a typical coalition. The two states have, for example, used the double veto more often than before to block US- and EU-initiated draft resolutions. As only one veto would be enough to block a draft resolution, this kind of behaviour can be interpreted as an act of opposition against the dominant Western coalition.

The Sino-Russian treaty of friendship signed in 2001 lifted the bilateral commitments to a new level in its Article 9: "When a situation arises in which one of the contracting parties deems that peace is being threatened and undermined or its security interests are involved or when it is confronted with the threat of aggression, the contracting parties shall immediately hold contacts and consultations in order to eliminate such threats". Perhaps the most significant step on the bilateral front occurred in 2008 when the two countries managed to peacefully resolve their border dispute. In the same year, Chinese and Russian defence ministers also established a direct phone hotline. When Xi Jinping came to power in 2013, he chose Russia as the destination for his first state visit, and became the first foreign leader to visit the Russian military command centre in Moscow. The fact that Xi and Vladimir Putin seem to get along well at a personal level helps in enhancing cooperation, which has become more intimate in comparison with Hu Jintao's years.

After the start of the Ukraine crisis in 2014 followed by Western economic sanctions against Russia, Sino-Russian strategic interests became more congruent. China and Russia have problematic relations with the West, although these relationships represent very different levels of difficulty. Both countries try to diminish Western influences in their respective domestic contexts visible in emphasising traditional values, changing educational policies and increasing censorship. Both must also deal with Western interference with areas regarded as China's and Russia's spheres of influence in these countries. While China named support for multipolarity and anti-hegemonism as its foreign policy goals decades ago indicating that it does not accept the US-dominated international order, its various national interests do not make it possible to give unconditional support to Russia in its dealings with the West. Thus, China supported Russia in the Ukraine crisis tacitly for the most part, as its economic interests were against openly siding with Russia. Sometimes Chinese sources close to the military were more openly anti-US describing it as a hegemon unwilling to adapt to a changed world with newly emerging powers. According to such commentaries, the declining US fights to maintain its primacy by strengthening alliances in the Asia-Pacific region to counter China and by pushing for NATOs eastward expansion to counter Russia. However, Russia's recent actions evoke mixed feelings in China even without the US factor. Justifying the annexation of Crimea based on a popular vote is not exactly a model that China would like to promote considering its problematic domestic situation in autonomous areas such as Tibet and Xinjiang. Regarding the Taiwan question, the Crimean case can be interpreted from multiple perspectives. It can be seen as an example of action based on voting, which would not be in China's interests in a scenario in which Taiwan would declare independence based on a referendum. Alternatively, Crimea could be taken as a case of a stronger state taking over the territory of a weaker party without much opposition, which could be a useful precedent for China's future Taiwan policy.

Despite somewhat different interests, closer cooperation with China can partly compensate Russia for the difficult international position it has been in, especially since 2014. For China, symbolic support from Russia in the international context can also be useful. Concrete examples of Sino-Russian win-win cooperation are the military parades organized in both countries in 2015. Most high-ranking Western politicians boycotted both events, but China and Russia gave each other face by sending their top men to attend each other's parades. Xi Jinping was the guest of honour in Russia's Victory Day parade in May 2015, celebrating the 70-year anniversary of the end of World War II. For China, it was important to have President Putin attend its military parade in September 2015 when most Western countries only sent diplomats or state officials below the top leadership to the event.

The China-Russia relationship is arguably better than it has ever been, manifested in political cooperation in key issues of world politics. Since April 2015, the two countries have held regular meetings under the title of the Sino-Russian Northeast Asian security dialogue in response to US and South Korean negotiations on supplying the Terminal High Altitude Area Defence missile defence system to South Korea. In July 2017 Xi Jinping was in Moscow on a state visit when North Korea conducted its first intercontinental ballistic missile test. After the launch, China and Russia issued a joint statement calling on the United States, South Korea, and North Korea to acquiesce to a "dual freeze" solution: North Korea would freeze its nuclear and ballistic missile testing in exchange for a cessation of conventional exercises by the United States and South Korea. Although this initiative received little support internationally, according to the Chinese foreign ministry, China and Russia will strengthen their coordination on the issue. It is rare for China to issue such joint statements. The country's joint statement with Russia in July 2017 was the first of its kind in ten years issued under the name of both Chinese and Russian Foreign Ministries.

MILITARY ACQUISITIONS FROM RUSSIA

Improved bilateral relations facilitate cooperation in the security realm, although the history of military equipment sales from Russia to China has had multiple twists and turns in recent years. Since the Tian'anmen Square protests of 1989, China has been under an arms embargo from the US, the EU, Australia, Canada, Japan and South Korea. Moscow and Beijing signed an agreement on military technology cooperation in 1992, and since then China has bought more military equipment from Russia than from all other countries combined. Chinese orders accounted for 34–60 per cent of Russian major weapons sales between 1999 and 2006. Russian arms transfers to China peaked in 2005 to the tune of 3.1 billion USD, when China accounted for around 60 per cent of Russian deliveries. After 2005 sales declined sharply, however, falling to 0.6 billion in 2016. There were several reasons for these developments. In the 2000s China had more resources to invest in its military, and its domestic defence industry became more developed than before, decreasing the need to buy equipment from Russia. Russia for its part feared Chinese reverse engineering and refused to sell its most advanced technologies to China. There were accusations that China had copied Russian technologies and sold them to African countries and elsewhere.

While the increasingly sophisticated Chinese defence industry is a stable factor continuously decreasing Chinese needs to buy equipment abroad, the fact that China and Russia managed to gradually overcome the copyright issues related to defence equipment improved trade relations. One step towards further cooperation after a low tide occurred when China and Russia signed an agreement on intellectual property in 2008 to prevent the illegal copying of technologies. After the copyright agreement, and especially since 2015, Russia has gradually agreed to sell China its most advanced military technologies. Siemon Wezeman presents two alternative reasons for Russia's willingness to sell its most advanced products to China, which also currently competes with Russia in arms sales in third markets. Either this was the last chance for Russia to engage in selling military equipment to China or it could be a result of improved bilateral relations. There may be elements of both factors involved. A higher level of trust must have been reached as the parties have been able to move towards joint production in limited areas. In 2011 Russia and China established a joint venture for servicing all Russian-made helicopters operating in China. In 2016, this cooperation was upgraded into a project developing a jointly produced heavy-lift helicopter for China. The two countries have also developed LADA-class submarines, which helps the People's Liberation Army (PLA) improve its noisy submarine fleet. Moreover, China and Russia have signed several research and development agreements on aero-engine technology, the production of space components and satellite navigation systems.

Deals since 2015 include China's purchase of Su-35 fighter jets, ten of which were delivered in 2016 and the second batch in 2017 with the remaining four scheduled for delivery this year. China has also made an advance payment to Russia for S-400 Triumph missile defence systems as Russia's first foreign customer to receive this product. The S-400 units will considerably improve China's anti-access/area-denial capability, which refers to capability consisting of interrelated missile, radar and other technologies designed to deny hostile forces access to the Chinese (coastal) territory. The S-400 could also facilitate China's installation of an air defence identification zone in the South China Sea, which China also threatened to do in the summer of 2016. In addition, the S-400 improves China's position with regard to Taiwan, as well as in the East China Sea where China has an air defence identification zone overlapping with those of Japan and South Korea. Depending on where China places its S-400 systems, they will have the potential to alter the balance of power in multiple Asia Pacific hotspots.

Naturally, China is intent on becoming self-sufficient in military technology as quickly as possible. In the September 2015 military parade, China showcased its advanced domestic technologies such as the so-called "carrier killer" Dongfeng-21D antiship ballistic missiles. In February 2017, the Chinese Ministry of National Defence reported on China's successful trial launch of an intercontinental ballistic missile carrying Multiple Independently Targetable Re-entry Vehicles (MIRVs).

China is also developing hypersonic glide vehicles, which can enhance its anti-access area denial capabilities. China's domestically produced fifth generation fighter jets (J-20) became operational in September 2017 according to Wu Qian, spokesperson for the Ministry of National Defence.

Although there are still areas in which China benefits from Russian sales, it appears that the time for further trade deals may be limited. In non-traditional security fields, however, China and Russia may find areas in which cooperation benefits both parties in the future as well. Online censorship, for example, is a key policy priority for both governments, and China has lengthy experience with its great firewall. This could benefit Russia, which seems to be taking steps towards decreased liberty in Russian cyberspace. In April 2016, the first China-Russia cyber forum was held in Moscow.

JOINT MILITARY EXERCISES

Cooperation with Russia helps China to advance its maritime strategy. China's wider security posture concentrates on improving its maritime strategy and points towards increased overseas engagement as outlined in China's first military strategy published in 2015. The navy is being formed into an elite force for the People's Liberation Army. Other examples of maritime concentration include building of new aircraft carriers and the naval base in Djibouti, which was opened in the spring of 2017. The first indigenously built carrier is estimated to be operational in 2020.

The 2015 Military Strategy states that "China's armed forces will further their exchanges and cooperation with the Russian military within the framework of the comprehensive strategic partnership of coordination between China and Russia, and foster a comprehensive, diverse and sustainable framework to promote military relations in more fields and at more levels". In June 2017 the two countries signed a general plan for bilateral military cooperation for the years 2017–2020. China and Russia have held joint military exercises frequently since the 2005 Peace Mission, which was their first joint exercise involving land, sea and air units. For some years, China and Russia have held their exercises jointly with other countries in the region using the SCO as the organizing body.

There has been qualitative improvement since the first two exercises in 2005 and 2007, moving towards interoperability: in 2009 the final stages of the drills involved joint action and in 2013 the air forces trained together for the first time. Joint military exercises give both countries a wider geographical scope than would otherwise be possible. In most of these exercises, the official agenda has been "anti-terrorist" although the implementation has not always matched such scenarios. Moreover, China and Russia have not shied away from politically sensitive geographical areas: the 2014 exercises were held in the East China Sea where Sino-Japanese tensions were running high at the time. The 2016 drills were held in the contested South China Sea. According to Ethan Meick's report, Russia sent three surface ships, two supply ships, two helicopters as well as amphibious vehicles to these 2016 drills. In addition, training areas have involved the Mediterranean, which is far away from China's territorial waters. In July 2017 Chinese and Russian troops held a joint naval exercise in the Baltic Sea, followed by another exercise in the Sea of Japan in September.

For China, joint maritime exercises have multiple motivations. In addition to political reasons for enhanced cooperation with Russia, China needs to secure shipping lanes as its commercial interests are widespread across the globe. China became the world's number one crude oil importer in 2017 and PLAN may need to participate in securing commercial or energy shipments in the future. The largest oil suppliers to China are Middle Eastern countries such as Saudi Arabia, Iran, Iraq and Oman, as well as Angola and Russia. From Russia, there are direct pipelines to China but part of the Russian oil sales are still transported via sea routes. PLAN also has a lot of catching up to do in operating in seas far away from its own coastline. China has participated in anti-piracy operations near Somalia since 2008, but beyond that PLAN has little experience of operating out of Asia.

THE RUSSIA-CHINA-INDIA TRIANGLE MOVES FORWARD

Soon after Russian Prime Minister Yevgeni Primakov arrived in New Delhi on Dec. 21 for a two-day official visit, a sensational piece of news sounded across the globe: Primakov had publicly called for the formation of a "strategic triangle" among the three giant nations of Russia, India, and China.

Encouraging India to see itself more as a world power, and calling for closer relations not only between India and Russia, but also between India and China, Primakov reportedly stated, "A lot in the region depends on the policies pursued by India, Russia, and China.... If we succeed in establishing a triangle, it will be very good."

As the Indian newspaper The Hindu commented, "The concept of a 'strategic triangle' covering India, China, and Russia, spelt out by the visiting Russian Prime Minister, Mr. Yevgeny Primakov, is of immense significance since this is perhaps the first time that a senior leader from Moscow has made such a statement."

Wasting no time to research the real background of Primakov's remarks, Western and other media were quick to impose their own distorted, mechanistic interpretation. The new "strategic triangle"—they intimated—was Russia's reply to the U.S.-British bombardment of Iraq, the attempt of the weakened and frustrated former superpower to put together a new, anti-Western bloc. When a spokesman of the Chinese Foreign Ministry, reacting to such press reports, emphasized China's strictly independent foreign policy and China's policy not to participate in any sort of blocs or alliances, the headlines of the British press proclaimed triumphally: "You see! China rebuffed Primakov"!

In reality, the Russia-China-India triangle is no new invention made under the pressure of the Iraq crisis, but a crucially necessary feature of the entire Eurasian Land-Bridge development strategy, as repeatedly emphasized by Lyndon LaRouche and others in the pages of EIR. For competently informed persons, the actual emergence of the "strategic triangle" Russia-China-India, became virtually inevitable no later than Chinese President Jiang Zemin's historic speech at the Russian Science City Akademgorodok in Novosibirsk on Nov. 24, 1998.

There, Jiang Zemin put forward the basic principles of a policy to harness Russia's enormous scientific and technological potential, as typified by the "closed cities" of the military-scientific-industrial complex, for the economic development of the entire region. This policy, as Jiang emphasized, is integral to creating a "new, just, and rational world economic order," guaranteeing the sovereign economic rights of the world's developing countries. That same concept was affirmed in the official declarations of both the Chinese-Russian and Russian-Indian summit meetings.

The most appropriate comment to these developments, interestingly enough, came in the pages of China's official foreign press review, Reference News (Can kao xiaoxi) on Dec. 24. Reference News published on its front page a detailed summary of a speech given by Helga Zepp-LaRouche in early December at a conference in Mexico City.

Her speech laid out the background and implications of Jiang Zemin's Novosibirsk speech, and predicted that Primakov would push for the inclusion of India in the new China-Russia development partnership during his (then forthcoming) visit to New Delhi.

What was most significant in the Reference News coverage of Mrs. LaRouche's remarks, however, was her emphasis on the difference in attitude between the Chinese government—which paid attention to LaRouche's analysis and warnings on the financial crisis—and the attitude of most other governments. That fact, indeed, uniquely coheres with China's role as a centre-point of a growing circle of nations devoted to real development around the Land-Bridge policy, at a time when the United States and western Europe are plunging toward a self-imposed "dark age" of financial and socio-economic collapse.

Collision ahead?

It is only in this context, and not from some mechanistic geopolitical standpoint, that can one speak of the Russian-Chinese-Indian triangle as an "answer" to what is increasingly perceived in Asia and elsewhere as a dangerous pattern of insanity coming from the West. The turning-point in that perception was doubtless the outrageous, disgusting performance of Vice President Al Gore at the Kuala Lumpur meeting of the Asian Pacific Economic Cooperation (APEC) forum on Nov. 17. Gore's "globalist" ravings and his brazen attack on Malaysia for asserting its sovereignty against international speculators, are increasingly viewed in Asia as a signal for the same insane, destructive policy and mind-frame, which characterize the Anglo-American attack on Iraq and the closely related escalation of the fraudulent "legal coup" against U.S. President Clinton. All add up to an unprecedented assault against the very institution of the sovereign nationstate—including, emphatically, against the constitutional system of the United States itself. Going handin-hand with a major escalation of British geopolitical destabilizations in the Near East and elsewhere, and a coming, new global financial earthquake of unprecedented dimensions, that assault has already brought the world closer to nuclear war, than anyone could have imagined a mere 12 months ago.

One should not forget, that it was China and India's stubborn insistence on maintaining their sovereignty in the face of "financial globalization," that has so far permitted those two countries to weather the so-called Asian financial crisis, while less prudent nations went under. The striving to restore to Russia a modicum of national sovereignty, is key to the constellation of forces behind the Primakov government. It is above all this issue of national sovereignty and economic development that is placing China, Russia, India, and other Asian nations—despite the repeated, and doubtless sincere affirmations that their growing partnership is not directed against any third party—on a collision course with the "globalist" policy championed by Gore.

The sharp reaction to the Iraq bombing, by Russia and China particularly, is a mild foretaste of what may come. Unequivocal condemnation of the Iraqi bombing was a major point of the Russian-Indian joint declaration signed during Primakov's visit. In an unprecedented action, Russia recalled its ambassadors from the United States and Great Britain, while at the same time calling a limited military alert.

Soon afterward, Russia gave the world a pointed reminder of its continued existence as a nuclear superpower, by deploying the first of its new generation of mobile, high-precision ICBMs. China's representative at the United Nations did not mince words in ripping apart the fraudulent basis for the whole operation, naming UNSCOM director Richard Butler in public. And after the Dec. 28 incident in which U.S. planes enforcing the so-called "no-fly zone" fired on an Iraqi anti-aircraft position, the speaker of the Chinese Foreign Ministry, Zhu Bangzao, declared: "The Chinese side has many times declared that the sovereignty, territory, and independence of Iraq must be fully respected.

China regards the action of creation of a 'no-fly zone' in Iraq as contrary to the United Nations Charter and to standards of international relations." Another, increasingly angry message is implicit in the sharp statements and actions of the Chinese government, in dealing with the Western-supported political opposition movement in China itself.

A growing community of interest

Russia, India, and China make up 22% of the world's land area and over 40% of its population. As the world's largest and most populous developing nations, whose very maintenance requires enormous inputs of science and technology, India and China have a strong common interest in stabilizing and developing Russia. Russia, for its part, can only survive by bringing its scientific and technological potentials into full economic play, which in turn requires large and stable markets for the kinds of industrial goods it can best produce. All three nations have a vital joint interest in Central Asia, and so forth.

They also share, in different ways, the experience of significant joint development in the 1950s. At that time, both India and China profitted greatly from close scientific and technological cooperation with the former Soviet Union—a partnership which was also key, in its direct and indirect effects, to the relatively rapid rates of industrial growth in the Soviet Union in that period. In a limited, but significant way, the transfer of industrial technology and know-how from the Soviet Union to China and India, in that period, helped shape the Non-Aligned Movement's later striving for a "new, just world economic order."

For all these and other reasons, a profound community of interest now exists among the three giant nations. That community of interest is by no means limited to the three alone, but explicitly includes the concept of joint cooperation in other developing countries. It should be noted, for example, that the Russian-Indian agreements signed during Prime Minister Primakov's visit, provide for joint exploration and exploitation of oil and gas resources not only on each other's territories, but also in Kazakstan, Central Asia, and Iraq. Iraq has already been an important oil supplier to India, and India and Russia both have considerable interest in developing petroleum resources there.

But the pathway to consolidation of the Russia-China-India triangle is by no means an easy one. It will be necessary to overcome a long heritage of British geopolitical manipulation in Eurasia. That heritage is lodged above all in false axioms and habits of thinking among the elites, which have permitted the nations of the region again and again to be manipulated against each other in the name of falsely defined, so-called "competitive national interests." The earlier triangle was effectively smashed in the late 1950s and early 1960s, by geopolitical manipulations whose fruits included the Sino-Soviet split, the Sino-Indian war, the apparently "insoluble" Indo-Pakistan conflict, and so on.

One of the notable tools in those British-directed manipulations, incidentally, was none other than the late Armand Hammer, sponsor of the Gore family and supposed "great friend" of the Soviet Union. Some painful rethinking of old mistakes will be needed on all sides, if Russia and its partners want the "Great Triangle" to succeed today. That means above all gaining a more competent under-standing of the historical conflict between the United States and Britain—or in other words, why Lyndon LaRouche has the friends and foes he has.

LaRouche's ideas circulate in Russia by Rachel Douglas

One new publication and one reprint, issued in Moscow at the end of 1998, have put key strategic writings of Lyndon LaRouche into circulation among Russian-speakers.

Bulletin No. 8 of the Schiller Institute for Science and Culture (Moscow) is headlined "Russia's Relation to Universal History," and features LaRouche's "Letter to a Russian Friend," which was published under that title in EIR of Nov. 29, 1996. The subject-matter resonates with Chinese President Jiang Zemin's recent address to Russian scientists at the Novosibirsk centre of the Russian Academy of Sciences, as LaRouche develops why the greatest strength of Russia, defining its potential to make a decisive contribution to saving mankind, is the quality of bold, "dissident" thinking by the Russian scientific intelligentsia. The preservation of Russian science and collaboration with Russia on "such great projects of reconstruction and progress as are urgently wanted for the benefit of both Russia itself and Eurasia more generally," LaRouche writes, is in the vital interests of every nation, especially the United States.

Pictured here is the other justissued publication, a reprint of the proceedings of the April 24, 1996 round table held at the Free Economic Society in Moscow, at which LaRouche was hosted by Academicians Leonid Abalkin and Gennadi Osipov, to speak on "Russia, the U.S.A., and the Global Financial Crisis." The 92-page booklet is published by the Institute of Social and Political Research (ISPI) of the Russian Academy of Sciences, with an introduction by ISPI's director, Academician Osipov. In his keynote at the round table, LaRouche developed the need to revive Franklin Delano Roosevelt's design of collaboration among the United States, Russia, and China for genuinely post-colonial development of nations after World War II.

RUSSIA-INDIA PARTNERSHIP LIFTED TO NEW HEIGHTS

This visit reinforced interests of both states in maintaining their traditionally close and friendly relationship and in strengthening a multipolar world order. In recent times, both India and Russia have been pursuing a multi-vector approach in their foreign policies. This visit was Indian Prime Minister Modi's second visit to Russia within a year's time; his first visit was in July 2015 to Ufa (Russian Federation) to participate in the BRICS (Brazil-Russia-India-China-South Africa) and SCO (Shanghai Cooperation Organisation) Summits.

The bilateral relationship between India and Russia was revived with the declaration of a Strategic Partnership between the two countries during the visit of President Putin to India in the year 2000. Since then the Indo-Russian relationship has diversified enormously and today it is uniquely strong and also expanding in the areas of defence, nuclear energy, hydrocarbons, space research, science & technology. Prime Minister Modi's recent visit re-activated the ties between two countries. During this visit India and Russia signed number of significant agreements, including the agreement for manufacturing of Kamov 226 helicopters in India. This is going to be the first project for a major defence platform under Modi's 'Make in India' policy, and also to enhance the defence partnership between Russia and India. Cooperation on number of other significant defence projects would also boost defence cooperation.

Bilateral cooperation in nuclear energy is increasing over the years. India and Russia made progress regarding twelve Russian nuclear reactors at different sites. The agreement on nuclear cooperation will increase Indian manufacturing content for these reactors. This also supports Prime Minister Modi's 'Make in India' mission. Other benefits from this agreement would include research and development, construction of nuclear plants and reprocessing of spent fuel. The signing of this landmark inter-governmental agreement on the peaceful use of atomic energy between the two countries has the potential to expand the horizon of nuclear relationship between the two Nations.

Prime Minister Modi mentioned that Russia being world's largest reserves of hydrocarbons can be a critical source of energy security for India; hence, the agreements signed for Indian investments in Russian hydrocarbon sector will enhance energy cooperation between two countries. Agreement for cooperation for geologic survey, exploration and production of on-shore hydrocarbons between Rosneft Oil Company, Oil India Limited and Indian Oil Corporation Limited has been signed during this visit.

India and Russia are also moving towards expanding the economic relationships which is the weakest link in the bilateral cooperation. It has been observed that in spite of accelerated growth and immense opportunities in each other's economy, statistics show business transaction is much less than the real potential. Promises had been made by the leaders of both countries earlier, but not much has happened. However, to put these words into practice and strengthen the economic relationship, India has created a special notified zone to facilitate direct trade between the world's largest uncut diamond exporters (Russia and India process 90% of the world's uncut diamonds and will now cooperate in this sector successfully).

Also the work on logistics is going on to make trade and economic cooperation faster. The Green Corridor project took off and the International North South Transit Corridor (INSTC) through Iran is expected to significantly reduce transportation time and cost. Now India and Russia are also moving forward to fulfil the India-Eurasian Economic Union (EEU) Free Trade Agreement. This will also benefit to connect Central Asia easily. The agreements and the announcements made during this visit gave confidence that now India and Russia will see huge increase in investments and trade from both directions.

Prime Minister Modi and President Putin assured strong commitment to deepen the cooperation in the international arena too. Prime Minister The leaders agreed that early political settlement through dialogue in West Asia is essential for restoring stability and containing extremism in the region. There is a close synergy in Indo-Russia perspectives. The joint declaration reinforced the warmth that exists between the two countries. Although differences arise over certain issues on certain occasions, the overall parallelism in the India-Russia relationship definitely symbolizes the trust that still exists between the two nations.

RUSSIA-INDIA STRATEGIC PARTNERSHIP: HAVE WE HIT A PLATEAU?

The President of the Russian Federation achieved yet another success while treading the "three seas" at the BRICS Summit in Goa, especially for large Russian companies that are growing their businesses in India. However, despite the fact that Moscow and New Delhi were able to reach new agreements on military and technical cooperation and energy, both countries will have to take a serious look at their approach to building relations if they want to take their partnership to the next level.

The BRICS Summit took place in Goa on October 15–16 and reaffirmed yet again the close partner ties enjoyed by Russia and India. In keeping with tradition, the BRICS platform was chosen as the venue for preliminary agreements and contracts on military and technical cooperation and energy to be signed. However, despite the impressive set of documents signed in Goa, it would seem that cooperation between Moscow and New Delhi has lost its former dynamism and, in terms of size and import, is far from the declared "Strategic Partnership" that has characterized Russia–India relations since 2000. The latest summit can serve as a convincing reason to try and discover exactly what it is that could threaten the partnership between Russia and India in the future and what is preventing this relationship from moving to the next level.

A Farewell to Arms

As always, the recent BRICS Summit was fruitful for the Russian defence industry. Military and technical cooperation traditionally serves as a driver of the Russia–India partnership. Moscow is the largest supplier of military equipment to India, with contracts worth more than $5 billion signed since 2012. At the same time, India is the world's biggest importer of military equipment, and it is little surprise that Russian suppliers are facing increasing competition on the Indian market.

An intergovernmental agreement was signed in Goa on the supply of modern Russian S-400 missile systems to India. A contract worth somewhere in the region of $4.5 billion is expected to be signed in early 2016. The sides also signed an agreement on the purchase by India of Russian naval ships. In addition, an agreement has been reached between Russia's Rosoboronexport and the Indian company HAL on the creation of a joint venture to localize production of Kamov Ka-226 helicopters in India.

Although India has been the leading purchaser of Russian weapons since 2007, Russia's share in the Indian arms market has been shrinking gradually in recent years. The trend is unmistakable. The first hints appeared in 2012, when the Russian MiG-35 lost out in a tender for the purchase and localization of production of 126 fighter jets for the Indian Air Force to the French *Rafale*. By the end of 2014, Russia had relinquished its position as India's leading arms supplier to United States

The most recent tenders have demonstrated that tactical and technical products may not be enough in the long term to secure the custom of the Indian side.

Russian companies have failed primarily because India considers developing its own defence industry to be a priority, while the Russian side is not prepared to accept all of the conditions connected with localizing arms production, including as part of the *Make in India* programme to stimulate industrial production. The Indian Armed Forces are also unhappy with the fact that delivery deadlines have been missed. One of the most high-profile examples of this was the late delivery of the *Vikramaditya* (formerly the *Admiral Gorshkov*) aircraft carrier. It is against this background that the Indian political establishment is keeping a close, and rather exasperated, eye on the supplies of advanced weapon systems to China and the burgeoning military and technical cooperation between Russia and Pakistan.

Considering the amount of weaponry sold to India throughout the 2000s, it could be argued that Russia does not need to worry about losing the Indian market in the foreseeable future, as the Armed Forces are heavily dependent on supplies of Russian components. However, the most recent tenders have demonstrated that tactical and technical products may not be enough in the long term to secure the custom of the Indian side. New Delhi will expect foreign suppliers to make lucrative offers that involve the transfer of technologies so that it can create its own production base and develop the Indian defence industry.

Oil in Exchange for Investments

Energy is another source of pride in the Russia–India strategic partnership. In the long term, this could be of even greater benefit that the arms trade. And nuclear energy has been on the agenda of bilateral relations for a long time now. The official ceremony to mark the commissioning of the Kudankulam Nuclear Power Plant was held during the Summit in Goa, and the ground of units 3 and 4 was broken. In addition to nuclear energy, the oil and gas sector is also showing increasing promise in terms of bilateral cooperation. India has always shown great interest in purchasing Russian oil and gas, but the logistical difficulties, coupled with the fact that India could satisfy its energy needs by purchasing oil and gas in Europe, meant that Russian suppliers saw no benefit in developing such projects. However, it would be short-sighted to ignore the Indian market at a time like this: energy prices are low, and the Indian economy is stepping up oil imports faster than any other country, including China.

It would be short-sighted to ignore the Indian market at a time like this: energy prices are low, and the Indian economy is stepping up oil imports faster than any other country, including China.

Rosneft announced at the BRICS Summit that it has signed a deal, alongside its partner, the major independent oil trader *Trafigura*, to purchase the Indian company *Essar Oil* for around $13 billion. As part of deal, Rosneft will receive a 49-per cent stake in the Vadinar Refinery, the second largest refinery in India in terms of volume, as well as a chain of 2700 *Essar* gas stations. The oil will most likely be delivered from Venezuela, where Rosneft has production and exploration operations, and sold primarily on the Indian market, or exported from there to South Asia and South East Asia. The deal has strategic importance for the Russian company: the acquisition of *Essar* will give it a presence on the world's fastest growing oil market, with 70 per cent of its requirements coming from imports. Moving forward, it may be able to apply pressure on suppliers from the Gulf, which have rushed to fill the void left by Russia after it was forced to withdraw from the European markets following the sanctions.

While Russian oil companies, faced with falling prices and international sanctions, are interested in foreign processing companies, the Indian side is doing the exact opposite, seeking to gain access to the sources of raw materials. In May 2016, the Indian company *ÎNGC Videsh* bought a 15-per cent stake in the Vankor Field from Rosneft, and in September it signed an agreement to purchase another 11 per cent. At the same time, Rosneft is discussing the possibility of selling a further 23.9 per cent of the field with a consortium of Indian investors that includes *Oil India, Indian Oil Corporation* and *Bharat Petro Resources*. Vankor Field will account for the largest amount of Indian investment in oil production in Russia since Indian companies purchased shares in Sakhalin-1.

The role of India as a potential investor in the Russian oil and gas industry is growing. This much is clear from information coming out of India (but which has yet to be confirmed in Russia) suggesting that Moscow is considering India as a possible participant in the upcoming partial privatization of Rosneft.

Getting Russian gas onto the Indian market appears to be a much more difficult proposition. The contract between Gazprom and GAIL for the supply of 2.5 million tonnes of liquefied natural gas starting in 2018/2019 for a period of 25 years was signed back in 2012. However, development of the Shtokman field, which was to supply the raw materials, has been frozen, and Gazprom does not currently have the output capacity to fulfil its obligations. It is expected that the gas will be delivered to India from the Yamal LNG plant, the first train of which is planned to be commissioned in late 2017. In addition to the technical difficulties, it seems that Gazprom will also be faced with commercial risks: the fall in gas prices has caused India to re-examine the delivery prices in its long-term contracts.

Have We Hit a Plateau?

Unfortunately, the isolated successes of Russian arms dealers and energy companies in India that were covered in glorious detail during the Goa Summit do not alter the fact that the strategic partnership between Russia and India has seemingly hit a plateau. And without serious political will, this plateau will not be overcome in the near future.

When the Declaration on Strategic Partnership between the Republic of India and the Russian Federation was signed in 2000, the trade turnover between Russia and India was a modest $1.5 billion. The foreign trade departments of the two countries decided then to increase this rather embarrassing figure to $10 billion (which is far more fitting of a strategic partnership) by 2010. That goal was reached only in 2012, however, which turned out to be the peak year in terms of trade turnover between Russia and India. Trade dropped to $7.83 billion in 2015, which falls well below Moscow's expectations of its cooperation with New Delhi.

Unfortunately, the isolated successes of Russian arms dealers and energy companies in India that were covered in glorious detail during the Goa Summit do not alter the fact that the strategic partnership between Russia and India has seemingly hit a plateau.

The devaluation of the rouble obviously had an impact on this drop in 2015. But this should not divert our attention from the systemic problems: the old model of partnership based on cooperation in strategic industries (or, in simpler terms, in industries where the government has a big presence), has exhausted its growth potential. India has been paying special attention to its relations with developed countries ever since the current government under the leadership of Narendra Modi came to power – the United States, Japan, Australia, France, Germany and the United Kingdom. As far as the Indian leadership is concerned, these countries are sources of investments, investments that India sorely needs in order to modernize its infrastructure and speed up economic growth. With this in mind, relations with Russia are no longer a major priority in India's foreign policy objectives. And there may not be enough administrative leverage to further stimulate the development of an economic partnership on orders from above.

The old model of partnership based on cooperation in strategic industries has exhausted its growth potential.

In order to bring economic ties to a new level, it is necessary to expand the product range. This will allow private companies and ordinary citizens, and not only state corporations, to contribute to the trade turnover between the two countries. Relations between Russia and the other Asian giant, China, are developing according to this model. To compare: trade turnover between Russia and China totalled roughly $68 billion in 2014. And we are not just talking about arms and raw materials here. Russians spent around $3.5 billion in Chinese online stores in 2014, which is around the same price as the contract for the supply of the S-400 missile systems to India. And customers spend an average of less than $20 on these online orders.

If the partnership between Russia and India does not go beyond the "strategic" sectors in the near future and does not expand to include goods and services, then relations between Moscow and Delhi risk being reduced to an investment and economic partnership of little note.

RUSSIA AND INDIA: TOWARDS A NEW AGENDA IN TRADE AND ECONOMIC RELATIONS

The Indian economy has entered a complicated period of development, despite the fact that the country avoided the impact of the 1997-1998 Asian crisis and was able to maintain high growth rates. It is agreed for India that a minimum or "politically secure" level of economic growth is at least 7 percent per year. Any growth rates below this threshold are regarded as "critical" while the "politically desirable" economic growth rates are 9 percent or above. Although in 2012 economic growth fell below 6 percent, the Indian economy is expected to pick up in early 2013.

India's economic potential has grown significantly. The country is trying to achieve two objectives simultaneously, both to complete "classical" industrialization while also continuing to develop heavy industry (chiefly the power industry), and expanding scientific and technological innovation services, information and communication technologies, scaling up outsourcing, expanding the banking sector, and cooperating with international high-tech companies. India's interest in modernization technologies amounts to a clear trend in India's economic development. Meanwhile, international companies are predominantly using licensing and service provision contracts in their operations with India (due to persistent limitations on foreign direct investment and local subcontractors' rapidly increasing capacity). The long-term government policy that refrained from criticizing India's citizens, including skilled specialists and researchers, for going to other countries has produced good results. The government made efforts to maintain regular ties with them. In 2010, net cash transfers to India from this foreign diaspora totalled $53.124 billion.

Deteriorating global trade conditions in the context of the Indian economy's increasing openness to global economic trends and processes has a negative impact on the prevailing mood in Indian society. One of the manifestations of the country's declining foreign economic vigour is the growing mutual disappointment within Indian and U.S. business communities with the prospects and results of joint activities aimed at "opening" their respective markets.

One of the new political and socio-economic factors expected to gain influence in the medium term is India's middle class (numbering between 100 and 400-500 million people). One of the likely outcomes of this phenomenon is the growing role to be played by small-and medium-sized businesses on India's political field.

Medium-sized businesses are mainly entrepreneurs who entered the market thanks to reforms carried out in the 1990s. They typically view the idea of the Soviet Union's role in Indian industrialization as a myth; many of them were educated in Western countries, and have little interest in business relations with Russia, which is to a certain extent due to unclear foreign economic policies pursued by Russia with regards to India.

Problems and Prospects of Bilateral Trade and Economic Relations

Despite the "privileged political partnership" status between Russia and India, trade and economic ties are still the weakest link in bilateral relations. One impediment is Russian foreign economic players' limited awareness of qualitative shifts in India's economy and a relatively low level of mutual trade operations. To maintain the "privileged" status of Russia-India relations, it is important to outline guidelines for our foreign economic activities. Practice shows that good economic and socio-political motivation providing a positive impetus for maintaining bilateral relations can be achieved at a minimum level of trade turnover reaching at least $17-18 billion.

It is necessary to strengthen ongoing work done by bilateral committees and raise the efficiency of control over how decisions that are made by these bodies are implemented. The final documents often reiterate one goal, for example, reaching the target figure of $10 billion in trade turnover between Russia and India, while this indicator has been well below the declared target for many years. It is quite obvious that reinvigorating traditional approaches to cooperation can boost trade and economic relations: upgrading enterprises built in India with Soviet assistance, military and technical cooperation, and nuclear power industry. In 2011 the volume of Russia-India trade turnover amounted to $9 billion. This low indicator can be explained, above all, by logistics problems. Therefore the volume of foreign economic ties between India and, say, China ($73.9 billion) should not be used as a benchmark, as the share of trans-border trade and exchange operations is quite significant in that relationship.

Unblocking transport routes linking Russia and India could become a powerful incentive for the growth of Russia-India trade and economic ties. This implies primarily "unfreezing" the North-South international transport corridor. What is needed here is streamlining multimodality, developing linear maritime traffic, building container trains and a uniform transportation system at fixed tariffs within the declared transit time spot, and granting customs benefits. Interaction with Iran could lend an impetus to reestablishing the Moscow – Tehran – Delhi geo-economic triangle. The existing visa regime remains an important problem blocking the strengthening of trade and economic ties. It appears that, with the relevant political will displayed by Russia, the visa regime could be liberalized in the near future.

A preferential trade agreement with India seems quite a realistic prospect, and could even be signed in the near future, facilitating an increase in Indian exports. As the world leader in diamond cutting, India is keen to receive Russian diamonds directly and is ready to set up joint companies for jewellery exports. In the pharmaceutical industry it is the Russian consumer that will definitely reap the benefits from Russia-India cooperation, as high-quality Indian drugs are significantly cheaper as compared to other imported equivalents. In the power industry, the greatest hopes have been related to the development of nuclear energy. However, cooperation in this area has failed to achieve the desired goals: after the Fukushima disaster anti-nuclear sentiment was running high in the Indian population, nourished by Russia's competitors (primarily from the United States). In effect, India adopted a law on nuclear power station builders' responsibility for any damage incurred during the facility's operation. Given the volume of contracts operated by Rosatomstroi, India has more to gain from this cooperation than Russia. Therefore, Russia must adopt a firm stand and suspend cooperation in this area. In the meantime, there is a clear need to build partnerships with Western companies (Germany's Siemens is probably the best choice in this respect) and major Indian private businesses, as India will soon pass a law allowing private capital investment in this sphere (Indian companies such as Larsen, Tubro and Tata could be potential partners). In the medium-term it would be advisable to start cooperating with India in the area of building fast neutron reactors, as Russia so far has no competitors in this area. Russia's position on India's nuclear market could be strengthened by vigorously stepping up production within Russia of small and medium capacity plants (for large Indian cities) in cooperation with Indian partners.

There are few prospects in hydropower energy due to the fact that Russian Federation has stopped manufacturing equipment for small and medium capacity hydropower stations, which are the focus of India's interest. It would be equally important for Russia to continue efforts aimed at expanding gas supply systems in India. According to existing estimates, gas consumption in the country will increase 70 percent by 20205.

It is also important to participate in India's electrification. It appears quite reasonable to sign in the coming year an agreement on creating joint ventures to supply gas to Indian brown coal to generate electricity powered by gas turbines. Hydrocarbon supplies to India are unlikely to yield many benefits due to the considerable delivery distances involved. There is therefore a need to identify new supply patterns. One such pattern involves creating new hydrocarbon production joint ventures in Russia (based on Sakhalin-1 example) and in third countries (chiefly in Central Asia). The hydrocarbons received via these channels could be sold by India to its partners. It would be advisable to review swap deals in this sphere.

The anticipated sharp rise in the size of the middle class (600 million people by 2030) with a consumption level comparable with that of Europe and environmental problems will push India to identify new ways of providing food supplies. Russia could be a natural partner in this area, helping to resolve this problem. Bilateral cooperation in the agricultural sector might open up Russia's path to the widely acclaimed achievements of Indian agricultural science. Russia is especially interested in raising India's investment in the Russian agro-industrial sector. India has to date retained high import duties for agricultural produce (the average duty on farm produce in the fiscal year of 2010-11 stood at 33.2 percent, compared with import duties on other kinds of produce, which stood at 8.9 percent). That is why there is a clear need to develop joint projects rather than relying on exporting finished products.

In particular, a pilot project on cooperation between our countries' breadbasket areas – Russia's Stavropol and Krasnodar regions and India's Punjab and Haryana states – looks very promising. Russia could offer to lease out land plots for farming in exchange for new jobs in Russia and Indian farming technologies. The prospects of building further links between Russian research (and its resources) and India's engineering skills (which can be witnessed already in the military realm) supplemented by low-cost Chinese labour with sufficient quality level look extremely promising.

Bringing together India's software production capacity with Russian hardware and software exports also has potential to deliver positive results. In the innovations sphere it would also be rational to explore the possibility of targeted support for Russian projects in the Skolkovo Innovation Centre. It is important to consider various different approaches to boosting Indian investment where it has the potential to support Russian innovation projects that will eventually gain a presence on the Indian market.

RUSSIA-INDIA RELATIONS: NEW AGENDA IN MILITARY-TECHNICAL COOPERATION

India is one of the world's largest national arms markets, behind the United States, Saudi Arabia, and (until recently) China. However, India's military-technical cooperation (MTC) with foreign countries pursues the exclusive aim of strengthening its own security, and therefore is unlikely to have a negative impact on regional security in South Asia. India's elites (supported by a significant proportion of the society) are keen to continue substantial "supplementary arming" of India, considering it a deterrent to the "geopolitical expansion" of China, a country that has experienced problematic relations with India following the border conflict in 1962, and as a means of implementing the military-political doctrine of India that aims to transform the "Elephant" into a leading force in the area from "Suez to Singapore."

India is diversifying the products supplied on the Indian market by a variety of foreign manufacturers, working towards saturating its defence-industrial complex with science and technology capacities, including broad based "naturalization" of foreign ideas and R&D. The main purpose of this is to stimulate the creation and development of domestic original ideas and solutions. The main feature of India's MTC is the trend aimed at purchasing weapons systems that are manufactured in accordance with individual requirements of Indian customers. Almost all newly-purchased air and sea platforms feature cockpit equipment and armaments from various manufacturers. As a result, India has enjoyed access to the maximum number of technologies that are available on the market.

Due to the stable trend in India's MTC towards focusing on the quality and technological prowess of purchased products the importance of price factors has declined. For several decades, India has been purchasing large consignments of armaments together with licenses allowing domestic production. However, the Indian industry is currently experiencing considerable difficulties as it tries to develop licensed production of high-end weapons systems. The country's defence industry does not seem able to substitute arms imports in the foreseeable future.

Since the early 1980s, India has been trying to implement its own national programs to manufacture major weapons systems. To date, most projects have not entered serial production, with the results India has demonstrated in creating an advanced national defence-industrial complex being far from encouraging. Limited success has been achieved only in ballistic missiles production.

Meanwhile, the practice of organizing tenders for arms and military equipment purchase as a means of internal political struggle has emerged in India. The domestic political opposition invariably declares that tender results do not serve the country's best interests and has accused the ruling party of corruption. This practice has now resulted in extreme delays around tender procedures: the bidding process can last a very long time due to fears it could trigger a political crisis or that tender results could be cancelled and the tender reopened.

STATUS, PROBLEMS AND PROSPECTS OF RUSSIA-INDIA MILITARY-TECHNICAL COOPERATION

Russia is a major exporter of arms and military equipment to India. Russia accounts for 55.3 percent of all purchases made by India in this area in 2008-2011. Overall the portfolio of orders contracted for March 2013 amounts to $10.3 billion.

*For reference. The United Kingdom was the second-largest exporter of military equipment to India in 2008-2011 at $2.007 billion. Orders booked in 2003-2010 comprise $4.094 billion. Israel ranks third at $1.839 billion and has an order book of $3.452 billion. The United States ranks fourth with $1.144 billion (and $3.986 billion on order), while Italy comes fifth with $690 million (and an order book of $4.23 billion). Overall, India imported armaments from 14 countries in 2008-2011*6.

In 2012-2015, Russia's share in the Indian arms market will fall to 37.5 percent, whereas maintaining leadership in absolute figures. This is related to several factors:

- India's diversification policy;
- Russia's inability to compete with other countries on a full range of purchased arms and military equipment (while India increases the number of areas for MTC);
- Our main competitors' consent to supply licenses for military production and the most advanced weapons to India (which they often refused to do previously);
- Indian armed forces' efforts to acquire the most combat-effective systems with payment issues being moved to the background.

The Indian party has consistently raised issue of state control over the quality of products and after-sales services exported expressing dissatisfaction with the "superfluous" (intermediary) links in the Russia-India military-technical cooperation.

MTC with India may have a favourable effect on the industrial structure of the national economy due to the programs' long-term nature and consistently significant purchase volumes. There is a clear need to approach the Indian market with unique solutions and technologies on operations and sub-strategic levels (in the area of missile defence, missile warning systems, nuclear-powered submarines, and missile technology) along with the opportunity to link these deliveries with conventional arms procurement. Russia may also join the Indian program to build INS Arihant nuclear submarines (multiple flaws were identified after the first submarine was built).

It is necessary to find a breakthrough branch in military-technical cooperation with India. This could be a major project for a national missile warning system and air defence development (the Indian system is based on outdated Soviet technology). The Indian party is very interested in developing a modern AMD system. This is an area in which the Russian Federation is in a position to offer India new developments, particularly in long-range air defence systems demonstrating extensive anti-missile potential, such as the Antey-2500 military air defence system, the Tor-M2E-2 and Buk-M2E anti-aircraft missile systems, and new modifications such as the C-400 (C-500 for the future). The Russian party could facilitate the joint design and production of a fifth-generation light fighter, given the advanced aviation know-how that already exists in the national defence complex.

The two countries' participation in joint projects involving third countries (chiefly Israel) seems a promising and profitable avenue for both parties to explore. Criticism consistently levelled by the Indian side over delays in spare parts delivery for imported Russian military equipment is largely caused by the Russian side's cumbersome bureaucracy. Claims to Russian enterprises go through Rosoboronexport, resulting in delays that may last several months. Reputable companies should be selectively allowed to perform independent operational interventions.

The time schedules followed by Western competitors should be used as benchmarks (replacing a unit normally takes 3-4 days). There is also a clear need to align servicing operations and provide technical maintenance for Russian equipment through to the end of service life, as other vendors do when dealing with India.

It would also be advisable to establish and finance an adequate and aggressive information support strategy for military cooperation, neutralizing the negative propaganda funded by Russian companies' competitors. Particular attention should be paid to Indian professional defence and technology sector magazines, while special emphasis should be placed on working with them. These magazines play a crucial role in shaping the opinion of the national military elite and that of the individuals that make decisions on MTC.

CONCLUSION

The three areas of cooperation discussed above demonstrate a trend of increased and enhanced Sino-Russian coordination.

Russia has sold China its most advanced military technologies, and although weapons sales have their limits due to China's rapid domestic development, future cooperation in the form of joint production is possible in areas not restricted to helicopters. Moreover, cooperation is already underway in areas of non-traditional security, such as cyber security.

Asia is a large and important market for the Russian military industry and Russia naturally avoids placing all of its eggs in one basket by continuing to sell arms to India and Vietnam, which is not in China's interests. Russia also conducts military exercises with other Asian countries in addition to China. Nonetheless, recent sales of military equipment to China combined with sophisticated military exercises taking a wider geographical scope than ever before serve as an efficient form of geopolitical signalling.

Despite deepened cooperation, China and Russia are not allies and any formal military alliance between the two countries is not in sight either. This is mainly due to the widening gap between the two countries' respective global power positions. China's relative rise will continue, whereas Russia's position is likely to decline. A formal alliance in the foreseeable future under the increasingly asymmetrical power balance would push Russia to adopt a subordinate role, which it will be unlikely to accept. However, as long as opposing the US or the West more broadly forms congruent interests, the Sino-Russian marriage of convenience will prevail.

5

Relations between Russia, China and Pakistan in Context of Russian-Indian Partnership

According to Nandan Unnikrishnan, no country should object to another country's collaboration with a third country if it does not affect its strategic interests. "If Russian military sales to Pakistan or China do not upset the existing balance of power of these countries with India then India should not object. Similarly, if India is seeking a closer military relationship with the United States it should not be a matter of concern to Russia as long as Russia' strategic balance vis-à-vis the US is not upset", the expert said.

However, it must be noted that while Russia and the US do not have currently any direct territorial dispute, that is not the case with China and Pakistan vis-à-vis India. "India has a direct long standing dispute with these two countries, which effectively makes them India's enemies. Therefore, it is natural that Russia's collaboration with them is a matter of intense concern for India", the expert noted.

"Russia clearly has a pragmatic leadership which would not want to jeopardise a multi-billion dollar relationship with India for a few million dollars' deals with Pakistan. As for China, it is natural for Russia to want to sell weapons, because that window may close after another couple of years given China's advances in developing its own technologies. But, that does not mean that India has to like it", the expert said.

COOPERATION IN THE ARCTIC

Nandan Unnikrishnan recalled, that president Vladimir Putin in an article to Indian media wrote that "the possibilities for the participation of Indian companies in joint hydrocarbons exploration and production projects in the Russian Arctic shelf are currently under consideration".

"India certainly is exploring the possibilities of cooperation with Russia in the Arctic region. Currently, the focus is primarily on two areas – natural resources and transport connections. India is also an observer in the Arctic Council and would be interested in being actively involved in the work of this organization", the expert said.

According to C. Raja Mohan, over the last decade and more India has closely followed the developments in the Arctic region amidst the new opportunities and challenges emerging for the international community. There is special concern about the melting of the Arctic ice cap and its environmental, economic and strategic consequences. "Russia is of course a major littoral county of the Arctic and is a natural partner for India. During their last meeting at the end of 2016, Prime Minister Modi and President Putin had discussed the prospect for participation of the Indian companies in the development of the energy resources of the Arctic shelf. The two leaders should take that discussion forward for a more comprehensive and strategic collaboration in the Arctic",the expert said.

PROBLEMS OF CULTURAL AND HUMANITARIAN COOPERATION BETWEEN RUSSIA AND INDIA

Russia is perceived as a potential geopolitical ally capable of helping boost India's status in international relations. Concepts that are popular among the Indian audiences such as BRICS and (to a lesser degree) the Russia-India-China "triangle" contribute to a positive perception of the prospects for bilateral relations. Based on this premise it seems reasonable to note that Russia-India relations are characterized by equal partnership, while economic cooperation is not limited to trade but in effect amounts to full-fledged cooperation, the exchange of knowledge and technology.

The positive image of Russia mainly results from its leading positions in space exploration, nuclear energy and military equipment production, which creates favourable conditions for cooperation in these areas. However, outside these areas, Russia is perceived in India as falling behind in economic development.

Bilateral cultural cooperation operates against a backdrop of fierce competition over influence on India in which the United States has a considerable advantage. In recent decades Russia has been losing the advantages it enjoyed previously with regard to India, mainly due to the lack of information and communication tools. This creates certain prerequisites for Delhi's shift towards greater interaction with other states. The main negative factor in Russia-India relations is that Moscow continues to treat India as a secondtier nation, invoking a similar response from Delhi. In the Indian *Nonalignment Report 2.0: India's Foreign Policy and Strategy in the 21st Century,* released in 2012, in terms of its importance to India, Russia is listed as a third tiernation. Although the report is not an official document it nevertheless reflects the prevailing sentiment in India.

Views about Russia are mainly based on information obtained during the Soviet period. More than half of India's population believes that Russia and the Soviet Union is one and the same country, and that only the name has changed. Less than 50 percent of respondents are familiar with the basic facts, while only a tiny proportion of the audience has any detailed understanding of the country. This pattern is characteristic of all social groups including the most educated and economically active strata. An acute shortage of information is apparent: people in India receive virtually no information about Russia via conventional channels. Taking into account the growing popularity of the RIAC website abroad, it would be appropriate to exploit it in dealing with the Indian expert community as a relevant target audience. The Russian and Indian mass media both fail to perform its primary function of unbiased coverage of events that take place in two countries. Attention is primarily focused on negative events and problems in bilateral relations, particularly when it comes to defence-tech cooperation. Meanwhile, reports about meetings between the two countries' leaders have all but vanished from the headlines. Monitoring the mass media in order to determine the accuracy and relevance of information on India and its relationship with Russia should help overcome this problem; journalistic mistakes damage Russia's image in India.

The events of the early 1990s had a negative effect on Russia's image in India. In addition, during the years of rapid economic development, a noticeable change in the values system of Indian society became apparent: market pragmatism trends have noticeably strengthened. In effect, today we observe a very low level of interpersonal contacts between citizens of these two countries and between members of business communities in Russia and India. The level of affection for and interest in Russia remains high among the younger generations. The inventory of means available in Russia to exert soft influence on India (such as associations of Russian universities' graduates, etc.) would allow to form an adequate interaction algorithm with India's youth audience, as well as with Russian expat community in India and Indian expat community in Russia. It is important to build separate communication formats with the Indian youth and to perform segmentation of Russian mass media target audiences in India.

The enrolment of Indian students in Russian universities should be revived. To this end, a group to identify bottlenecks should be created and a program for the large-scale admission of Indian students should be developed with financial support from Russian universities. It could also engage Indian professionals who studied at Soviet universities and now hold influential positions in the Indian education system. This is an extremely important area both from the perspective of Russia's image and in terms of enhancing Russian universities' commercial appeal. To this day there is a very real appreciation within India of the value of Russian higher education, particularly for medical and engineering professions; however the dearth of adequate information about the Russian higher education system, the continuing lack of clarity over the international recognition of Russian diplomas, and personal safety concerns make Russia less competitive on India's education market. Conducting annual "trade fairs" for Russian universities, primarily federal universities, in India could be one way of overcoming this problem. Higher education ties should be strengthened, while Russian universities should be geared to expanding comprehensive cooperation with their Indian partners (teacher and student exchanges; joint conferences and seminars, joint publications in Russian and English).

Under these parameters, there is also a need to promote more vigorous cooperation between scientists. It is especially advisable to organize regular expert conferences on foreign policy and political and military subjects on bilateral and multilateral levels, in particular within the framework of the SCO, RIC and BRICS. In order to improve Russia's image in India, there is a clear need to streamline and organize activities aimed at the public promotion of projects that Russian companies and corporations implement in India. The emphasis should be placed on both large and medium-sized businesses.

Increase RIA Novosti's range of activities in India, with the main focus on creating a positive image of Russia. Additional agreements must also be signed with major Indian newspapers covering the provision of Russian materials. An English-language Russian online publication for India is also a good option. The opportunity for Indian media to open Moscow offices or bureaus should be permanently on the table. It is important to step up journalist exchange programs. Funds should also be allocated to cover costs incurred in providing Russian materials to the Indian press in areas of special importance to Russia. Expansion of the Voice of Russia radio broadcasting in India could be another good option, however the target audience must first be identified. The emphasis should be on programs of interest to the Indian audience thereby resulting in an increase in the audiences of Indian radio stations.

The promotion of popular Russian books, movies, and TV shows should not rely solely on government financing. It would be reasonable to raise private funds for this. It would be appropriate to offer our Asian partners the opportunity to conduct regular largescale cultural festivals in Russia and India to promote better mutual understanding. During cultural activities special attention should be given to publicity campaigns. So far the Indian public is generally not very well informed about upcoming events.

PAKISTAN, CHINA UNDERPIN INDIA'S SECURITY DOCTRINE

Any national security doctrine of India has to cater to the possibility of threats from two sources-China and Pakistan.

The threat from China was rated high until 1988 because of the unresolved border dispute between the two countries, the clandestine military and nuclear assistance given by the Chinese government to the Pakistani armed forces in order to keep the Indian security forces preoccupied on two fronts, and the support extended by the Chinese intelligence agencies to the tribal insurgent groups of India's Northeast. The border dispute led to a war between the two countries in 1962. Between 1967 and 1979, many of these insurgent groups went to Yunnan in China via north Myanmar and were trained and armed by the Chinese intelligence.

The visit of Rajiv Gandhi, the then Indian prime minister, to China in 1988 and his meeting with Deng Xiaoping set in motion the process of improving bilateral relations. In 1988 and thereafter, the two countries agreed on a number of confidence-building measures, set up a joint working group to discuss the border problem on a sustained basis and decided not to let the pending border dispute come in the way of an improvement in relations in the economic, cultural and other fields.

The Chinese intelligence, which had already started reducing its clandestine assistance to the tribal insurgent groups from 1979, totally stopped it after 1988. Despite this, China continues to pre-occupy the attention of India's national security managers due to the following reasons:

The very slow progress of the talks on the border issue, giving rise to misgivings that Beijing probably wants to keep this issue alive till it has totally pacified Tibet to its satisfaction. Though there is no more unrest in Tibet, which has been developing economically, the Dalai Lama still enjoys a large following there. The Chinese are determined that when the present Dalai Lama dies, his successor will be a man of their choice. They appreciate that this could give rise to serious unrest, which could be exploited by the Tibetan Diaspora in India and elsewhere. By keeping the border issue alive, China wants to retain a pressure point which it can exploit should India show reluctance to keep the Tibetan refugees under control. In national security matters, the Chinese, unlike the Indians, work on a long-term basis and try to develop today options that they may need years hence should circumstances so warrant. For example, China's continued clandestine assistance to Pakistan in the military nuclear field and in the acquisition of a missile-based delivery capability.

Even as Beijing was entering into an agreement with Rajiv Gandhi on improving bilateral relations, it was secretly entering an agreement with Islamabad for assistance in the missile field. Another example is China's decision in 2001 to assist Pakistan in the construction of the Gwadar port on the Balochistan coast, which will reduce Pakistan's present dependence on Karachi port, which is within easy reach of the Indian navy, and give the Pakistani navy a greater operational flexibility. The threat from Pakistan, meanwhile, has always remained and will continue to remain of a very high order due to the following reasons:

- Pakistan's inability to reconcile itself to the loss of Jammu and Kashmir and its obsessive urge to gain control of this territory by hook or by crook.

- Its equally obsessive urge to avenge its defeat at the hands of India in 1971 and its loss of the then East Pakistan.
- The predominant role of the revenge-seeking Pakistani army in its national security management, with practically no role for an elected political leadership in this matter.
- Its refusal to work for a reduction of tension and for the improvement of relations in other fields until a negotiated solution could be found to the Kashmir question.
- The complexes and the feelings of insecurity from which the Pakistan army suffers vis-a-vis its Indian counterpart.
- The role of the pan-Islamic extremist elements in moulding perceptions towards India, whether in the civil society or in the national security apparatus.

Its 1971 defeat at the hands of India brought home to Pakistan the ground reality that it could never hope to achieve its territorial objective through a conventional war on India. It therefore embarked on a policy of waging a proxy war through the use of terrorism as a weapon against the Indian state.

Pakistan had been using terrorism against the Indian state since 1956 when the Naga insurgency broke out. Whereas its use of terrorism against India before 1971 was a defensive measure to keep the Indian security forces preoccupied with internal security duties so that they could not pose a threat to it, its use after 1971 was an aggressive measure having the dual objective of continuing to keep the Indian security forces bleeding and preoccupied with internal security duties and achieving its strategic objective of annexing Jammu and Kashmir without the direct use of its army in a conventional war. Until Pakistan achieved a military nuclear capability in the late 1980s, which was subsequently openly demonstrated in the Chagai nuclear tests of 1998, it kept its proxy war restricted to the training and arming of Indian separatist groups, whether in Punjab or Kashmir, which had taken to arms against the government of India due to various grievances.

The acquisition of the military nuclear capability made the Pakistani military leadership conclude that the possibility of an Indian-imposed conventional war in retaliation for its proxy war had been reduced considerably, if not largely eliminated, and hence it could further escalate its proxy war by training, arming and infiltrating into India its own nationals under the guise of jihadi volunteers from different pan-Islamic organizations to intensify the jihad against India. Until 1995, the role of these mercenaries was largely confined to Jammu and Kashmir, but since then Pakistan's Inter-Services Intelligence has been using them in other parts of India too.

Pakistan looks on its nuclear arsenal and its missile delivery capability not as a weapon of deterrence to deter India from using its nuclear capability against it, but as a weapon of intimidation to prevent India from retaliating against it through its armed forces for its proxy war and as a weapon of psychological pressure by creating fears of a possible nuclear holocaust and thereby moving the rest of the world, particularly the US, to exercise pressure on India on the Jammu and Kashmir issue.

Its consistent refusal to subscribe to the no first use of nuclear weapons declaration and its repeated reiteration of its readiness to make first use of its nuclear weapons to prevent the Indian army from over-running its large cities and crushing its army are part of its intimidatory tactics.

The nuclear threat from Pakistan is compounded by the presence of pan-Islamic jihadi elements which justify the use of the weapons of mass destruction to protect Islam, if necessary. The possibility of the nuclearization of terrorism originating from the terrorist hub of Pakistan is a matter of great concern not only to India, but also to the international community as a whole, confronted with the threat of pan-Islamic jihadi terrorism.

Since President General Pervez Musharraf seized power on October 12, 1999, Pakistan has embarked on a policy of overprojecting its nuclear and missile capability in order to reassure its own population of the adequacy of its capability and to intimidate India and prevent a retaliatory conventional strike against its proxy war.

A GROWING ALLIANCE BETWEEN CHINA AND PAKISTAN

The small town of Gwadar, for example, was a forgotten end of the earth, filled with dust-colored cinder-block houses that lined trash-strewn streets and ringed by cliffs, desert and the Arabian Sea. Yet this sleepy fishing town has erupted with development over the past few years. A Chinese delegation inaugurated its sparkling new container port in early April, as part of a deal by which China will build and have rights over the port.

China has agreed to spend an extraordinary $46 billion in investment throughout Pakistan, far more than the annual U.S. aid budget for the entire world. This is now Beijing's biggest commitment to any one country. Pakistan is also the largest recipient of Chinese weapons, and Beijing increasingly relies on it to help contain militants in China's western provinces.

Pakistan holds a unique position in Chinese diplomatic circles. The Chinese state media describes Pakistan as China's only "all-weather strategic cooperation partner." Though it is the largest beneficiary of Beijing's investment, it is not a client state, as North Korea is. Rather, in a neighborhood where many countries either distrust China, feel beholden to it or both, Pakistan is the closest thing to a real ally and friend that Beijing possesses.

This means that China and Pakistan sometimes cooperate in ways that concern the United States and India. Washington and New Delhi worry that all this largesse will bring Pakistan firmly into China's orbit. With subtle diplomacy, however, all four countries may be able to create a workable balance.

The Gwadar port is just one example of China's "One Belt, One Road" initiative. This effort is by far the most spectacular example of Beijing's strategic policy of combining aid, trade and foreign direct investment to build goodwill, expand its global political sway and secure the natural resources it needs to grow.

Declaring that the Chinese-Pakistani friendship is "sweeter than honey," and "stronger than steel," Beijing announced last year that it would finance a 1,800-mile-long superhighway and a high-speed railway from the Arabian Sea over the Himalayas to China's Xinjiang province. In addition, it would fund an oil pipeline route to the inland Chinese city of Kashgar. This network of infrastructure, including the Gwadar port, would help Pakistan grow, while pushing back against the growing power of regional competitors like India.

Helping Pakistan so dramatically also fits into China's overall economic strategy. With a deep-sea port in the Arabian Sea and a land route to remote western China, some of Beijing's Middle Eastern oil could travel the short route through Pakistan, instead of 6,000 miles through the Malacca Straits to Shanghai. That's the route more than 80 percent of China's oil and natural resources now have to take.

The infrastructure projects allow China to invest its large, if dwindling, foreign currency reserves, and also buy goodwill with its neighbors. Chinese state-owned companies get additional work, and the many energy projects that are part of the deal offer strong financial returns.

The initiative even has the convenient side effect of annoying India, Pakistan's archenemy and China's potential strategic rival. Chinese engineers have already begun digging tunnels and building bridges to improve safety along the legendary Karakoram highway, one of the highest paved roads on earth, which links Pakistan to China. In addition, China is Pakistan's largest trading partner and allows Pakistan special trade preferences through a free-trade agreement signed in 2006, though the volume of trade with Pakistan remains a drop in the bucket for Beijing. As another sign of the growing alliance, Pakistan and China are close partners militarily, and their cooperation has increased in recent years. Pakistan accounts for more than a third of Chinese weapons sales.

In just the past seven months, Pakistan and China have conducted joint military exercises in Pakistan, China and, for the first time, in the East China Sea. China also built six nuclear reactors in Pakistan over the past two decades and expects to help build at least two more. This is raising concerns with the Nuclear Suppliers Group, an institution that supervises the export of global civilian nuclear technology.

In the 1980s and 1990s, China helped develop Pakistan's nuclear weapons program. Some intelligence suggests that Beijing even helped with Pakistan's new frightening miniature "battlefield" nuclear weapons, and with its first weaponized drone.

Many in India and the United States are alarmed about what they see as a China-Pakistan axis. They worry that China's largesse means that Western nations will have little leverage to shape Pakistan's actions on militants or nuclear weapons, or in supporting peace in Afghanistan. Another concern is that China would protect Pakistan when, for example, it refuses to cooperate with India and the West on handing over dangerous militants Washington should indeed monitor the China-Pakistan relationship closely, but the signs are not all bad.

There is still much the world can do to prevent South Asia from splitting into two hostile China-Pakistan and India-U.S. camps, which is in no one's interest. The West should cautiously welcome China's lavish economic investment in Pakistan because more development helps stabilize the country, a positive result for everyone.

Although China considers Pakistan an ally and a convenient access route to western China, China has broader interests in the region that may cause it to moderate Pakistan's more worrisome tendencies. China trades more with India than with Pakistan and shares with it a long, sometimes contested border. So despite sometimes touchy relations, China cannot afford to really antagonize New Delhi. More broadly, addressing Islamic militancy is a serious goal for Beijing because small groups of Uighur militants have launched violent attacks in China and at times allied with the Pakistani Taliban, Islamic State and others. This alliance means that China is likely prodding Pakistan to do more to crack down on militants there. It could also have a positive effect for Afghanistan, where China has become engaged in pushing for peace talks, and just announced a small security aid package.

The United States, India and others should keep in mind that — weak as it is — Pakistan is one of China's only real partners. They should engage both Chinese and Pakistani officials on economic development in the region, as well as terrorism and Afghanistan's future. They should make clear, again and again, that Washington wants good relations with all states in the area. As long as India and the United States have a seat at the table, all four may be able to work out a satisfactory balance.

RUSSIAN-CHINESE RELATIONS: A STUDY IN CONTEMPORARY GEOPOLITICS

The disappointment which a number of Russian politicians feel over the way their country's relations with the West evolved in the decade following the end of the Cold War, has led many of them to discuss various „eastern options". Since 1994, one hears the talk of new axes, alliances and partnerships with countries ranging from India to Iran to Iraq, but above all, with China. This harkens back to a traditional adage of Russian diplomacy: when checked in the west, look for opportunities in the east. This largely self-contained elite discussion received much wider attention in December 1998 when then Prime Minister Evgenii Primakov casually mentioned the need for creating a „strategic triangle" consisting of Russia, China and India. The offer found no immediate takers and was subsequently downplayed by Primakov himself, but it left a trace. Never before had a senior Russian leader been so explicit about the idea of counterbalancing the global domination of the West, led by the

United States, by means of a Eurasian alliance. A few months later, during the Kosovo crisis, Russia and China moved even more closer together in their opposition to U.S. "hegemonism". Symbolically, as the Russian military forces were holding their first major exercise dubbed „West-99" which for the first time in a decade again designated NATO as the enemy, a visiting high-level Chinese military delegation was given unprecedented access to Russian nuclear bases. Moscow and Beijing are beginning to live up to the notion of a strategic partnership through taking a common position on the issue of theatre missile defenses in Asia, which they oppose. There are signs that Moscow is relaxing its self-imposed restrictions regarding the quality level of the arms and technologies it sells to China.

Only recently, the Sino-Russian relationship was carefully analysed and found to be of rather limited nature. Is this changing now? Is a new geopolitical realignment in the works? Will the current Moscow-Beijing entente eventually lead to an alliance? Or, conversely, are the inherent constraints in the bilateral relationship strong enough to keep China and Russia from forming an anti-Western bloc? Or, to completely reverse the discussion, can it be that the present improvement in the Moscow-Beijing ties is only a short-term phenomenon, and in the medium and long term the two countries will collide again, as China becomes more powerful and assertive? What, in short, are the prospects and limitations of the geopolitical relationship which is likely to be among the most important and complex anywhere in Eurasia?

Geopolitics, of course, is only one aspect of the broader Russo-Chinese interaction. Economic relations, cross-border migration, contacts at regional and local levels, and not least among ordinary people, the impact of information technology and the exponential growth of communication, leading to cross-cultural influence, i.e. everything which is usually associated with the world of the future, is not covered by geopolitics. A narrowly geopolitically-focused perspective is not just deemed to be old-fashioned and plainly obsolete, it can be distorting and misleading. Still, it is highly useful for a number of important reasons. First, much of the government-to-government bilateral relationship between Beijing and Moscow today is about geopolitics. There is little else, at least for the moment, to back the claim of a „strategic partnership". Second, the bulk of Chinese and Russian elites are keen students or at least admirers of geopolitics, which informs many of their actions. Third, for much of the outside world it is the prospect of a geopolitical realignment of China and Russia – and not, say, the chances for their economic cooperation-which evokes the most intense interest.

This chapter starts with an assessment of the new status quo between Russia and China, the vaunted correlation of forces between them, which has undergone dramatic changes in the last ten years. It then proceeds to take stock of the geopolitical gains resulting from the improvement in the bilateral relations. Lastly, it examines the potential for geopolitical cooperation and conflict between the two countries in the future.

Role Reversal

The starting point for any discussion of contemporary Sino-Russian geopolitics is recognizing and assessing the new standing of the parties vis-a-vis each other. The first fundamental change concerns the position that Russia and China hold in Asia.

Most Russians lamenting the passing of the Soviet Union usually compare their country's decline with the apparent new omnipotence and omnipresence of their erstwhile global rival, the United States. Still, the change of fortunes between Russia and China is only slightly less dramatic. In 1989, when President Gorbachev came to Beijing to repair the 30-year old Sino-Soviet rift, the USSR still included the five Central Asian republics; Mongolia was a loyal Moscow ally, and home to some 75,000 Soviet military personnel; so was Vietnam, with its strategic naval and air facilities. Laos and Cambodia were Soviet clients. India was a quasi-ally, under the 1971 treaty. In Afghanistan, even after the Soviet withdrawal, a pro-Moscow Najibulla regime continued to hold Kabul. As long as Soviet aid flowed, Moscow retained a measure of influence in Pyongyang.

Ten years later, along the former Soviet border, China has four neighbours, and Russia is only one of them. The others, Kazakstan, Kyrgyzstan, and Tajikistan, the new Moslem states, are engaged in a careful balancing act between Russia, China and the West. The Commonwealth of Independent States (CIS), a most useful framework for the dismantlement of the Soviet Union, has turned out to be virtually useless as a tool for post-Soviet integration. Mongolia, having shaken off Moscow's tutelage, has for the first time in its recent history adopted an independent foreign policy posture. Vietnam and its neighbours in Indochina have gravitated toward the ASEAN.

Ironically, Russia was constrained to become a supporter of the Afghan coalition which had ousted Najibulla, but the coalition has been defeated by the Taleban forces which now control at least three quarters of the country, including the capital. In 1997, many Russian political leaders and top military commanders sincerely feared that the Taleban would march across the former Soviet border and take over the entire region up to the Volga delta. These fears have since been proven false, but even without the Taleban, Russia finds it increasingly difficult to help maintain stability in the once dormant Central Asia. To add insult to injury, Moscow has found itself excluded from both the Korean nuclear energy (KEDO) project and the Korea peace talks. The ties to India have grown stale and deteriorated. In short, Russia has ceased to be a political superpower in Asia and it faces a hard task of asserting itself even as a major regional player.

China, by contrast, has gone some way to becoming a regional power in Asia-Pacific. The „gathering of Chinese lands" has achieved important results. In 1997, Beijing achieved a historic reunification with Hong Kong, to be followed by reabsorption of Macau at the end of 1999. After this, only Taiwan will remain on Beijing's reunification agenda. China's claims to the South China Sea have been repeatedly reasserted. Beijing's diplomatic stature has also grown. From Kashmir to Korea, its influence is acutely felt and often sought by the local and regional forces. Whether it is nuclear proliferation in South Asia or the stand-off on the Korean Peninsula, Beijing is a key outside player. In Central Asia, it is quietly supplanting Russia's waning influence as it moves to diversify its sources of energy supply and to protect its rear. Beijing diplomats have been issuing statements on the conflicts in the Persian Gulf and the Balkans. In a symbolic recognition of its new role, China has evidently become the single most important country from the perspective of the world's only superpower, the United States.

The change in the relative economic weight between Russia and China is equally, if not more drastic. In 1989, the U.S.S.R. was still the world's third largest economy, after the U.S. and Japan. It produced substantially more goods and services than China. Ten years later, Russia has been demoted to the 16th place, in terms of its GDP. By contrast, China, due to its phenomenal growth rate since the start of Deng Xiaoping's reforms, has been able to surpass its former mentor several times over. Even if Russia starts to grow again at a decent annual rate of 3-4%, which is not yet in sight, its relative decline vis-a-vis China will continue. By 2010, the margin of difference between them can be tenfold. Even in per capita GDP terms the gap is fast closing. Thirty years ago the Soviet Union dominated China in this respect by approximately seven to one. Currently, China accounts for about 60% of Russia's level, and some of its coastal provinces have surpassed Russia's national average. Russia's technological lead over „backward China", historically the source of Moscow's pride, is also becoming history.

In 1989, the Soviet army was the most potent military force in both Europe and Asia. In the following years, it has gone through unprecedented decline. In 1997, e.g., it was officially admitted that the Russian military did not possess a single army division that was combat-ready. The quantity and quality of the forces deployed in the Far East have gone down significantly. Their power projection capabilities have been drastically reduced, and problems with the discipline abound, as weapons arsenals catch fire and blow up, and conscripts take to the taiga to escape hazing. The defeat of Moscow's attempt to subdue rebellious Chechnya by military force has become an emblem of a thoroughly new phenomenon – Russia's military weakness. By and large, Russia has missed on the revolution in military affairs. As a result, many have become convinced that, in any hypothetical major military conflict Russia would probably lose if the war remained conventional. Consequently, reliance on nuclear weapons for national defence has never been more pronounced in the Russian military doctrine and strategy. Clearly, this has implications not only for the West, but for the East-i.e. China – as well. Some Russian military officers privately admit that in a conflict with China the main Russian defenses along the border, including all the principal cities, will be overrun in a matter of days, leaving the General Staff with few options other than going nuclear.

China, for its part, has been steadily, if slowly modernizing its vast, although still primitive armed forces. Since 1992, it has been able to do this with the help of steady Russian transfers of arms and military technology, at the average annual rate of about $1 billion. In a pathetic symbol of the changed fortunes of the two states in the defence area, Russian military enterprises have been constrained to sell their products to China – or face closure. Recently, the People's Liberation Army has been buying more Russian-made combat aircraft than the Russian Air Force itself. Even in the nuclear field, there are projections that China may get even with Russia in the next 10-15 years if the latter continues on its path of decline and Beijing adopts an ambitious nuclear build-up policy.

In 1989, the last year of the Soviet census, the country's population reached 282 million, which made it the world's third largest. In 1999, when Russian census was cancelled due to the lack of funding, the country's population dropped to 146 million – two million less than when the USSR was dismantled. This figure roughly equals the combined population of China's three northeastern provinces which border on the Russian Far East. As to the Far East itself, its population has been declining faster than the national average, about 9% in the last decade of this century. Across the Amur and the Ussuri rivers, some 5 million Russians are facing around 130 million Chinese. Even if the entire population of Russia were resettled along the Chinese border, that would redress the imbalance with North-East China only temporarily. The population decline in Russia will continue unabated, and the country may lose as much as 10% of its current population in the next three or four decades. China's population will continue to grow from the current 1.2 billion, and Beijing's family planning policy will only moderate that growth, not arrest it. It has become commonplace in Moscow and Vladivostok to refer to the huge Chinese demographic „overhang" in the border area as a prime security concern.

Thus, the collapse of the Soviet Union, which itself was a result of a quarter of a century long decline, has dramatically reversed the geopolitical dynamics of Eurasia as a whole. Long an assertive and expanding centre, Russia has been on the defensive all around, losing ground to the historical rivals and to the new states which for centuries were its provinces. It strives to project an image of a still great power, to win time and restore the status quo, but it has found this increasingly difficult. China, by contrast, is not a status quo power. In the past 150 years it has suffered from too much humiliation at the hands of Europeans, including the Russians. It is now looking forward to coming back to the world stage as a strong independent force to be reckoned with. In the Sino-Russian relationship, roles have been reversed. Never since the two countries have established permanent contacts three hundred years ago, has Russia been the weaker, the less dynamic and the less confident of the two. This new distribution of power and influence, this newly prevailing „wind from the East" is more than a passing phenomenon.

Even assuming that Russia's economic crisis will be eventually overcome, and allowing for inevitable and increasing difficulties in China as its transformation deepens, it is unlikely that the traditional geopolitical relationship between the two countries – i.e., Russia's preponderance – will be restored. Russia's relative decline vis-a-vis China will probably continue well into the 21st century. This change in stature has wide-ranging implications for both countries, and for the outside world. For the time being, however, the reversal of roles has helped to establish a more equitable relationship from which both Russia and China have been able to draw important benefits.

Positive Gains

It would be absolutely wrong to argue that the new geopolitical environment in Asia, in the short to medium term, is inherently inimical, or even threatening to Russia. The end of the 25-year-long cold war between Moscow and Beijing has brought both countries important benefits. This concerns above all the 4,400-kilometer long common border, once the scene of bloody armed clashes. Since 1991, a series of agreements have been signed which led to the delimitation, demarcation and the partial demilitarization of the border. Of its entire length, only three river islands currently controlled by Russia remain contested. Beijing is no longer raising claims to some 1.5 million square km of territory annexed in the 19th century by Czarist Russia through „unequal treaties". The border which for three decades had been a source of tension and a likely site for large-scale conflagration has become a zone of tranquillity.

Both governments have felt confident enough to decrease and dealert their military forces facing each other. Confidence-building measures are in place. The nightmare of a Sino-Russian conflict has become remote. In fact, both countries' General Staffs have designated different risks and opportunities. Beijing's main axes of strategic interest run to the south and southeast; Moscow feels the pressure of NATO enlargement and NATO interventionism in the west and the heat of instability in the south. Instead of confronting each other face to face, as they did in the past, Russia and China are actually standing now back to back to each other and feel so much more secure.

What is more, the border agreements and the military detente have been extended to the three former Soviet republics in Central Asia. Together with Mongolia, from which all Russian forces were withdrawn in 1992, they now form a huge buffer zone between Russia and China in Inner Asia, limiting their direct contact to Chinese Manchuria and the Russian Far East. The rise of the new states lowers the prospect for the resumption of a Cold-War type confrontation, though it could revive the traditional schemes of the struggle for the zones of influence. For the time being, however, both China and Russia abstain from this kind of competition. Beijing and Moscow are concentrated on the domestic needs rather than outward expansion. Another major change is linked to the emergence of regionalism in both Russia and China. For the first time in 500 years, centralized political control in Russia is no longer absolute. Popularly elected provincial governors, legislators and city mayors are wielding real power and occasionally challenge the federal authorities. In a parallel development, China's provinces have been becoming more assertive vis-a-vis Beijing, eager to preserve their particular interests. As on the Russian side, these interests have much more to do with gaining (or preserving) economic advantages than with power politics.

Thus, although this may appear paradoxical, the dramatic reversal of geopolitical roles between Russia and China has resulted in a more peaceful and equitable relationship which is mutually satisfying and valued by both. Whether this relationship will continue depends on how the longer-term interests of the two countries will interact.

Convergence of Interests and Its Limitations

In their rhetoric, Moscow and Beijing employ many like-sounding formulae. However, a geopolitical tour d'horizon allows one to see both convergence of interest and important differences which limit cooperation and may even point to conflict.

Multipolar world

Both Russian and Chinese leaders use the concept of multipolarity as the shorthand for the desired state of international relations in the post-Cold War era. Yet, taken on its own merit, the concept in the longer term can probably suit Beijing much more than Moscow. China is on the way to become a regional power, whereas Russia's fortunes continue to decline.

Having ceased to be for the first time in history a self-contained and self-sustained universe, Russia will soon discover that its territory falls within the zones of attraction of several power centres, and, moreover, that some of Russia's own regions start to gravitate in different directions.

The North-West from Kaliningrad to Karelia to Kola, e.g., would move to „meet" the European Union, whereas Khabarovsk and Primorie would become part of China's „near abroad". It will require more than an average effort on behalf of the Russian leadership to respond to this new challenge creatively, and work out a new geopolitical model for the Russian state-both in terms of its domestic structural organization and its relation to the outside world.

This, however, is yet a task for the future. For the time being, Moscow and Beijing continue to use the rhetoric of multipolarity as a code word for their opposition to what they see as the domination of the world arena by the United States. This reminds one of the anti-hegemony platform that Washington and Beijing used to characterize their alignment in the late 1970s-1980s, when both perceived the Soviet Union as an adversary.

The United States

The Cold War-era triangular relationship has undergone a fundamental change, both in structure (with the diminishing of Russia's role) and in meaning (America no longer has a better relationship with China and Russia than these two have between themselves). In the early 1990s, when it briefly appeared that Moscow could become Washington's strategic ally, the Chinese grew concerned – for such a change would have meant, to them, a U.S. – engineered encirclement of the People's Republic. The failure of the Russo-American strategic partnership, which became evident in the dispute over NATO enlargement, brought relief to the Chinese government. By the mid-1990s, Sino-Russian relations reached the level of public cordiality which is no longer present in the U.S.-Russian case. In 1996, Moscow and Beijing agreed on a formula for a long-time partnership.

Having started with verbal expressions of opposition to „hegemonism", Russia and China have found it useful to work together on specific issues, such as Iraq, the Balkans and theatre missile defenses, in an attempt to contain U.S. assertiveness, or at least to get some leverage vis-a-vis Washington. In general, this has not worked, but has increased the self-confidence of both governments. After the Kosovo crisis, both countries' militaries have come to see themselves on the receiving end of American-led international interventionism. The NATO operation against Yugoslavia has resulted in the intensification of political and military contacts between Moscow and Beijing. The UN Security Council has become de-facto split with China and Russia routinely teaming up against the United States and its allies.

Still, all this cooperation, or even strategic alignment is likely to fall far short of an anti-American bloc. China, by culture and tradition, prefers to act alone; Russia would probably reject the role of a junior partner that it would be offered in any hypothetical coalition; most important, both countries, whatever their current differences with the United States and their opposition to the „unipolar world", need good relations with America for a host of economic, financial and other reasons. For Moscow, the most vital foreign policy issue is debt restructuring and relations with the international financial institutions, where Washington plays a paramount role. Russia's economic development is doomed without access to Western technology and capital investment. For Beijing, suffice it to mention that China's trade with America is worth ten times its trade with Russia.

Japan

It is still too early to speak about a „triangle" with Beijing, Moscow and Tokyo as its three corners: the level of mutual dependency among the three is far too low. However, from the Russian point of view a solid relationship with Japan is a necessary second pillar of Moscow's Asian policy, which otherwise would be too slanted toward China – to Russia's disadvantage. No meaningful economic integration of Russia into Asia-Pacific is possible without Japanese participation in the development of the Russian Far East. As for Japan, the rise of China is displacing it from the long-held position as the number one nation in Asia. From Tokyo's perspective, an active and successful policy of engagement toward Russia would serve as a hedge against a too dominant China.

Russia finds itself in a situation where the natural Sino-Japanese rivalry presents Moscow with an opening. It needn't make a choice between the two; rather, developing ties with one would strengthen its position with respect to the other, and vice versa.

Even though both Beijing and Moscow remain suspicious of a resurgent Japan, China's fear is much stronger. Even though Russia and China expressed concern over the expansion of Japan's role in the bilateral defence relationship with the United States, China is more worried. Russia, by contrast, has acknowledged the stabilizing effect of the U.S.-Japan security relationship which effectively places Japan's defence policy under American control– something which the Chinese are yet to recognize.

Moscow and Beijing have voiced their objection to the U.S.-driven plans for a theatre missile defence system in East Asia, but Beijing's interests are more directly implicated than Moscow's. Interestingly, however, China shares the Japanese view on the status of the Kurile islands – a vestige of the times when the USSR was regarded its chief adversary.

Korea

China and Russia, no less than America and Japan, are clearly interested in the successful management of the situation on the Korean Peninsula – both the stand-off between South and North Korea and the incipient crisis within the North. The two countries, however, are able to exercise very different degrees of influence on the situation on the Peninsula. Whereas Beijing is the only international player with a real access to the Pyongyang leadership, Russia can only watch the situation from the sidelines. China, unlike Russia, is also party to the Korea peace talks – by virtue of the 1953 armistice agreement. Moscow's pleas to broaden the talks to include itself (and Japan) have fallen on deaf ears in Washington as well as in Beijing. China is reluctant to give up its exclusive position as one of the two outside powers – alongside with the U.S. – involved in the peace process.

The Chinese hope that Korea, which historically used to gravitate toward China, will once again assume this familiar posture. In the future, however, a reunified Korea may indeed see its ties with Russia, the weakest major power in North-East Asia, as a natural and relatively benign counterweight to the domination by the two regional hegemons and historical overlords, China and Japan. If this happens, Moscow's relations with Beijing will become more delicate.

Central and Inner Asia

On their flanks, Russia and China border on a potentially very unstable region of the former Soviet Central Asia. Potentially, this is an immense powder keg. Ethnic and religious conflicts in that part of the world can spill over both to the north and the east. The new states in the region are all too fragile, with the post-Soviet regimes remaining vulnerable to domestic unrest inspired by political Islam. Faute de mieux, Beijing even prefers that for the time being Russia exercise a leading role in the region, through elite contacts, limited military presence and even the moribund institutes of the CIS. Interestingly, the post-Soviet border treaty, the confidence building agreement and the force reduction accord were negotiated and signed by China with the three Central Asian states and Russia simultaneously, as multilateral documents.

Russia, however, no longer has sufficient leverage with its southern neighbours. Like Beijing, Moscow sees the growth of Western influence at elite level and the spread of political Islam and Turkic nationalism at grassroots level in Central Asia as a cause for concern or even a threat (in the latter case). The Western presence in Central Asia is overwhelmingly of economic nature and is of private character. However, the Central Asians' participation in the NATO Partnership for Peace program, including the staging of joint exercises, and Uzbekistan's membership in GUUAM, a U.S.-backed loose association of former Soviet republics, is being read as a sign of growing American and European political and security attention given to the region. This Western geopolitical „trespassing", however, pales in comparison to the threat of domestic conflict, intra-state rivalry, and the spread of political extremism, coupled with the exponential growth of drugs trafficking from Central Asia.

Much like the West, China sees Central Asia primarily as a source of energy supplies for its growing economy. Ever since 1991, Beijing has been successfully cultivating ties with the governments in the region, winning their support for the Chinese pipeline projects. So far, Russian and Chinese interests in Central Asia do not collide. In the future, they might, especially if both governments continue to espouse the traditional form of geopolitical thinking with its emphasis on zero-sum gaming.

Since 1990-1991, Mongolia has been enjoying true independence – due in large part to the benign neglect simultaneously demonstrated toward it by China and Russia, each preoccupied with its domestic problems. On the other hand, pan-Mongolism, initially feared in both Russia– because of the two ethnically close republics – Buryatia and Tuva (of which the latter was an independent state between 1921 and 1944), and in China – due to the existence of the autonomous region of Inner Mongolia, has remained dormant and non-provocative.

If Mongolia manages to use this pause to construct a viable market economy and a durable system of political institutions, which would win it international recognition in America, Europe and Japan, it can become an anchor of stability in Inner Asia, a useful transit corridor and a meeting place for Russia and China. If, on the other hand, Mongolia fails to get on its feet, it will be a source of tension, likely to solicit both Russian and Chinese response. In the worst-case scenario, Mongolia may come under the domination of China, or turn into an area of competition between China and Russia.

The two other areas of Inner Asia worth mentioning are Xinjiang and Tibet. Both have an indigenous population which is distinctly non-Chinese, both have been subjected to a policy of Sinicization, both have political movements aiming at separation from China. Moscow, currently a champion of territorial integrity, gives moral support to Beijing. It professes little sympathy for the Turkic independence activists in Xinjiang and has no interest in interfering with Beijing over the human rights situation in Tibet. The domestic pressure in Russia in support of the Dalai Lama is very light, producing virtually no impact on the government's policy course.

Taiwan

Moscow's official view that Taiwan is part of China ruled from Beijing has remained unchanged during the decades of Sino-Soviet confrontation. Since then, Russia's ties with Taiwan have been carefully confined to economic, cultural and other non-political issues, never provoking a protest from Beijing. Throughout the 1990s, Beijing's support of the Russian position on Chechnya, including during the 1994-1996 war, can be regarded as a downpayment for Russia's understanding of any action the PRC may take with respect to Taiwan. At the end of the decade, in the wake of the crisis over Kosovo, both Moscow and Beijing strongly advocate non-interference in the internal affairs of states over secession issues.

Moscow is actually content that Beijing's strategic activism is directed at Taiwan, where Russia does not have any significant interests which could be affected by a crisis. Thus, China is likely to continue concentrating its military resources at a significant distance from the Russian border and for a very special kind of mission. The Taiwan issue, Moscow appreciates, is a permanent source of tension and mutual suspicions in Sino-American relations, preventing too close a collaboration between those two countries. Russia is happily providing China with arms and equipment which Beijing has been purchasing with an eye for the evolving situation across the Taiwan Strait. A continued stand-off in the area works to increase China's dependency on

Russian military supplies. Still, if and when push comes to shove, and Beijing resorts to military measures against Taipei, leading to U.S. involvement in whatever form, Moscow will face a hard choice, for openly becoming China's ally and military supply base will irreparably damage its relations with America and Japan.

South Asia

There is little justification at present for the new idea of an emerging Sino-Russo-Indian „triangle". All three countries are important players in Eurasia, and relations among them will help shape the future of the continent, but in the foreseeable future the specter of the strategic triangle will remain a figment of wishful thinking of those who would do anything to upset the „unipolar world".

It is important to note, however, that here, too, the Cold War confrontation lines have recently become relaxed. There is no longer a situation where two of the three countries were engaged in parallel stand-off with the third, China. Moscow and Beijing are no longer maintaining exclusive client relationships with New Delhi and Islamabad. India has normalized relations with China, and Russia has warmed up to Pakistan. Indeed, nuclear proliferation in South Asia warrants cooperation among America, China and Russia with the aim of preventing a nuclear war between India and Pakistan and helping the two countries to stabilize their strategic relationship.

The Russian Far East

Still, it is the Russian Far East, and not some third country, which may become a prime factor in the future Sino-Russian relationship. Unless Russia wants to de-facto lose the region, already semi-detached from the rest of the country, it will need to seriously develop it. Developing the Far East calls for a much more intimate relationship with China than heretofore – in particular where it concerns the import of Chinese labour. While at present there are few Chinese residents in the Russian Far East – 20.000 or so in Primorie, most of them temporary, their number is likely to grow, and not only east of the Urals. Even now, the number of Chinese semi-permanent residents in Moscow is roughly estimated to be around 50.000. Some projections assume that by mid-21st century the Chinese diaspora in Russia may reach 7 million, which will make them the second largest ethnic group in the country after the Russians themselves. A failure to construct a mutually satisfying relationship under such conditions could result in a conflict with ethnic and even racial overtones which in turn could lead to a full-fledged Russo-Chinese confrontation. This danger is very remote now, but it shouldn't be overlooked.

COOPERATION IN THE FIGHT AGAINST TERRORISM

India and Russia have very similar and long-standing understanding of terrorism and how it should be tackled. But, recently some tactical differences appear in the context of Afghanistan. "However, the two countries have a history of cooperating on Afghanistan and should be able to overcome their differences. Another important aspect to keep in mind is that we are going through a period of great uncertainty in international affairs. So, the appearance of differences is not surprising. What is important is to have frank discussions about these differences to narrow them down and not let them undermine the overall partnership," Nandan Unnikrishnan concluded.

CHINA, INDIA, PAKISTAN AND A STABLE REGIONAL ORDER

Three powers – China, India, and Pakistan – hold the keys to the future of south Asia. As the West withdraws from Afghanistan and US influence in the region declines, this triangular strategic relationship will become more complicated unless China and India – the two major powers – can define the parameters of a new regional order.

The strategic landscape of the sub-region is defined by the complex interactions between these three: a rising "superpower" with a commercially defined unilateral approach to the region's strategic fault lines; a reluctant emerging power unwilling to commit political or diplomatic resources to stabilise the region or even to preserve the status quo; and a deeply dissatisfied revisionist power intent on redrawing the regional order, with the not-so-explicit approval of the rising superpower.

China's engagement with the region serves as a good template for speculation on how its rise will change the international order. Will it begin to engage from a more normative and conflict-resolution perspective, or will it continue to approach the region from its unilateral, self-seeking, commercial and strategic positions? By reaching out to the Taliban, Beijing has demonstrated that it is not averse to sponsoring conflict-resolution processes, though this may be mostly aimed at safeguarding its own commercial interests in mineral-rich Afghanistan. Will China follow the historical trajectory of rising powers by attempting to dominate its "near abroad"? If so, how will India and other stakeholders in the region respond?

India's (in)security perceptions

For over three decades now, India's primary security concern has been Pakistan's attempts at destabilisation, be it in Kashmir, Punjab, or other parts of the country. Pakistan's inconclusive and unsatisfactory trial of the perpetrators of the 2008 Mumbai terror attack, and the intermittent ceasefire violations along the border, continue to dominate New Delhi's perception of its security situation.

Another of India's major security concerns is also linked to Pakistan – the issue of post-NATO Afghanistan, where Pakistan is attempting to control the Kabul regime through proxies, and where the Taliban is gaining ground. For New Delhi, the near-certain return of the Taliban to Kabul, in one form or another, brings back memories of the 1999 hijacking of Indian Airlines flight IC-814 by a Pakistani Islamist group, when the Indian People's Party (Bharatiya Janata Party, BJP) government was forced to release high-ranking terrorists in order to get its passengers released from Taliban-controlled Kandahar province. Another BJP government is in power today, led by the more resolute Narendra Modi, and it has stated more than once that New Delhi will deal with Pakistani aggression with far greater resolve.

Thirdly, India's disputed borders with Pakistan and China continue to generate insecurity for the country. No comprehensive agreement seems to be forthcoming, despite 18 rounds of border talks with China, and there have been occasional Chinese military incursions into Indian-controlled territory, increasing political tensions between the two capitals.

The border with Pakistan is far more complicated because sovereignty over an entire state (Jammu and Kashmir, J&K) has been historically disputed. Pakistan's attempts to directly and indirectly wrest J&K from India have not been successful, but it is unclear whether the Pakistani army has completely given up on its aggressive Kashmir policy.

Finally, Islamic State (IS) poses a potential threat to India because it has the ability to gain an ideological foothold in the country and provide a rallying call for disaffected, though disparate, elements. The jury is still out on whether Pakistan and Afghanistan would be a fertile breeding ground for the group, given the anti-IS stand taken by the Afghan Taliban and by the Pakistani government.

For many decades now, India has expressed concerns about the clandestine strategic engagement between China and Pakistan, through which Beijing has provided a great deal of assistance to Pakistan's nuclear weapon and missile programmes.

In recent years, however, it appears as if New Delhi has made peace with this, preferring to ignore the Sino-Pak partnership and strengthen its own strategic ties with the United States and various Western states, while improving its economic relationship with China.

What worries New Delhi today is the increasing Chinese presence in the Pakistani part of J&K, including Gilgit-Baltistan.

However, on a positive note for India, China has been less supportive of Pakistan's Kashmir policy.

Notably, it did not support its "all-weather friend" during the 1999 India–Pakistan Kargil conflict, either materially or politically.

The third aspect of contemporary Sino-Pak ties that bothers India is the strengthened three-way partnership between Pakistan, Afghanistan, and China. China is steadily increasing its influence in the region with its innovative "New Silk Road" strategy, and by offering economic and development assistance to Pakistan. Beijing is also increasingly engaged in regional "conflict management" initiatives, mediating between Kabul and the Taliban, and organising trilateral strategic engagements with Afghanistan and Pakistan. For example, in November 2014, representatives of the Taliban from its Doha-based office met in Beijing for talks. In February this year, China, Pakistan, and Afghanistan initiated a new trilateral strategic dialogue in Kabul. Then, in July, Pakistan hosted a meeting in Murree, as part of the "Murree Peace Process", between the Afghan government and representatives of Tehreek-e-Taliban Pakistan (TPP), the Pakistani branch of the Taliban, which was also attended by representatives of China and the US.

India's policy of limited engagement

Indian responses to the above events and developments have been suboptimal and poorly thought-out. New Delhi is used to adopting a strategy of limited engagement when it comes to dealing with China – whether it is resolving border tensions or finalising an agreement on the disputed border.

While on the one hand India seeks to engage China on the trade front, on the other hand it fights shy of engaging China on larger regional security issues.

With Pakistan, New Delhi also shows a tendency to indefinitely postpone the resolution of the troublesome issue of Kashmir. Limited engagement, then, seems to be New Delhi's preferred policy option when it comes to dealing with complex issues.

New Delhi also avoids addressing various emerging threats, failing to recognise them politically. For instance, IS hardly figures on New Delhi's list of strategic priorities, and nor does the geopolitical transformation of Afghanistan. This head-in-the-sand, inward-looking strategic posture is clearly not the exception but the rule in India's strategic thinking.

Policymakers in New Delhi also exhibit a tendency to deal with what they can, rather than with what they should.

New Delhi's response, for instance, to the two-pronged problem that it faces with Pakistan and China has been to give disproportionate attention to Pakistan, attempting to shame and isolate the country rather than engaging in a sustained and high-level politico-strategic engagement with China to normalise the strategic triangle.

A strategically wise leadership in New Delhi would have catered to Pakistani concerns in Kashmir and moved on to addressing bigger regional issues, rather than getting boxed into a never-ending action-reaction game of "*Tu Tu Main Main*" (a Hindi phrase for constant bickering) with Islamabad.

Finally, Indian diplomacy has failed to think beyond bilaterally engaging with its neighbours, or the great powers, for that matter. While India has engaged with Beijing on a variety of bilateral issues, it has not been able to join forces with China and other neighbours in fighting terror, stabilising Afghanistan, addressing the IS threat, or even bringing Iran into the mainstream. Modi's government has not yet brought pressing regional security issues to the table in its bilateral relationship with China.

A wider strategic perspective

India is uncomfortably placed at the heart of a geopolitical landscape – the India–China–Pakistan strategic triangle – that is beset with multiple strategic challenges. Even if one were to interpret China's attempts to engage in the reconciliation process in Afghanistan as commercially driven but benign, the perceived Indo-Pak rivalry in Afghanistan and the Sino-Pak partnership would effectively keep India out of the Afghan reconciliation process, hampering New Delhi's regional aspirations.

The question, therefore, is whether the Chinese leadership can think beyond the false necessities imposed by its partnership with Pakistan to consider the region as a security complex (i.e. acknowledging that the security of each state cannot be considered separately from that of the others), and manage its relations with India in a cooperative manner. Beijing's tacit approval of Pakistan's revisionist agenda could prove costly for China and may even hamper its rise. The Chinese leadership cannot ignore the need to pacify the region and stabilise ties with India while it pursues its global ambitions.

India, for its part, must view the region from a wider, long-term strategic perspective and avoid getting tied down in petty fights with Pakistan – for its own sake and for the sake of promoting a stable regional order. Such an order could lead to peaceful coexistence between India and China and conciliatory management of the region's problems. It could even produce the first signs of a peaceful Asian superpower on the rise.

Finally, Pakistan needs to adjust its strategic priorities, in light of its growing inability to act as a modern, functioning state. Its deep-seated obsession with India, and the use of non-state actors as a tool of statecraft, need to end if it wants to get back on its feet as a viable nation state and contribute to a stable regional order.

INDIA, RUSSIA WORKING TO RESOLVE AFGHAN CRISIS

The circumstance in Afghanistan is falling apart, with rising levels of brutality damaging prospects of peace coming back to that nation at any point in the near future. The meeting of senior authorities from nations in the 'Heart of Asia' or Istanbul process on Afghanistan, held in New Delhi on April 26, was huge, concurring as it did with Afghan President Ashraf Ghani's renouncement of drawing in with Pakistan to control the assault of the Taliban.

The 'Heart of Asia' or Istanbul Process was built up in 2011 to give a stage to urge provincial coordinated effort to handle the issues confronting Afghanistan, the "heart" of Asia. A gathering of 14 nations other than Afghanistan, which frame the center provincial association, talk about territorial issues, especially promising security, political, and financial collaboration among Afghanistan and its neighbors. This area drove discourse plans to grow pragmatic coordination amongst Afghanistan and its neighbors and territorial accomplices to confront earnest basic dangers, especially counter-fear mongering, counter-opiates, destitution, and radicalism.

HoA Consultations

Other than the appointment from Afghanistan, headed by Deputy Foreign Minister Hekmat Karzai, assignments from the 14 other part nations, Azerbaijan, China, India, Iran, Kazakhstan, Kyrgyzstan, Pakistan, Russia, Saudi Arabia, Tajikistan, Turkey, Turkmenistan, the United Arab Emirates and Uzbekistan went to the meeting in New Delhi. Likewise in participation were agents of 15 other supporting nations, including the US, and 11 supporting associations, including the UN, NATO, SCO and OSCE.

After the shut entryway meeting, a source in the Indian government said, "It was a consultative meeting, the primary this year, to examine needs and plan in 2016 paving the way to the Ministerial to be facilitated by India in December 2016."

As Co-Chair with Afghanistan, India "set forward specific recommendations to upgrade local participation inside Heart of Asia (HoA) to improve solidness, security and success in Afghanistan and in the district", an official source said.

These incorporate six HoA Confidence Building Measures (CBMs) and "expanding provincial network". Likewise, there was agreement on denouncing the April 19 psychological oppressor assault in Kabul which murdered and damaged mover 400 individuals.

More than 40 taking an interest nations and supporting nations and associations consented to keep on contributing to continuous political, security and monetary changes in Afghanistan.

The April meeting concentrated on advancing further exchange and participation and delivered a statement in backing of Afghanistan's improvement. Ambassadors and authorities discussed upgrading provincial endeavors in counter-fear mongering and counter-opiates trafficking, exchange advancement, and even the Turkmenistan-Afghanistan-Pakistan-India (TAPI) pipeline, and the extension of the travel halls under the Asian Development Bank's Central Asia Regional Economic Corridor (CAREC) Program.

Combating Terrorism

The most serious discussion, the source said, was the issue of combating the spread of Islamic State (IS) terrorists towards the region and checking the Taliban. Mechanisms to improve the quality of intelligence sharing were discussed. Russian diplomat Albert Khorev, who heads the Afghanistan department in the Russian Ministry of Foreign Affairs, provided several concrete suggestions on improved coordination during the HoA meeting, an official source told RIR.

Analysts, observers and officials opine that without major commitments and sustained support from regional neighbours like Iran, Russia, China and India particularly, it is difficult for the Afghan government to endure; economically, politically, or militarily; with the war against a resurgent Taliban at its current pitch and Afghan politics so fractured.

Afghanistan's neighbours in the region realise this, which is why countries like Iran and Russia have deepened their engagement with the insurgency. Iran has sheltered key Taliban factions in Mashhad, while Russia is increasing its diplomatic contacts with some elements of the Taliban in a bid to counter IS moves toward and gains in Central Asia.

Zamir Kabulov, Russia's special envoy to Afghanistan, recently acknowledged that "we and the Taliban have channels for exchanging information". "The Taliban interest," he said while speaking to Interfax, "objectively coincides with ours." He was referring to the IS, which is increasingly rivalling the Taliban in eastern parts of Afghanistan. No country wants to see a Taliban takeover.

India, a former senior official said, is stuck in a quandary and is unable to determine its way forward. Among its "red lines" is a refusal to differentiate between "good" Taliban and "bad" Taliban, hence it cannot engage with the insurgent group, certainly not officially.

Resolving Afghan crisis

Shashank Joshi, a Senior Research Fellow of the Royal United Services Institute, London, wrote in an opinion piece in the Hindu newspaper earlier this week that there have been various attempts at various forums to try and restore peace and stability to Afghanistan. Most recently, as violence raged, a Quadrilateral Coordination Group (QCG) of the U.S., China, Pakistan and Afghanistan was convened in January 2016 and met four times over the following month. This diplomatic initiative too has proved ineffective, and India has sought expansion of the quadrilateral to include three more members, Russia, Iran and India.

In his piece, Joshi wrote that the QCG's efforts to engage the Taliban collapsed when news of their leader Mullah Omar's death was confirmed by Pakistani authorities. The Pakistan establishment's "levers" to "pressurise and control" the Taliban have proved increasingly ineffective as incidents of violence escalated, with the Taliban even retaking control of Kunduz town last September and horrific incidents of violence in Kabul, Helmand and Kandahar. Between January and March 2016, civilian deaths rose by 13 per cent compared to the same period in the previous year, while the number of "complex and suicide attacks" rose by over a quarter. As a result of this Pakistani recalcitrance, Afghan President Ghani called off his 18-month-long engagement with Pakistan after the April 19 attack in Kabul.

"The result may be a short-term boost in India-Afghanistan ties, but longer-term trends are bleak. No one," Joshi wrote, "is fully committed to Afghanistan's dysfunctional government. Beijing is unwilling to use its leverage over Pakistan, Washington is distracted, while Moscow and Tehran are hedging their bets. The idea of a regional concert of powers to resolve the conflict", he said, "is implausible today." The HoA Process provides a new agenda for regional cooperation by placing Afghanistan at its centre and engaging countries of the region in sincere and result oriented cooperation for a peaceful and stable Afghanistan, as well as a secure and prosperous region as a whole.

RUSSIA LIFTING EMBARGO ON MILITARY SUPPLIES TO PAKISTAN

Russia has just announced a hugely strategic decision that may alter the regional power matrix and bug India at a time when the just-installed Indian Prime Minister Narendra Modi was looking to deepen ties with Moscow.

Sergey Chemezov, head of Russian state-run technologies corporation Rostec, announced on Monday that Russia has lifted an embargo on supplying weapons and military hardware to Pakistan. He also said that Moscow is negotiating the delivery of several Mi-25 helicopter gunships to Islamabad. *"The decision was taken and we are negotiating the delivery of helicopters,"* the Voice of Russia quoted Chemezov as saying.

Why this move and why now?

The Russian decision is indicative of a paradigm shift in Russian foreign policy, a kind of move which one sees once in several decades. Naturally, when a state takes such a decision it must not be without considering the pros and cons of the matter, the strategic takeaways and the possible pitfalls.

Two compelling reasons for the Russian move may well be Afghanistan and the Russia-West spat over Ukraine.

Like India and China, Russia too is waiting with bated breath the post-2014 Afghanistan as American/NATO are scheduled to pull out most of their troops from the land-locked country by this year end. The Taliban is in a resurgent mode. Everybody knows that during the Taliban rule (1996-2001), Afghanistan had become the most productive and flourishing factory of jihad in the world. Therefore, the withdrawal of American/NATO troops from Afghanistan by the end of 2014 may well turn the country into a tinder box again.

While Russia would definitely not like this scenario, it can hardly change the situation and counter the new situation with a Plan B. Pakistan's importance would increase enormously in the post-2014 situation in Afghanistan.

Improving relations with Pakistan would give an important leverage to Russia in the post-2014 Afghanistan. If Russia and China do not want the loose canons of the Taliban to unleash themselves at them, then it is Pakistan and no one else that can make it happen. The Russian move may be far shrewder than one can think. It may well be indicative of a China-Russia-Pakistan (CRP) axis, largely because of flawed policies of the Obama administration.

Russia and Pakistan have had a rather cold relationship, despite the latter's sustained attempts over recent years to mend the ties. Reasons for the Russian coldness toward Pakistan are not difficult to see. It is the India factor. India clearly does not favor Russia cozying up to Pakistan and Russia could not have afforded to annoy the Indians. Why, after all, Russia should play a zero-sum game in South Asia when it is having the best of relations with India, a sworn enemy of Pakistan?

That was the argument of most Russians who opposed the very idea of needling India, the largest importer of Russian weapons. But even this defense relationship received setbacks in the past two years as Russia lost out to other competitors like Israel, the United States and Europe on several big-ticket Indian defense deals.

The India angle

Let me begin the India angle in this context with two seemingly contradictory statements. One, the Russian decision of lifting its embargo on weapons supplies to Pakistan is a huge setback to India. Two, India and Russia will continue to do business together as both need each other immensely.

It is highly unlikely that the Russian move would have come as a complete surprise to the Indians. New Delhi has been aware of formal consultations between Russia and Pakistan in the trilateral format on Afghanistan – the third country being China. It is quite possible that Moscow may have taken the Indians into its confidence on its upcoming policy change and put forth its strategic compulsions.

Russia and India are working very closely in the Afghan theater and have embarked on a novel understanding wherein India pays for Russian arms supplied by Russia to Afghanistan for boosting Afghan armed forces' capabilities. Is there a possibility that the Russians have taken a sort of 'no-objection certificate' from the Indians for their unprecedented outreach to Pakistan?

One cannot rule out anything. Games such as these are often played on the strategic chessboards. What can be a bigger strategic chessboard than Afghanistan where all the top powers of the world are directly involved? Moreover, one should not expect an official statement from either Moscow or New Delhi on this issue. Games such as these are often played in the back alleys, far from the media glare. The statements, views and opinions expressed in this column are solely those of the author and do not necessarily represent those of RT.

NOTHING COMES WITHOUT CONDITIONS: CHINA'S RELATIONSHIP WITH PAKISTAN

In one of the many revealing anecdotes in Andrew Small's new book on the relationship between China and Pakistan, a Chinese expert describes worries about the Islamization of the Pakistan Army. "We're not worried about the generals, we're worried the brigadiers," the Chinese expert says.

The generals were old enough to have established their habits by the time military ruler Muhammad Zia-ul-Haq seized power in a coup in 1977 and promoted a militant strain of Islam in the country and its army. "They drink, they send their children to study in the United States or Great Britain. The younger ones are sending their children to study in the Gulf."

The comments highlight an often-overlooked ambivalence in China's attitude to Pakistan. Though Beijing has always been willing to use Pakistan to counter India, its support is conditional. Like the United States and India, China worries about the threat posed by the rise of violent Islamism to the outside world and to Pakistan itself. That makes it a potential ally in helping to stabilize Pakistan. As Washington and New Delhi forge ever closer ties—highlighted by President Barack Obama's visit to India—they will need careful diplomacy to avoid alienating China with talk of containing it and instead seek to enlist its help. In *The China-Pakistan Axis*, Small recounts China's role in helping Pakistan obtain nuclear weapons and nuclear-capable missiles by supplying technology and expertise—going as far as flying in supplies of highly enriched uranium—to help it keep pace with India's nuclear weapons program. But China has never committed troops on Pakistan's behalf, even during its many conflicts with India, and has often been more inclined to work with the United States to try to defuse a crisis than provide Pakistan with support.

As Small writes, "China would like to see the India-Pakistan relationship exist in a state of managed mistrust," one which keeps India tied down in its own neighborhood rather than challenging China across their long land border or competing with it in the rest of Asia. But, particularly since India and Pakistan conducted nuclear tests in 1998, China has also fretted about the possibility of an all-out war between the two.

Thus when Pakistan began a border conflict with India in the Kargil region of Jammu and Kashmir in 1999, China refused to provide military or diplomatic support. Significantly, Chinese officials were in regular contact with their U.S. counterparts during the Kargil crisis to ensure both Beijing and Washington delivered the same message to Pakistan about the need to pull back its troops. Those contacts would come as a surprise to many in Pakistan, which has tried to use its "all-weather friendship" with China to balance its often-antagonistic relationship with the United States, little realizing the two could also work together behind its back. Similarly, after the attack on Mumbai by the Pakistan-based Lashkar-e-Taiba (LeT) in 2008, China refused to use its veto in the United Nations Security Council to block sanctions against the Jamaat-ud-Dawa, the front organization for the LeT. It would, as Small notes, be ready to help Pakistan in the event of an unexpected Indian invasion. But there would be no blank check to underwrite Pakistani adventurism. "As with its enduring assistance to Pakistan's nuclear program, the most significant backing that China provides does not come in the midst of the latest crisis, but from the steady, long-term commitment to ensure that Pakistan has the capabilities it needs to play the role China wants it to," writes Small.

There is, of course, a level of trust and intimacy between China and Pakistan that comes from the sharing of military and nuclear secrets. China also worked closely with Pakistan to supply weapons, paid for by the United States and Saudi Arabia, to militants fighting the Soviet occupation of Afghanistan from 1979 to 1989. Until relatively recently, moreover, it was able to rely on Pakistan's Inter-Services Intelligence (ISI) agency to gain access to the Afghan Taliban and other Islamist militants to ensure Chinese interests were left alone and Uighur militants from its Xinjiang region kept in check. But as Pakistan began to lose its grip on Islamist militants, China also lost some of its confidence in Pakistan. At home, China has faced increased attacks from Uighur militants; while in both Pakistan and Afghanistan, Chinese workers have been killed. Hence its worries about the Pakistan Army: it is one thing to support a national military against India and quite another to supply one being eaten away from within by a virulent strain of violent Islamism.

China's concerns mean that while it had feared an outright U.S. victory in the Afghan war that would allow it to set up permanent military bases in the region, it also has common cause with Washington in its desire for regional stability. Indeed it was U.S. drone strikes rather than Pakistani troops that killed Uighur militant leaders wanted by China in the Federally Administered Tribal Areas (FATA) of Pakistan.

The coincidence of interests between China and the United States is perhaps best illustrated by their views of the potential threat posed by Islamist militants to Pakistan's nuclear weapons. Their views are not the same—Small writes that efforts by Washington to draw Beijing into discussions about contingency planning to secure nuclear weapons in the event of a crisis have been routinely rebuffed. But they do overlap. "Would we accept a U.S. intervention to seize Pakistan's nuclear weapons? No. Are we as worried as [the United States] about the security of Pakistan's nuclear weapons? No," Small quotes a Chinese expert as saying. "But China is willing to help Pakistan defend a Pakistani bomb. We won't help them protect an Islamic bomb. If it's under the control of a mullah, then everything changes. It's not unconditional."

China, like the United States and India, is obviously hoping it won't come to that. It is still making plans for an economic corridor through Pakistan that would link western China with the Gulf. Those plans could anchor Pakistan into a more stable framework of rising economic growth if security is improved enough to permit it. Small's book, however, is an important reminder that if Pakistan continues to slide into instability, China's help will be sorely needed. It should be compulsory reading for anyone too carried away by the euphoria of warming U.S.-India ties and tempted to believe China can be nudged out of the picture.

CHINA'S ROLE IN PROLIFERATION: NUCLEAR TRADE WITH PAKISTAN

China has recently done the basic minimum in order to facilitate its entry into the world of international "civilian" nuclear power. It joined the International Atomic Energy Agency

(IAEA) in 1984, signing some voluntary safeguard measures in 1988, and it signed the Nuclear Non-Proliferation Treaty in 1992. However, in 1991 the China Nuclear Energy Industry Corporation (CNEIC ~ a subsidiary of the CNNC) sold a 300 MW PWR based on Qinshan-1 to Pakistan, and construction began in August 1993 at the Chasma (or "Chashma") site, 200 km south west of Islamabad. By 1996, China had supplied the turbine-generator; the 60 metre concrete dome had been completed; but nuclear components had not yet been supplied. Pakistan optimistically hopes to complete the plant in 1999.

Chairperson of the Pakistan Atomic Energy Commission, Ishfaq Ahmad Khan, has stated that knowledge from the Chasma plan and the KANUPP reactor (sold to Pakistan by Canada), will enable Pakistan to launch an indigenous nuclear power program, although foreign assistance will be needed with "a few more nuclear power plants". In late 1995, the World Bank and Overseas Economic Co-operation Fund of Japan informed Pakistan that the $300 million Chasma plant was not part of a "least cost" solution for meeting the country's electricity requirements, and recommended an alternate development approach. Despite this recommendation, Pakistan has maintained funding for Chasma, estimated to cost over Rs 31 billion ~ about US $900 million.

A primary issue with Chinese/Pakistan nuclear dealings is the fact that Pakistan has been actively pursuing nuclear weapons capability for many years. Pakistan is in an unofficial sub- continental nuclear arms race with India ~ another "undeclared" nuclear weapons state. Along with human rights violations, Chinese dealings with Pakistan (and other states such a Iran and North Korea) have been the cause of a US nuclear trade boycott of China.

After the Tiananmen Square massacre in 1989, the US Congress passed further restrictions on nuclear trade with China. In 1992, allegations were raised that China was transferring ballistic missile technology to Pakistan. There have also been allegations that China is helping Pakistan build a plutonium production reactor at Khusab, and an associated plutonium separation facility.

In October 1993, the US negotiated a nuclear exports agreement with China that eased tensions when China agreed to restrict exports. In order to weaken the impact of the US nuclear trade boycott, the Chinese strategy has been to establish solid nuclear trade relations with companies from other western countries ~ notably Framatome (France) and now AECL from Canada.

In January 1996, evidence collected by the US Central Intelligence Agency (CIA) was released that indicated Chinese aid for Pakistan's uranium enrichment program at Kahuta. Similar allegations had been made in the mid-1980s. China has reportedly sold 5,000 magnetic bearing assemblies to Pakistan for use in gas centrifuges used to enrich uranium for nuclear bombs. The Kahuta complex was originally built using technology stolen from the Urenco corporation in the mid-1970s. This illicit trade was clearly a violation by China of the Nuclear Non-Proliferation Treaty , which allows trade of such technology only to states which have full-scope safeguards under the International Atomic Energy Agency (IAEA). China acceded to the NPT in 1992, but Pakistan is not a signatory.

However, the US nuclear industry is pressuring its government to end the boycott of China, and other US corporate interests eager to enter the Chinese market. The Clinton administration has therefore backed off from imposing trade sanctions, in exchange for a commitment from the Chinese that the nuclear sales to Pakistan would not be repeated. Congress, however, was not pleased with the President's actions, and on May 14, 1996, Congress amended the 1997 defense authorization bill saying that sanctions should have been imposed on China. Despite President Clinton's vacillation, it is clear that the US boycott on nuclear trade with China will remain in place over the short to medium- term. Adding more fuel to the fire, US intelligence sources disclosed in September 1996 that Pakistan was building a medium- range missile factory in Rawalpindi using Chinese designs and equipment. The factory is to build the Chinese M-11 nuclear- capable missile, with a range of about 200 miles. The missile deal is a violation of China's repeated pledges to observe the Missile Technology Control Regime ~ an agreement among about 30 countries.

China has also signed a contract with Iran for a 2X300 MW plant, and has also sold missile technology to that country. In addition, China has also exported a number of "research" reactors as noted above. These foreign sales have validated and strengthened China's reputation as a renegade in the dark world of nuclear weapons proliferation.

SINO-INDIAN RELATIONS: IMPLICATIONS FOR PAKISTAN

Since the beginning of the twentieth century or more precisely the start of World War I, the world has been witnessing an intensive and extensive competition for balancing of power among states. The situation is no different now, although the dynamics of the New World Order have added more variables in the balancing equation. The variables were less natural and more man-made but their outreach and influence have made it beyond the capacity and capability of any State (read human being) to regulate or constrain the unfolding developments. The Cold War was an intense period of international politics and its demise culminated in the emergence of the culture of interdependence – *security and economic*. The Third World states have been the focus of this culture and, further, China and India are two of the six main actors and emerging powers. It is interesting to note that the advent of the unipolar world brought economic interdependence and only two decades later the states are finding themselves intertwined into deep security interdependence as well, making the future of economic prosperity and peace perilous. The China-Pakistan-India trilateral relations have an interesting economic and security interdependence equation. It not only reflects their bilateral misgivings but also how extra-regional states influence is keeping the regional multilateral mechanisms handicapped. China is self-reliant in its security capability but interdependent on the world economies for its economic development.

In 2009, the U.S., Japan and India were ranked as first, second and tenth, respectively, top trade partners of China. India, on the other hand, has both economic and security interdependence. For economy it is dependent on China and the U.S. China is India's largest trading partner and the U.S. second-largest. For its security or military capability, India is dependent mainly on Israel, Russia, France and the USA.

Pakistan, at the same time, is also locked into economic and security interdependence. It is mostly dependent on China for security and partially for economy. China is Pakistan's largest defence supplier, but in economic terms, it is the fourth largest trading partner after Europe, the UAE and the USA. Nevertheless, its tilt has always been towards the USA, owing to the superpower's military and diplomatic prowess.

Diplomatic Support

Pakistan has been a major source of diplomatic support for China in almost every hour of need whether it has been the support for Chinese rights over Tibet, Taiwan and the Xinjiang province or in the world's criticism of alleged Chinese human rights violations. Islamabad has been lending its supportive hand to Beijing at all platforms.

Another very important aspect of Pakistan's diplomatic support to China is the facilitation of the American president's groundbreaking visit to Beijing in 1972. China largely owes Pakistan its opening to the world.

Acknowledging this support of Pakistan, Prime Minister Wen Jiabao, while addressing Pakistan parliament, said: "At the crucial moments when China sought to break the external blockade, restore its lawful seat at the United Nations and achieve the normalization of relations with the United States, we received valuable help from Pakistan. On those major issues related to Taiwan, Tibet and Xinjiang, we have enjoyed Pakistan's consistent and full support."

Energy Corridor

Pakistan's strategic location, which links it to the West and Central Asian States, becomes even more significant for China in securing energy routes amid its growing economy: it is the energy corridor which Islamabad has offered to China to pay back its time-tested friend.

In 2006, Pakistan developed the Gwadar port as a first step in an elaborate energy corridor proposal that is expected to ship Persian Gulf oil overland from Gwadar to China. Pakistan will expectedly generate US$60 billion a year in transit fees in the next 20 years, and China will secure a cheaper energy route.

The Gwadar Port, that has reinvented Pakistan as one of the region's largest energy players, is a highlight of a little-studied dimension of the global quest for depleting oil; the fact is being well gauged by Beijing. China is now the world's second-largest consumer of oil after the US. Its consumption is expected to double by 2025, with 70 per cent coming from the Middle East. Both India and China are competing for finite supplies. Gal Luft, executive director of the Institute for the Analysis of Global Security in Washington, once opined that Gwadar is the closest access point China has to the Persian Gulf. Pakistan is crucial to China's bid for regional influence. China is rapidly diversifying its sources (of oil transportation) by cutting billion-dollar deals from Sudan to Iran and scoping out alternative transport routes through Pakistan, Myanmar, Thailand, and Bangladesh.

Strategic Partnership

Their strategic partnership is a long-term, win-win commitment between the two nations with the objective to achieve specific goals by maximizing the effectiveness of either side's resources. This relationship is based on integrity, trust, dedication to common goals, and an understanding of each other's expectations and values. When President Pervez Musharraf when visited China in April 2006, Chinese President Hu Jintao proposed a "strategic partnership" with Pakistan to "consolidate and deepen bilateral relations." The proposal indicated the significance in which Pakistan is held by China as its strategic partner. Unfortunately, this partnership has been unable to avail its full potential. In this context, Prime Minister Wen Jiabao, during his December 2010 visit to Islamabad, pointed out, "the international and regional situations at present remain complicated. As all-weather strategic partners, China and Pakistan should communicate and cooperate closely and cope with challenges jointly ... China-Pakistan pragmatic cooperation is a key part of the bilateral strategic partnership and enjoys promising prospects. China expects to take concerted actions with Pakistan to bring more benefits to their people."

Military Cooperation: The Eye of the Tiger

Sino-Pak military ties can be described as the „eye of the tiger. They continue to flourish amid the Western criticism of Pakistan's nuclear weapons development; China has been Pakistan's largest defence supplier since 1965. Though China is investing heavily in a myriad of economic projects across Pakistan, including power and telecommunication projects in the troubled northern parts of the country, the bilateral military and defence ties surpass every other sector. China's *Sino-Indian relations: implications for Pakistan* 9 unabated military cooperation with Pakistan can be attributed to mutual rivalry with India and the latter's defence and nuclear cooperation with the US. In response to the Indo-US nuclear deal, China has "privately" agreed to follow a "step-by-step" approach to fulfilling Pakistan's aspiration for an expanded nuclear energy programme. In the joint statement issued at the conclusion of Prime Minister Wen Jiabao's visit in December 2010, the two States "reiterated that they will continue to enhance mutual trust and cooperation in the military and security field in line with the principles and spirit of the Treaty of Friendship, Cooperation and Good-neighborly relations ... This is conducive to peace, security and stability of the two countries and the region. ... (They) agreed to step up personnel training, joint exercises, training and cooperation for national defence, science and technology, and collaboration in defence production ... (and) maritime security."

GLOBALIZATION AND DECENTRALIZATION: GOOD GOVERNANCE FROM CHINA AND INDIA

The World Bank's *World Development Report for 1999-2000* asserts that globalization and localization are simultaneously transforming the development landscape. Globalization incites countries to reach out to international partners to manage the growing volumes of trade, financial flows and the global environment, while localization — defined as the push to expand popular participation in politics and to increase local autonomy in decisionmaking — promotes administrative decentralization.

The analysis of this influential volume considers globalization and decentralization as independent trends. The interrelationship between globalization and decentralization. I contend that globalization creates incentives to reorganize the structure of authority within states. The impact of globalization is complex. While globalization promotes decentralization by creating incentives for subnational governments to play a more active role in attracting foreign investment, promoting trade, providing infrastructure, and enhancing human capital, it promotes various forms of centralization by increasing the importance of macroeconomic policy levers, especially monetary policy and central banks. The outcomes of the changes incited by globalization are contingent on the previous configurations of authority and the relative development of capacities within a state. Centralizing tendencies are likely to be more salient in countries like the United States where intrastate authority was initially more decentralized while decentralizing tendencies are more salient in states that are initially more centralized like the Peoples Republic of China and India.

Regardless of the overall outcome, globalization has two important consequences for intergovernmental relations. First, the opportunities offered by increasing international flows of capital and trade enhance the incentives for autonomous action of subnational governments. They also provide them with resource flows that can support increased independence from central government authority. Second, globalization increases in the importance of subnational policy for economic development. The wave of economic liberalization that has swept the world is beginning to reduce the difference in central government policies, decreasing the importance of variation in national policy frameworks as a factor determining the location international investment and increasing the relative importance of locational advantages including human resources, infrastructure and innovative capacity, and local governments generally have predominant authority over the policies that affect these domains. Friedan and Rogowski (1996) offer a useful point of departure in understanding the relationship between globalization and the restructuring of intergovernmental relations.

They argue that the ?exogenous decrease in the costs, or an increase in the rewards, of international economic transactions? alters the policy preferences of socioeconomic actors in ways that enhance support for economic reform. Unfortunately, their analysis is closely tied to Stolper-Samuelson and Ricardo-Viner models of politics which simplistically portray the political process as being initiated by economic interest groups who pressure state officials to implement policies that reflect their changing interests. These models seem particularly inappropriate for developing countries where pressures for reform seldom comes from interest groups. Instead, policy makers have frequently implemented reforms with little direction from interest groups. Globalization creates incentives for political authorities as well as interest groups. The prospect of accelerated economic growth, enhanced revenues, increased patronage, and for some, new opportunities for corruption has been sufficient motivation for many policy makers to initiate reforms — especially in the wake of economic crises that have dramatically curtailed economic performance. The two cases under examination here demonstrate that globalization not only alters the matrix of incentives for policy makers at the national level, but that it can also lead central policy makers to implement reforms that change the decision-making incentives of policy makers at the subnational level by exposing them to the opportunities presented by globalization and by increasing their autonomy to take advantage of them.

The states in China and India possessed a formidable array of controls over subnational governments and the economy. In each case, the impetus for decentralization came from central government policy-makers. Globalization did not inevitably portend decentralization. In both China and India, policy-makers attempted to bolster centralized pre-reform regimes by accessing international capital and trade flows prior to implementing decentralizing reforms. In many cases, decentralized controls were discredited by economic crises. However, perceptive policy-makers could perceive that diminished policy-making authority could actually result in dramatic increases in resources under their control as the growth of the economy and government revenues accelerated following the reforms. Dillinger and Webb (1999) and Willis et al. (1999) highlight the party system as an important variable promoting economic reform. Partisan competition was also a factor promoting decentralization in China and India. Decentralization can be a valuable political resource that can bolster the support of central leaders who distribute its benefits differentially to reward their supporters. Shirk (1996) plausibly contends that Deng Xiaoping's economic opening selectively decentralized in a way that built his support among China's coastal provinces and light industry after Hua Guofeng attempted to access international resources to build his support in the inland provinces and heavy industry. Similarly, Bajpai and Sach (1999) and Weiner (1998) argue that the growing importance of regional parties in the formation of India's central government has promoted decentralizing reforms, although as we will see, even the Congress has sought to build support by promoting decentralization.

Globalization and Decentralization in China

As early as the mid 1970s, China's political leaders began to see the opportunities provided by globalization. The remarkable economic progress in East Asia had eroded China's skepticism regarding involvement in the international economy and impressed upon its leadership the need to accelerate its development, especially after 1972 when travel abroad restrictions were eased after China's rapprochement with the U.S. The rapid development of Japan, Taiwan, Hong Kong, and Korea meant that these economies were moving up the product cycle and were beginning to establish international production chains in order to outsource labour intensive production to low cost producers. China with its cheap labour, potentially huge domestic economy, and personal contacts with the overseas Chinese community was an especially attractive location for developing trade and foreign investment. Diplomatic entreaties from the United States promised China access for Chinese exports to the American market.

As early as 1975, Deng Xiaoping, then vice-chairman of the CCP and first vice-premier, began developing a reform strategy that advocated accelerating Chinese industrial development by increasing advanced technologies from abroad and utilizing foreign credits to pay for them. He argued that China should not adopt a closed-door attitude and refuse to learn from the good things of foreign countries. Hua Guofeng's Ten Year Plan initiated in 1978, which proposed to accelerate the development of China's heavy industry through increased petroleum exports, was also a response to the opportunities presented by globalization even though its objective was to strengthen state-owned enterprises (SOE's) rather than reform the economy. However, Hua's plans were doomed when it became clear that China's oil reserves had been overestimated and that local officials had begun to sign a binge of deals that threatened to obligate China to a larger hard currency debt than it could manage.

The promotion of foreign trade has been an important element of China's reforms. Central to China's trade reforms has been the decentralization of the central government's control over foreign trade and foreign exchange in an effort to create more incentives to export. Prior to the reforms, the Ministry of

Foreign Trade (renamed the Ministry of Foreign Economic Relations and Trade often referred to by its acronym, MOFERT) monopolized trade through about 10 to 16 foreign trading corporations under its control. Reforms were implemented in 1980 that led to the proliferation of foreign trading corporations, and by 1994 there were 9400 foreign trading corporations. Central government ministries, provinces, municipalities, and a few large SOE's set up these trading corporations. Guangdong alone had 900 trading enterprises by 1987. Changes in the national trade plan also gave subnational governments more autonomy. The scope of the plan shrank from approximately 90 percent of all trade before the reforms to 43 percent at the end of the 80s, and the plan was divided into mandatory and guidance components with local trading corporations falling under the non-binding general targets of the guidance plan instead of the mandatory plan. The trade regime was also decentralized in the sense that SOE's, joint ventures, foreign-owned, collective and private firms were allowed a growing share of China's foreign trade and by 1994 their share grew to more than half.

China's reforms also attempted to promote exports by decentralizing control over foreign exchange during the 1980s. Prior to the reforms, the Ministry of Foreign Trade controlled foreign exchange through its trading corporations. Beginning in 1979, the central government introduced the ?foreign exchange retention system? allowing export-producing enterprises and their superordinate level of government to control a share of the foreign exchange they earned through exports. In 1982, the State Council replaced differential rates for products with rates for different regions with coastal provinces Guangdong and Fujian securing higher rates. In 1985, the state began a two-tier system in which above-plan exports were subject to a preferential retention rate. The value of retained foreign exchange was increased when enterprises with rights to foreign exchange were allowed to trade them in 1980. Foreign exchange markets quickly appeared in Guangzhou and Shanghai even though the first officially sanctioned foreign exchange 'swap center' was established in Shenzhen in 1985. The advantage of these centers for exporters is that they could sell their foreign exchange for rates substantially higher than official rates. By 1988 thirty-nine foreign exchange centers had sprung up with trading valued at more than $6 billion.

During the 1990s, China became by far the largest recipient of foreign direct investment (FDI) in the developing world, receiving 40 percent of developing country FDI in 1997. Chinese FDI in 1997 and 1998 — at approximately $46 billion — accounted for more than 25 percent of all domestic investment and added some 16 million new jobs annually. (World Bank, 1999a, pp. 22, 102; 1997 p. 21) Reforms of FDI regulations have also promoted decentralization and increased the autonomy of subnational governments. They began cautiously with the passage of the Joint Venture Law in 1979. Special economic zones offering tax concessions were opened in Shenzhen, Zhuai and Shantou in Guangdong and Xiamen in Fujian in 1980. Access to foreign investment was gradually extended to different localities and the entire country was open to foreign investment by the end of the 1980s. Subnational governments were gradually devolved authority over FDI. Authority was extended to provinces on different terms. By the end of the 1980s, nine provinces, five cities, and the SEZ's could sanction projects valued at up to $30 million without the central government approval while most interior provinces and cities could sanction projects up to $10 million in value. By the end of 1991, township and village enterprises (TVE's) had attracted 12 percent of total committed FDI.

During the 1990s reforms were implemented to entice foreign investment into infrastructural sectors. The Chinese proposed an investment program requiring $600 billion for a decade beginning in the mid-90s, and it is unlikely that the needed resources can be raised domestically, FDI is especially attractive. The Chinese opened the electric power generation sector to FDI in 1992, and they encouraged build-operate-transfer (BOT) projects in the sector. Foreign investment was also permitted in road, air and rail transportation. Port development and the oil sector also secured major foreign investment projects.

Attracting FDI to industrial and infrastructure sectors were extremely important to subnational governments efforts to promote economic growth. Localities fiercely competed for FDI by tax concessions and other measures to make the investment environment attractive. Measures taken by local governments to protect and promote industry within their jurisdiction has created inefficiencies by truncating the domestic market and supporting sub-optimal scale projects. Localities established — what were in some cases pseudo — joint ventures to gain direct access to the international market and avoid having to accept the dictated by foreign trading corporations which were substantially less than those on the international market. They also used joint ventures to circumvent tariffs and import licences to gain advantage on the domestic market. The preferential treatment accorded to foreign capital has led to the practice of ?roundtripping? whereby enterprises and subnational governments transfer funds offshore — most often to Hong Kong — only to return it in the guise of FDI. According to some estimates, roundtripping may account for 20 percent of all Chinese FDI.

Progress in enacting reforms to attract foreign portfolio investment, while much more limited that the changes in the FDI regime have also showed decentralizing tendencies. Stock exchanges were created at Shanghai in 1990 and Shezhen in 1991 and regulatory authority was devolved to the China Securities and Regulatory Commission in 199?. However, the restriction of foreign investment to a some 72 companies who have issued ?B shares? exclusively for foreigners has limited foreign portfolio inflows, and regulation was lax until the National People's Congress passed the Securities Law in December 1998. Chinese companies have been allowed to access European and American capital markets through global depository receipts and American depository receipts, but the capital raised through this method has been limited.

China has achieved greater access to the international bond market. The China International Trust and Investment Company (CITIC) was chartered to raise funds on international capital markets in 1979. Other international trust and investment companies were established beginning in 1980 by provincial governments in Shandong, Liaoning and Guangdong by major municipalities such as Guangzhou, Xian and Dalian as well as by smaller cities such as Changjiang in Sichuan Province. The Guandong International Trust and Investment Corporation (GITIC) became the China's second largest debt-issuing international trust and investment company. It accumulated approximately $3 billion in assets and $5 billion in liabilities before the government authorized its liquidation in 1999. China raised $4 billion through international bond issues in 1996. The extent of decentralization in the flow of funds from international bonds is indicated by the fact that by 1996 CITIC and along with two other companies accounted for 30 percent of the total

Globalization and Decentralization in India

The surprising policy reversal of 1981 was one of the earliest manifestations of the impact of globalization on India's economic policy. India's balance of payments position deteriorated after the second oil shock. At the same time, India's worst drought since independence sliced agricultural production by 15 percent and contributed to high inflation ? 17 percent in 1979-80 and 18 percent in 1980-81 ? and growing fiscal deficits — 8.1 percent of GDP in 1980-81. (Joshi and Little 1994, pp. 58-9, 177-78) In contrast, to previous economic crises when India responded with import controls and fiscal conservatism, India responded to its problems of 1979-81 with a strategy of ?expansionary adjustment? which included increased investment in domestic oil production and infrastructure along with incentives to increase exports. The considerable growth in foreign remittances, that in large measure came from Indian workers in the Middle East following the hikes in oil prices demonstrated that the international economy could be a source of valuable capital. India's expansionary adjustment also depended on a $5.8 billion loan from the IMF.

As the 1980's progressed, the government increasingly took advantage of India's high credit rating to borrow from private commercial sources. Long-term debt to private creditors rose from $1.7 billion in 1980 to $22.8 billion in 1990. Short-term debt rose $1.3 billion to $8.5 billion. India's total debt jumped from $21 billion to $84 billion in 1990, later peaking at $103 billion in 1994 The Indian government's resort to foreign finance during the 1980s, not only funded its current account deficits, but facilitated unprecedented fiscal deficits. Central government deficits grew from an average of 4.9 percent of GDP for the last five years of the 1970s to an average of 8.6 percent of GDP for the last half of the 1980s.

India's resort to foreign borrowing should be understood in the context of the evolution of its political competition. Since 1967, Indian politics at both the national and state levels have become increasingly competitive. By the 1980's, the Congress had developed into an office-seeking party that attracted most of its supporters by dispensing government largesse. During the 1960's, subsidies accounted for less than ten percent of central government expenditures. Subsidies increased to almost a fourth (24.1 percent) of all government expenditures by 1989. In the 1980's, Congress leaders also turned to foreign investors and contractors for illicit contributions to fill the party coffers. India's opening to foreign credit and capital was in no small measure driven by the Congress party leaders desire to build support by distributing state patronage.

Like China, India attempted to exploit globalization to bolster its previous economic regime before deciding to reform it. Although Rajiv Gandhi initiated some modest reform measures in the 1980s, India's reform program began in earnest only after its balance of payment's crisis in 1991. The 1991 crisis made it clear that if India was to continue to take advantage of the opportunities offered by expanding world markets and increased international capital flows, it would have to implement major changes in the Nehruvian economic regime. Many of India's reforms following the 1991 crises were responses to the changes brought about by globalization.

Some of these reforms, for instance the decline in the average tariff rate from more than 120 percent in 1991 to 35 percent in

1997 did not produce much decentralization. Two categories of reform, however, have introduced important measures of administrative decentralization: 1) India has attempted to attract foreign capital in financial and infrastructural sectors by creating independent regulatory agencies which limit central government intervention and curtail its arbitrariness, and 2) India virtually abolished its industrial licensing regime thereby increasing the autonomy of its states to compete for foreign and domestic investment.

The creation of independent regulatory agencies can be understood as movement from distributive to procedural regulation. (Echeverri-Gent 1999; Rudolph 1999) Prior to the reforms, central government agencies used various forms of regulation to intervene in the market to alter distributive outcomes. Reforms, to a greater or lesser degree, curtailed these interventions and established independent regulatory agencies that regulated, not market outcomes, but the procedures by which the market operated. For instance, prior to 1992, India's stock exchanges were regulated by the Controller of Capital Issues, (CCI) an agency within the central government's Finance Ministry. The CCI regulated what firms could access the country's stock markets and the prices for their initial public offerings. In 1992, the CCI was abolished and the Securities and Exchange Bureau of India (SEBI) was given legal sanction. SEBI's objective has been to develop general procedures and norms for accessing and trading on India's stock exchanges in a manner that increases domestic and foreign investment by curtailing arbitrary interventions and enhancing predictability and calculability. (Shah 1999; Echeverri-Gent 1999) Similiarly, the Telecom Regulatory Authority was established to regulate the bidding of firms for contracts to provide telecom services in India. Its creation has curtailed the power of the Government of India's Ministry of Telecommunications which prior to the reforms served as the major provider of telecommunication equipment and services and the primary regulator of the sector. Other independent regulatory authorities recently have been set up in power and insurance sectors. While each of these agencies has been established in sectors where the state has attempted to accelerate investment and enhance the efficiency of its allocation, the effectiveness of these agencies varies and is rapidly evolving.

While the transition from distributive to procedural regulation curtails central government effort to dictate market outcomes in the short run, in the long-run it is likely to enhance the autonomy of subnational governments by contributing to the development of India's market for the bonds of state and local governments.

Currently, state governments and parastatal organizations issue a limited number of bonds. Ahmedabad bond issue in 1996 is the first instance of a municipality issuing bonds in recent memory. Reform in the financial sector and greater fiscal responsibility by central and state governments are essential for bond market development in India.

More effective regulation of capital markets by SEBI has already made modest contributions to developing the debt market and India's mutual fund industry. Proper regulation of the insurance industry will increase the country's investment pool, and improved regulation of various infrastructural sectors will enhance their attractiveness for domestic and foreign investors. By developing India's bond market, these reforms could make a major contribution to helping subnational governments meet India's infrastructural needs.

The rollback of India's system of industrial licensing beginning with the modest measures under Rajiv Gandhi and the reforms that followed the 1991 crisis ? has greatly enhanced the role of subnational governments in attracting foreign and domestic investment.

Ever since the Industries (Development and Regulation) Act of 1951, capitalists had to secure a licence from the central government before it could invest in new undertakings or expand existing ones. The virtual elimination of industrial licensing by 1991, greatly reduced central government control over the location of new investment. Rather than competing for the favour of the central government politicians and bureaucrats to win new investments, state governments now compete for investments by providing an attractive investment climate.

Virtually all Indian states have established industrial development corporations to encourage private investment. Regardless, of their ideology, the leaders of India's states travel abroad and meet with domestic business leaders to solicit their investment. They have engaged in bidding wars to win investment projects. As central government reforms begin to transform state governments' traditionally soft budget constraints, the state's quest for capital has begun to transform of state level politics. State-level political leaders like Chandrababu Naidu in Andhra Pradesh and Digvijay Singh have taken steps away from the populism that has predominated the politics of most Indian states to a more developmentalist approach whereby state governments attract private investment by providing efficient infrastructure and a well educated labour force.

The economic and political success of Chandrababu Naidu in particular, may provide a model that encourages state-level leaders to discard populism and pursue a developmentalist political strategy.

PAKISTAN HOPES FOR RUSSIA , CHINA , IRAN & PAKISTAN AXIS TO COUNTER US .INDIA , JAPAN

"There is a face to the factors determining South Asia's geostrategic shape, which is derived from [Indian Prime Minister Narendra] Modi's 'Act Asia' strategy [editorial note: the Indian policy is called 'Act East,' having evolved from 'Look East'] and Obama's 'Pivot to Asia' policy. In reality, the gist of the two strategies is the failed policy adopted in the aftermath of 9/11. The objective of the India-U.S. Strategic Partnership prepared in 2005 is to establish India's hegemony in the region from Afghanistan [through Pakistan] to Bangladesh. This was the thinking behind the declaration of Afghanistan as part of South Asia; India benefited from this thought, and by joining hands with the allies [in Afghanistan] thrust the scourge of terrorism [on Pakistan] and established centers of espionage against all neighboring countries, especially Pakistan.

"In 2005 itself, a civil-nuclear pact was agreed [between the U.S. and India], to get that which India voted against regarding the Iranian nuclear program [in a resolution at the UN International Atomic Energy Agency in November 2009]. And by allying with America and its allies, [India] was emboldened to play its role against the growing dangers of Islamic extremism in the region. Sadly, America and its allies were badly defeated in this objective [as the Taliban thrived in Afghanistan]. Recently, Modi has given a new geostrategic direction to the region by befriending America... By rejecting its ideology as a member-country of the Non-Aligned [Movement], India has adopted an *aligned* identity, getting tied in a long-term military relationship from the Gulf of Aden to the Straits of Malacca. This agreement will be effective for ten years. Besides, signatures have been put to defense, technical, and trade agreements, as per which India will become capable of building aircraft carriers.

"India has also become part of the Asia Pacific Economic Cooperation Forum, established by America and Japan, under which it is practically bound to break up China's New Silk Road Partnership. In addition, India is also bound to counter the growing influence of China. Therefore, China has obtained many advantages [via agreements] through the Euro-Asian Land Bridge land route built by it and the String of Pearls ports in several countries which are spread from the Middle East to China [through the Indian Ocean]. China's growing influence and reach is unacceptable to America, India, and their allies.

"Modi's important goal is to help the fruits of economic progress reach the poor people. Modi's goal is not to make the fruits of economic progress reach people as per the 'trickle down' principle behind the established international economic system; his goal is to make the fruits of 'trickle up' progress reach the poor class for which it will be essential to depend on goods manufactured within the country [hence, the 'Make in

India' strategy adopted by Modi]. Obama's goal, too, is to make India an important power in Asia by enabling its economic progress because America considers India's power as important to the achievement of its objectives. For the achievement of this goal, the supply of American technology [to India] will be very beneficial, a fact that Modi understands well."

"The Clear Target Of India-U.S. Strategic Partnership Is To Limit The Growing Power Of China"; "But In Response To It, An Environment Of Understanding In Military And Economic Relations Between China, Pakistan, And Russia Is Being Smoothened"

"Therefore, India and America have set a goal to take their bilateral trade from $100 million to $500 million [sic, actually: $100 billion to $500 billion], which equals bilateral trade with China. Additionally, the purpose of Obama's visit to India [to be the chief guest at the January 26 Republic Day parade in New Delhi] was to find a formula under which concerns since 2005 about India's atomic law [which require economic costs for foreign companies in the event of nuclear disasters] could be addressed and India could be supplied with atomic technology. An agreement has been reached to this effect."

"[...] On the contrary, during the 1950s, which was the era of Cold War, Pakistan was forced to become the ally of America, but as a result of its policies it had to go through difficult experiences because its powerful partner used Pakistan to suit its needs, and when there was no need [for Pakistan] turned its eyes away. The worst example of this was set in 2001 when Pakistan was told [after 9/11]: 'either you are with us or against us.' Scared, Pakistani took an immoral and illogical decision to participate in the American war against the brother Islamic nation of Afghanistan, as a result of which Pakistan had to bear irreparable losses, and continues to bear them even now. Situations emerging in recent times are extremely difficult for Pakistan, especially since terrorism and political fragmentation has spread inside the country, and there is a situation of war on our north-western borders [along Afghanistan].

"However, even in this entangled scenario, there are hints of hope which require us to make decisions with understanding and foresight, and derive full advantages from these opportunities. At the logical level, it is correct to say that the clear target of India-U.S. strategic partnership is to limit the growing power of China.

Surely this is a cause of worry for China, but in response to it an environment of understanding in military and economic relations between China, Pakistan, and Russia is being smoothened, which will open new paths for Pakistan's security. At the 'Heart of Asia Conference' organized in Beijing [in October 2014], Afghan President Ashraf Ghani announced that decisions for the future of Afghanistan will be made in a unique way, for which he has established close relationships with the six neighboring countries – Pakistan, Iran, China, Russia, and [some] Central Asian countries; and excluded from this are India and America, due to whose conspiracies the situation of civil war was born in 1990s Afghanistan. Therefore, the Afghan nation has now decided that it would not enter anyone's deception...

"This is a precious moment for Pakistan to pave the way for new foundations of Pakistan-America relations based on mutual respect and interests. Therefore, it is essential to keep this point in mind that America is not just any other country, but it is a superpower that has made the world a dangerous land. In the recent past, wherever America intervened it has only left behind destruction, and such that even a dictator would not have caused. The examples of Afghanistan, Iraq, Libya, and Syria are in front of us. Therefore, this is important for us to understand how soon we leave America's strong sinew (bear hug) and establish a confidence-full relationship so that it becomes possible to breathe freely in a free atmosphere."

6

Sino-Russian-India Relations and Cold War

The period from March 1999 to September 2001 was marked by new, hitherto unseen challenges in the international environment for Moscow, Beijing, and Washington alike. During this period, China and Russia had the strongest common interests and the greatest need for cooperation (Cheng, 2009: 152). Accordingly, two crucial factors paved the way for the Sino-Russian rapprochement at the beginning of the new millennium: (1) U.S. aggressive foreign policy and (2) political change in Russia. First, U.S. military strikes against Iraq and increasing American presence in the Central Asia; plans for creation of U.S.-Japanese Theatre Missile Defence (TMD) and National Missile Defence (NMD); NATO expansion into the Baltics; and, ultimately, bombing of Yugoslavia, during which the Chinese embassy in Belgrade had been destroyed.

All these developments reflected Moscow and Beijing's concerns over growing American influence, inasmuch as many of the above-mentioned events directly affected Russia and China's spheres of national interest. Second, Russia's new leader, former Prime Minister Vladimir Putin, started to pursue a course aimed, *inter alia*, at working towards a multipolar system of international relations and creating a favourable environment for Russia's economic development upon assuming the presidency in 2000. One of the main tenets of Putin's foreign policy, delineated in the Foreign Policy Concept of June 28, 2000, was maintaining good-neighbourly relations with the country's neighbours, and Russia's relationship with China (on a par with India) was defined as "one of the most important" directions of Russian foreign policy in Asia (Leksyutina, 2010).

In July 2000, Vladimir Putin paid his first official visit to Beijing, where Russian President and his Chinese counterpart issued a joint communiqué, "the Beijing Declaration," on the Anti-Ballistic Missile problem. In light of Washington's plans of withdrawing from the ABM Treaty signed between the United States and the Soviet Union in 1972, Vladimir Putin and Jiang Zemin China confirmed their strong opposition to the U.S. plans of deploying missile systems and agreed upon the essence of the U.S. National Missile Defence and Theatre Missile Defence programs, which, according to the parties, was to seek "unilateral military and security advantages" (Wilson, 2004: 161). One year later, during Jiang Zemin's visit to Moscow in July 2001, Russia and China signed a historical agreement, the "Treaty for Good Neighborliness, Friendship and Cooperation," under which Moscow and Beijing agreed to develop long-term relations of friendship and equal partnership. Furthermore, the Treaty prioritized strengthening confidence in the military area and enhancing security between countries, while providing framework for moving towards a more stable regional and international environment.

Under the pact, Moscow and Beijing expressed their will to uphold the strict observance of generally recognized principles and norms of international law against any actions aimed at exerting pressure or meddling in the internal affairs of the sovereign states. In addition, Russia and China agreed to develop mutually beneficial cooperation in trade, military, energy, transportation, scientific and technical spheres, and other fields. Ultimately, the parties to the Treaty voiced their determination to fight terrorism, separatism, extremism, organized crime, drug trafficking, and illegal migration in the following twenty years.

Another significant achievement in Sino-Russian relations during this period was the establishment of the Shanghai

Cooperation Organization, in June 2001. Building upon the Shanghai agreement of 1996, China, Russia, Kazakhstan, Tajikistan, Kyrgyzstan along with the new member, Uzbekistan, further consolidated their relations by setting up the Shanghai Cooperation Organization with the declared objectives of strengthening mutual trust and good-neighbourly friendship among the member states; encouraging effective cooperation among the member states in political, economic and trade, scientific and technological, cultural, educational, energy, communications, environment and other fields; devoting themselves jointly to preserving and safeguarding regional peace, security and stability; and establishing a democratic, fair and rational new international political and economic order (Bailes et al., 2007).

Despite increasing cooperation between Moscow and Beijing resulting in the new Sino-Russian Treaty and the establishment of the Shanghai Cooperation Organization, both agreements lost their tremendous significance, albeit for a short period of time, in the wake of the post-9/11 realignment in global politics (Kutchins, 2010: 41). After the collision of U.S. and Chinese planes in April 2001, increased arms sales to Taiwan, and U.S. President George W. Bush's remarks about defending Taiwan by all means, Sino-U.S. relations reached their nadir prior to the 9/11 events. Likewise, U.S.-Russian relations exacerbated after the "espionage" scandal in early 2001, and were further damaged by plans of the NATO enlargement and U.S. withdrawal from the ABM treaty. For these reasons, the improvement of relations with the United States was on top of China and Russia's foreign policy agendas in the aftermath of the terrorist attacks on the United States. Accordingly, both countries sought to take advantage of the momentum in order to improve their relations with Washington during this period, but Russia even more so.

After Vladimir Putin supported the United States in its efforts to combat the Taliban in Afghanistan, Russia's President expected Washington to provide more room for negotiation on such divisive issues in bilateral relations as the second round of

NATO expansion and termination of the ABM Treaty. However, just like at the beginning of the 1990s, Russia's "honeymoon" with the United States appeared to be short-lived: the Bush Administration provided too little in return for the Kremlin's support. China, for its part, also sought to resuscitate its relations with the United States after September 11. During the informal summit of the Asia Pacific Economic Cooperation (APEC) in Shanghai in October 2001, President George W. Bush and Jiang Zemin reiterated that both countries attached great importance to Sino-U.S. ties, vowed to work together to build a constructive relationship, and agreed to establish long and medium-term mechanisms for combating terrorism (Mao, 2003: 85). Nonetheless, the U.S. invasion in Iraq in 2003, spread of the "color revolutions" into the post-Soviet states, and the third round of NATO expansion in Europe made Moscow rethink its approach to relations with the United States and focus on further developing of the "strategic relationship" with China.

During Vladimir Putin's visit to Beijing in October 2004, Russia and China concluded the supplementary agreement on the Eastern section of the Sino-Russian border, which was subsequently ratified by the countries' parliaments in 2005. Furthermore, during this summit, Vladimir Putin and Hu Jintao approved the implementation guidelines of the Sino-Russian Treaty of 2001 for the next four years (Cheng, 2009: 161). Subsequently, in July 2005, the Chinese and Russian leaders issued a joint communiqué on the "International Order in the 21st Century," which reaffirmed the common goals of working toward a multipolar world previously stated by Moscow and Beijing.

During the Shanghai Cooperation Organization's Astana summit in 2005, Russia and China along with four Central Asian states released a declaration, which declared that "a rational and just world order must be based upon consolidation of mutual trust and good-neighbourly relations with no pretense to monopoly and domination in international affairs" (Bailes et al., 2007). Russia and China participated in joint military exercises under the SCO's Peace Missions in 2005 and 2007, which were aimed at combining efforts at preventing a possible ethnic conflict in a third country and countering terrorism (Wishnick, 2009: 20). However, in light of the Georgian crisis and ensuing split of Abkhazia and South Ossetia in 2008, China did not express support for Russian policy toward Georgia due to dangerous ramifications of the of the republics' cessation. During the presidential meeting in Dushanbe following the Russian-Georgian conflict, China's Hu Jintao expressed his concern to Russia's President Dmitri Medvedev about the conflict and voiced his hope that the disputing parties would be able to resolve the conflict through dialogue and consultation (Yuan, 2011: 12). Nonetheless, Moscow's recognition of the breakaway regions was not welcomed by Beijing due to its concerns over the Taiwan issue and separatist movement in Xinjiang.

SINO-INDIAN RELATIONS: A GROWING UNEASE

The dramatic rise of two Asian giants set against the backdrop of a troubled diplomatic history has propelled India and China into a trajectory that will likely prove difficult to navigate in the coming years. With the world riveted by Chinese aggression against Japan and Southeast Asian states in recent months, one country was not surprised: India. After all, New Delhi has been grappling with the challenge of China's rapid rise for some time. Bilateral ties between China and India nosedived so dramatically last year that Indian strategists were even predicting 'the year of the Chinese attack on India'; it was suggested that China would attack India by 2012 primarily to divert attention from its growing domestic troubles. This suggestion received widespread coverage in the Indian media, which was more interested in sensationalizing the issue than interrogating the claims.

Meanwhile, the official Chinese media picked up the story and gave it another spin. It argued that while a Chinese attack on India is highly unlikely, a conflict between the two neighbours could occur in one scenario: an aggressive Indian policy toward China about their border dispute, forcing China to take military action. The Chinese media went on to speculate that the 'China will attack India' line might just be a pretext for India to deploy more troops to the border areas.

A Growing Unease

This curious exchange reflects an uneasiness that exists between the two Asian giants as they continue their ascent in the global inter-state hierarchy. Even as they sign loftily worded documents year after year, the distrust between the two is actually growing at an alarming rate. True, economic cooperation and bilateral political, as well as socio-cultural exchanges are at an all time high; China is India's largest trading partner. Yet this cooperation has done little to assuage each country's concerns about the other's intentions. The two sides are locked in a classic security dilemma, where any action taken by one is immediately interpreted by the other as a threat to its interests. At the global level, the rhetoric is all about cooperation, and indeed the two sides have worked together on climate change, global trade negotiations and demanding a restructuring of global financial institutions in view of the global economy's shifting centre of gravity. At the bilateral level, however, mounting tensions reached an impasse last year, when China took its territorial dispute with India all the way to the Asian Development Bank. There China blocked India's application for a loan that included money for development projects in the Indian state of Arunachal Pradesh, which China continues to claim as part of its own territory. Also, the suggestion by the Chinese to the US Pacific fleet commander last year that the Indian Ocean should be recognized as a Chinese sphere of influence has raised hackles in New Delhi. China's lack of support for the US-India civilian nuclear energy cooperation pact, which it tried to block at the Nuclear Suppliers Group (NSG), and its pro-Pakistan position on anti-India terrorist groups operating on Pakistani soil, including the orchestrators of the November 2008 Mumbai attacks, have further strained ties.

Sino-Indian frictions are growing, and the potential for conflict remains high. Alarm is rising in India because of frequent and strident Chinese claims about the Line of Actual Control in Arunachal Pradesh and Sikkim, where Indians have complained of a dramatic rise in Chinese intrusions into Indian territory over the last few years, most along the border in Arunachal Pradesh, which China refers to as "Southern Tibet". China has recently upped the ante on the border issue. It has been regularly protesting against the Indian prime minister's visit to Arunachal Pradesh, asserting its claims over the territory. What has caught most observers of Sino-Indian ties by surprise, however, is the vehemence with which Beijing has contested recent Indian administrative and political actions in the state, even denying visas to Indian citizens of Arunachal Pradesh.

The recent rounds of boundary negotiations have been a disappointing failure, with a growing perception in India that China is less willing to adhere to earlier political understandings about how to address the boundary dispute. Even the rhetoric has degenerated to such an extent that a Chinese analyst connected to China's Ministry of National Defence claimed in an article last year that China could "dismember the so-called 'Indian Union' with one little move" into as many as 30 states.

Pakistan, of course, has always been a crucial foreign policy asset for China, but with India's rise and US-India rapprochement, its role in China's grand strategy is bound to grow even further.

Not surprisingly, recent revelations about China's shift away from a three-decades' old cautious approach on Jammu and Kashmir, its increasing military presence in Pakistan, planned infrastructure linking Xinjiang and Gwadar, issuing stapled visas to residents of Jammu and Kashmir and supplying nuclear reactors to Pakistan, all confirm a new intensity behind China's old strategy of using Pakistan to secure its interests in the region.

India's Formidable Challenge

While it has not yet achieved the economic and political profile that China enjoys regionally and globally, India is increasingly bracketed with China as a rising or emerging power-

or even a global superpower. Indian elites who have been obsessed with Pakistan for more than 60 years suddenly have found a new object of fascination. India's main security concern now is not the increasingly decrepit state of Pakistan but an ever more assertive China, a shift that is widely viewed inside India as one that can facilitate better strategic planning.

India's defeat at Chinese hands in 1962 shaped the Indian elite's perceptions of China, and they are unlikely to alter them anytime soon.

China is thus viewed by India as a growing, aggressive nationalistic power whose ambitions are likely to reshape the contours of the regional and global balance of power with deleterious consequences for Indian interests. Indian policymakers, however, continue to believe that Beijing is not a short-term threat to India but needs to be watched over the long-term. However, Indian defence officials are increasingly warning in rather blunt terms about the disparity between the two Asian powers. The Indian naval chief has warned that India neither has "the capability nor the intention to match China force for force" in military terms, while the former Indian air chief has suggested that China posed more of a threat to India than Pakistan.

China's recent hardening toward India could well be a function of its own internal vulnerabilities, but that is hardly a consolation to Indian policymakers who have to respond to an Indian public that increasingly wants the country to assert itself in the region and beyond. India is rather belatedly gearing up to respond with its own diplomatic and military overtures, setting the stage for a Sino-Indian strategic rivalry. Both India and China have a vested interest in stabilizing their relationship by seeking out issues on which their interests converge, but pursuing mutually desirable interests does not inevitably produce satisfactory solutions to strategic problems. A troubled history coupled with the structural uncertainties engendered by their simultaneous rise is propelling the two Asian giants into a trajectory that they might find rather difficult to navigate in the coming years. Sino-Indian ties have entered turbulent times, and they are likely to remain there for the foreseeable future.

The Indian and Chinese Experience

One of the cruel ironies of today's world is that India which is applauded as the world's largest democracy has the largest number of poor and destitute in any country, and China which has achieved, a steady rise in people's living standards and has also acquired the status of a world power has failed to develop democratic institutions and practices. It is also interesting to note that despite the absence of liberal democratic freedoms the West has a deep fascination with China which is reflected not only in the tourist inflow to China but also in the flow of foreign investment and government good will. Operation of democratic institutions such as free and fair elections, existence of competitive politics and dissent do not particularly attract either Western tourists or Western capital to India. On the contrary the geopolitics of South Asia has been governed by the US and other Western countries as compared by India's pre-eminent position and therefore they have followed by an large a policy of containment of India vis-a-vis its neighbours. The functioning democratic system of India has had little effect on their policy. The experience of India and China have put the theory of democracy to a severe test. Two old questions need to be asked again about democracy. In addition, two new questions have to be raised. Do formal political institutions and practices constitute democracy or does it involve appropriate socio-economic conditions which enable citizens to exercise their political rights. On this issue India scores poorly with nearly forty per cent of its people below what is statistically called a "poverty line". China has asserted that it is engaged in creating better living conditions for its people after overthrowing semicolonial and semifeudal domination. Today, however, this dichotomy between economic and political conditions of democracy is seriously questioned. Their mutual dependence is emphasised. Therefore both India and China have to achieve yet more conditions of democracy.

The other familiar question relates to equality and freedom. Western liberal democratic theory asserts the priority of freedom over equality even though the radical stream in liberalism stresses that gross inequalities are detrimental to the exercise of freedom. On this criterion pre-Reform China scored higher marks than India. Social inequalities were reduced in China to a very large extent with the abolition of landlordism and formation of cooperatives and Communes and also takeover of the bourgeoisie owned industries by the state. The wage system was directed towards promoting equality and limiting income differences within the six point grade system. In India too there were a number of measures taken in the early decades following independence to curb monopoly in industry, abolish zamindari system and carry out land reforms. In both the countries the stress on equality declined in the 1980s and almost disappeared in the 1990s. In the past decade or so equality has been a low priority in both China and India. The "equalitarianism", "theory of eating from the iron rice bowl" and such ideas of the Cultural Revolution were severely criticised by the Chinese reformers as being obstacles to the development of the productive forces. The perspective of the present day leadership in China is to "allow some people to get rich first" so that the general level of growth is raised steadily. In India the introduction of the Structural Adjustment Programme promoted the ideology of profit and the egalitarian programmes of social transformation took the back seat.

The two new issues arise from the great democratic upsurges of the past few decades, namely the social movements such as the women's movements, the environmental movement, the autonomy movement and the human rights movements. One question posed by them is to concretise freedom as freedom from multiple forms of domination so that freedom to realise the potentialities of the human being is advanced. Patriarchal domination continues substantially in all the countries of the world as evident from the deliberations at the Fourth World Congress of Women in Beijing and as documents in the 1995 *Human Development Report*. China and India have only marginal difference among them. As to ethnic self-determination there has not yet been a scientific measurement. But both the countries have fairly centralised regimes and both have regions manifesting popular discontent. The caste hierarchy and disabilities in India are targets of public attention and social action. There is no comparable social problem in China though new forms of social stratification have emerged in the recent years.

The other issue is response of the modern state to these expanding democratic demands. All ruling elites would like to have an appearance of being popular and responsive to the demands of the various unprivileged groups. And they engage in innumerable measures of legitimation to create a climate of acceptability among the people. Thus the modern state is coercive, responsive and legitimative at the same time. For this purpose it has developed sophisticated systems of management of society, complex methods of propaganda and innovative techniques of manipulation. Today the technology of repression and the vast networks of communication allow the formal democracy to continue while the citizens remain helpless. There is a new authoritarianism in the modern societies including those of the West which make the basic notion of democracy nominal. The tragedy is that while failing on the scores of either political or socio-economic freedom both India and China have fast accumulated the resources of modern authoritarianism. These tools include modern capitalist preoccupation with consumerism promoted through advertisement. Sensate entertainment that commefcialises culture in the global scale on the one hand and building up security forces of all kinds to suppress democratic movements on the other. It is this process which is strengthened by the forces of capitalist globalization. The alliance of Western capitalists and the native elites has intervened to assimilate the rest of the third world into the Western model of capitalist political economy. The alternatives which the socialist revolutions and the anticolonial struggles had presented have been defeated in course of the battles of the recent decades. The socialist experiments adopted the same economic goals as capitalist systems and failed to promote socialist democracy. The anticolonial struggles such as India's which centred on the comprehensive concept of *Swaraj* failed to institutionalise after Independence.

The result was the crisis of the state and crisis of development in the third world to tackle which the elites leaned on the West. Thus today on the one hand there is an expanding demand for multidimensional freedom while on the other hand there is a an advancing tide of global hegemony by the capitalist West. The experiments in India and China are caught in this historical conjuncture. With these comparative notes let us look at the democratic prospects in China.

RUSSIA'S CURRENT PERCEPTIONS OF ITS RELATIONSHIP WITH INDIA

This analysis would be incomplete if current Russian perceptions of its relationship with India are not taken into account before reaching conclusions. Leaving aside political statements of Russian leaders, a sampling of views by Russian political analysts are quoted below to highlight the emerging trends:

Vladimir Baranovosky

"In an era of massive realignment, Russia appreciates India's continuing insistence with non-aligned status and its caution and restraint in development of ties with the United States of America, especially in the area of arms transfers."

"India's ascendance to the status of a declared nuclear weapon power has produced mixed feelings in Russia... However, the very fact of India going 'nuclear may be seen by Russia as devaluing its own nuclear arsenal which is almost the sole remaining symbol of its great power status and an important bargaining chip in the international arena."

"It seems clear, however, that both powers assign each other considerable roles in their respective foreign policy calculations. In particular, the rapprochement is generated by

India's search for higher international status and Russia's desire to prevent further erosion of its global role."

Vladimir Moskalenko & Tatiana Shaunna

"The appearance of two new possessors of nuclear arms in South Asia is a serious challenge to Russia's National Security."

At the same time an improvement of Russia's relations with Pakistan as the second party in the South Asia confrontation seems possible and must run in parallel to further expansion and strengthening of relations with India."

Felix N Yurolov

"With the emergence of a new President of the Russian Federation, it has to strengthen its eastern policy by making it more concrete, more substantial, and more dynamic. Russian-Indian bi-lateral relations and international cooperation between the two countries must be a very important part of this policy."

The signing of the 'Declaration of Strategic Partnership' between Russia and India should not be further delayed."

"It is also in Russia's interests to call for support of India's entry to UN Security Council as a permanent member.

"In any case we have to admit that the fundamental changes in the world balance of forces have had a direct bearing on Russia-India relations.

While formulating their strategy of national interests and security, Russia and India should fully take into account the radical changes that have taken place in the international system. They cannot ignore the new realities."

These are very interesting Russian thoughts, but somehow they seem to compartmentalise Russia. India focus to South Asia only. The Russian analysts are also silent on the strategic coalition that has emerged between Russia and China and how it impacts on the India-Russia relations. Felix Yurolov (the last named Russian analyst) seems to be conceding that by implied analysis, namely, each country to take into account its own national interests and security.

Concluding Analysis

In state craft and foreign policy formulations, as Lord Salisbury once stated that there are no permanent friends or foes, only permanent interests. The same dictum applies to India-Russia relations also. The changed parameters of Russia's foreign policy according an overriding priority to its China relationship and building up a Russia-China coalition aimed at the United States unipolarity, imperatively demands that India too carries out a re-appraisal of what was once a strategic relationship between India and Russia.

When Russia made a conscious decision to enter into a strategic coalition with China, it could surely not have been oblivious to India's threat perceptions about China. It could have been foreseen that Gorbachev's concessions to China would release her from her Pacific preoccupations and permit additional Chinese military formations for deployment on its Southern Peripheries complicating India's security problems. Russian upgradation of Chinese offensive capabilities cannot be exclusively confined for use against USA; they could be used elsewhere. However, Russia in its defence could argue, that these determinations were made in Russia's national interests. Similar India prerogatives need to be conceded by Russia, without rancour.

While Russia in pursuance of its national interests and security has cast its lot with China, India's national interests and security needs demand that:

* India moves away from its erstwhile strategic relationship with Russia and exercise alternative options.
* India drastically reduces its military dependency on Russian weapon systems and spares. Immediate diversification is the answer.
* India unambiguously declares that it is not interested in creation of any multi-polar structures and especially not the kind being advocated of a Russia-China-India triangle. There are many other 'poles' which will emerge in the natural evolution of the global structure.

* Many years ago, USA gave an assurance that American arms given to Pakistan in aid will not be used against India. Pakistan did use the same. There is no guarantee that Russian arms given to China will not be used against India in any future India- China conflict. India must take into account enhanced Chinese offensive capabilities arising from Russian arms supplies.

India and Russia can surely continue to have good friendly relations based on their proximity of the past. India and Russia can surely look for convergence of interests in the international field. However, seeking convergence with Russia cannot be at the expense of India's quest for newer strategic cooperative link with countries like USA, France, Israel, Vietnam, Japan and South Africa. More realistically, and in tune with the emerging international system, it is Russia which would need to be more accommodative in seeking strategic convergence with India. India needs to be aware of the many alternative strategic options open to her, other than Russia, which the emerging international security environment provides her. India should be ready and have the will to play the 'India card'.

SINO-RUSSIAN RELATIONS IN A CHANGING WORLD ORDER

The nature of the relationship between China and Russia is a major determinant of stability in Eurasia and the Asia-Pacific region. Sino-Russian relations also shape the broader world order and, hence, are important for the security of the United States. Because China, Russia, and the United States have a degree of influence in nearly all major regional and strategic issues, the US-Russian-Chinese triangle is a complicated game, and Washington must take this triangle into account when formulating policy. In light of the Snowden affair, some commentators saw a greater willingness of Russia and China to snub the United States. Leslie Gelb and Dmitri Simes wrote in July 2013 that "Russia and China appear to have decided that, to better advance their own interests, they need to knock Washington down a peg or two." This is due to Moscow and

Beijing's common interest in reducing the influence of the United States in world affairs. While the Chinese-Russian strategic partnership is substantive and productive, it is based on both dissatisfaction with a US-led world order and very practical considerations. The relationship is not grounded in a shared long-term positive vision of world order, and the conditions that have given rise to the partnership will also limit it and perhaps even erode it in the long term, as seen in disagreements over energy, weapons sales, and Russia's annexation of Crimea. This article examines the Chinese-Russian strategic partnership, focusing on the drivers of this relationship as well as its points of friction. It then examines Chinese-Russian interactions in the realms of economics, security, and Central Asia and considers the implications of the Chinese-Russian partnership for the United States.

CHINA, RUSSIA, AND WORLD ORDER

In 1996, China and Russia proclaimed a strategic cooperative partnership, which was subsequently anchored in the Treaty for Good Neigh-borliness, Friendship, and Cooperation signed in 2001. In 2008, both countries ratified an action plan to implement the treaty. In 2011, the nature of the relationship was raised to a "comprehensive strategic and cooperative partnership," the highest level of cooperation from China's perspective. Since the 2001 treaty, Chinese and Russian leaders have signed more than 50 additional bilateral agreements. When Russian president Dmitry Medvedev attended the Shanghai Expo in 2009, he proclaimed that Russian-Chinese relations had achieved their "highest point in history." This partnership has been characterized by frequent visits between high-level leaders, growing cooperation in energy, expanding trade, Russian arms sales to China, expanded people-to-people contacts, and some level of diplomatic cooperation over the Middle East and other issues.

The partnership between China and Russia is motivated by two broad factors: common views on what they object to in the contemporary world order and practical concerns. Regarding world order, both countries hope to end what they have seen as US hegemony and institute a more multipolar system. This would involve a stronger role for the United Nations Security Council (UNSC), where Russia and China both have a veto, in dealing with pressing security issues. There is, of course, some irony in the fact that the "liberal" United States has reservations regarding the United Nations while China and Russia embrace this institution. A more multipolar world order where China and Russia had greater influence would raise their status and better protect states that raise the ire of the West but where China and/or Russia have important interests, such as Iran, Syria, and North Korea. In March 2014, Russia used its veto in the UNSC to defeat a draft resolution condemning the referendum by which residents of Crimea voted to join Russia.

Another element of the current world order that China and Russia wish to undermine is the liberal emphasis on human rights and minority self-determination and the resulting erosion of sovereignty that these entail. Russia and China believe that human rights are primarily an issue for state governments, not the world community. This view stems in large part from domestic politics. Russia wants freedom to do what it sees as necessary with Chechnya, the Caucasus, and most recently, Ukraine. China is determined to suppress all dissent in Tibet, Xinjiang, and other restive regions, as well as recover Taiwan. Moreover, both China and Russia believe in maintaining geographic spheres of influence. For Russia, this means having decisive influence in the foreign policy of the states of the "near abroad," or republics of the former Soviet Union. For China, this means a privileged position for its territorial claims in the South China Sea and the maintenance of a friendly government in North Korea. For both China and Russia, preventing revolutions in Central Asia or other former Soviet republics that would bring democratic, pro-Western governments into power is a priority.

Another relevant world order issue for Russia and China is reform of international institutions. Interestingly, this does not include the UNSC. Neither country is eager to see an expansion of the Security Council or loss of its veto power there. However, it does include reforms to financial institutions such as the World Bank and International Monetary Fund (IMF), giving a greater share of authority in those institutions to non-Western states. It also includes the development of multilateral organizations that exclude the West, such as the BRICS (Brazil, Russia, India, China, and South Africa) and the Shanghai Cooperation Organization (SCO).

Nevertheless, Russian and Chinese views on world order diverge in important respects as well. It is unclear what kind of world order China ultimately will seek, but there are numerous voices on foreign policy being heard in China today with multiple views on the proper direction of foreign policy. While Hu Jintao insisted that China's development is peaceful, recent aggressive policies in the East and South China Seas lead China's neighbours to doubt these assurances. Some in China, including some People's Liberation Army (PLA) officers, push for a triumphalist foreign policy that seeks Chinese hegemony. Other thinkers envision a return to an "all under heaven" system consisting of a hierarchical world order led by a benevolent Chinese imperialism. Most of these views of world order envision a more powerful international position for China that could undermine important Russian interests.

Putin's view of world order is more limited, but also challenges the status quo. Putin demands that Russia be treated as a great power. While attempting to build closer ties with Europe, Russia still insists on keeping the former Soviet republics in its orbit, a policy some compare to the Monroe Doctrine and others describe as imperialism. While this has mainly disrupted the international system in Europe, with Russian military force used in Ukraine and Georgia, it also confronts Chinese interests in Central Asia.

The Chinese-Russian relationship is also built on very practical issues. The first is economics. Both Russia and China place a high priority on domestic economic development. One result is that mutual trade and investment are important to both sides. As Russia has an abundance of oil and other natural resources while China is an importer of such products, the energy trade is a practical way in which both sides benefit. In addition, the Russian Far East (RFE) has an undeveloped economy that Moscow cannot afford to expand alone. Economic growth in the RFE has been a goal of Russian-Chinese cooperation, although one that has been less successful. Overall, the levels of trade and investment outside the energy sector have been disappointing.

Security is another important issue. Threats and border clashes led perilously close to war in the late 1960s and early 1970s. By the 1980s, both China and Russia were absorbed with domestic concerns. A secure Russian-Chinese border was imperative for both sides. After a series of negotiations, the last border dispute was resolved in 2008 and the border demilitarized. In addition, throughout the 1990s and early 2000s, the Russian defence industry was desperate for orders and cash. China wanted advanced weapons systems, and both sides benefited from Russian weapons sales to China, including fighter planes and submarines.

In politics, economics, and security, the Sino-Russia "comprehensive strategic and cooperative partnership" is driven by mutual interests, not mutual affection. Dmitri Trenin, a well-regarded analyst of Russian politics, observes, "There has never been a spirit of camaraderie about Russo-Chinese summits. The leaders do not take off their ties or use first names. And there have been few truly strategic conversations. But the summits are invariably business-like and results-orientated."

In a similar vein, Andrew Kuchins asserts that Russia has "profound ambivalence" toward China, but acts in a pragmatic fashion. Trenin's conclusion from his study of Chinese-Russian relations is that "while both countries need each other and would benefit from a stable political relationship and close economic ties, both Moscow and Beijing lack the long-term strategies to create such a bond."

The foundations of the Sino-Russian partnership may not be stable for the long term. As China rises in power, its conception of the ideal world order is likely to diverge from Russia's viewpoint. For example, Leszek Buszynski argues that Russia has been eclipsed by China in the Asia-Pacific region. Russia is being marginalized, and its partnership with China has not been in Russia's best interests. Moreover, there may be increasing conflict between China and Russia over spheres of influence that overlap, especially in Central Asia. In sum, world order is driven by values but also power, and as China's power increases relative to Russia's, there will be a divergence of views on such an order.

Even practical issues change character over time. Growing Chinese military capabilities may make Russia rethink its border security. Russian concerns about being primarily a provider of resources to China may dampen economic ties, as may Russian fears about Chinese dominating the RFE. Thus, it is worth exploring issue areas to understand where China and Russia cooperate and where they have conflicts.

Russia's annexation of Crimea in March 2014 illustrated tensions between the Chinese and Russian worldviews which also affect practical issues. Russia's move put China in an uncomfortable position. China's foreign policy declarations (if not always its actions) have long rejected outside interference in the internal affairs of any state. China has often criticized the United States for violating this principle, and Russia clearly violated the noninterference principle in Ukraine. Moreover, China has important interests in Ukraine. It imports Ukrainian weapons and military technology, it has agricultural interests in Ukraine, and Ukraine is the linchpin for Chinese investment plans in Eastern Europe. Most seriously, the Crimean referendum provides an unwanted precedent that residents of Taiwan, Tibet, or Xinjiang might refer to in calling for similar referenda.

On the other hand, Russia is an important strategic partner of China, and Putin clearly counts on Chinese support. The Chinese government saw advantages in a Western setback, while the Chinese press went further in praising Putin for being strong and poking the West in the eye.

Moreover, China had much to gain in a confrontation between Putin and the West that make Russia more dependent on China for energy purchases and economic growth.

In the end, China refused to commit to either side. It abstained on a UNSC draft resolution condemning the Crimean referendum. It issued bland statements that were fairly noncommittal and tried to muddle through in a way that would not offend Ukraine or Russia. However, clearly practical considerations and realpolitik overrode a firm stance on principles.

CHINA-RUSSIA SPECIFIC INTERACTION

As noted, a number of very practical issues affect the Chinese-Russian relationship in various ways. Most significant among these are economics, security, and shared and/or competing interests in Central Asia.

Economics

The most important economic exchange between Russia and China involves energy. Russia is a major energy exporter, while China's imports grow each year. Moreover, China has become a profitable market for Russian oil. Nevertheless, creating the necessary energy infrastructure and reaching concrete agreements on energy supplies and pricing has not gone smoothly, exacerbated by infighting among Russian energy companies and mutual mistrust and misunderstanding between China and Russia. This has led to frustration, especially in China. After years of negotiations and Russian efforts to play off China against Japan, in January 2011, Russia began shipping oil to China through the East Siberia–Pacific Ocean (ESPO) pipeline. This was enabled by a 2009 agreement that provided a $25 billion Chinese loan to Russia's oil and pipeline companies, Rosneft and Transneft, with an agreement for Russia to provide China with 300 million tons of crude oil over a 30-year period. However, in the first two months of the pipeline's operations, Russians charged the Chinese National Petroleum Corporation (CNPC) with underpaying for oil by $100 million. The dispute was settled the next year. Moreover, when Chinese president Xi Jinping visited Moscow in June 2013, China and Russia signed an additional crude oil deal worth $270 billion.

Natural gas, however, has yet to flow from Russia to China, in spite of a 2006 memorandum between Gazprom and CNPC that pledged 30 billion cubic meters of gas to China via a western route and 38 billion cubic meters across a route in the east, as well as an additional 2009 agreement. Russia and China have been sharply divided on the price of gas, and as a result, the necessary pipelines have not been built. This is due, in part, to issues in Chinese politics related to CNPC. Some analysts speculated that a loan deal with Gazprom would eventually lead to a resolution, similar to the oil deal. However, it seems that gas exports will no longer be a monopoly of Gazprom. Rosneft now has plans to sell liquid natural gas (LNG) to Japanese companies from a terminal on Sakhalin, while Novatek, an independent gas producer, has partnered with CNPC to sell China LNG from the Arctic. Finally, at the May 2014 summit between Vladimir Putin and Xi Jinping, China and Russia agreed to a 30-year gas deal that will begin delivering gas from Russia to China in 2018 after the necessary infrastructure is completed. The price of that gas is referred to as a "commercial secret."

In a related issue, Russia has clear economic and political interests in further developing the RFE, where it needs to reassert its control over the region and form a stronger basis for international influence in the

Asia-Pacific region. Energy plays a role in these goals, but there are other aspects to this challenge as well. After the fall of the Soviet Union, the RFE was virtually ignored while the new leaders of Russia attempted to put the state back together. Since 1991, the population in the area has shrunk by 20 percent, to 6.28 million, and is projected to drop further to 4.7 million by 2025.24 However, in recent years Russia has paid new attention to the RFE, due in part to the growth of China and dimming prospects for economic growth based on European trade and investment. Thus, in 2009 the Russian government approved the "Strategy for Socio-Economic Development of the Far East and the Baikal Region until 2025 (Strategy 2025)" to promote the development of its eastern regions. The 2012 Asia-Pacific Economic Cooperation (APEC) summit in Vladivostok also served as a catalyst for Moscow's attention, with the Russian government reportedly spending over $20 billion to upgrade Vladivostok's infrastructure.

Russia has a dilemma in developing the RFE. On the one hand, it needs the assistance of China and other Asia-Pacific powers to spur economic growth. The Russian government does not have the resources itself, and corruption and bureaucratic inefficiency stymie much of its efforts. On the other hand, Russia does not want the RFE to become an appendage of China. It is uncertain if Russia will be able to successfully walk this line. In August of 2013, the Chinese State Development Bank announced that it may spend $5 billion in the RFE to finance Russian development programs. Moreover, Chinese workers reportedly now farm 40 percent of arable land in the Jewish Autonomous Region of the RFE, while Chinese farmers grew 90 percent of vegetables sold in the RFE in 2012.26 In sum, the RFE provides numerous opportunities for economic cooperation that would benefit Chinese and Russians. However, these opportunities also provide a potential liability to the Russian state as it seeks to establish a firm grip on its eastern regions.

China and Russia are also finding areas of cooperation on trade and investment. In 2010, China became Russia's biggest trade partner, and Russia's Micex exchange began trading the yuan and ruble as China and Russia sought to reduce dependence on the dollar in international trade. Nevertheless, Russia's place in China's overall trade is still modest. According to Chinese data published by the IMF, Chinese exports to Russia rose from $13.21 billion in 2005 to $44.07 billion in 2012, more than tripling. Nevertheless, calculations show that Chinese exports to Russia as a percentage of total exports only rose from 1.7

percent in 2005 to 2.2 percent in 2012. For sake of comparison, Chinese exports to Russia in 2012 were only 12.5 percent of Chinese exports to the United States. From 2005 to 2012, Chinese imports from Russia rose from $15.89 billion to $43.95 billion, although the percentage of total imports remained at 2.4 percent.

Russian data provided to the IMF shows that Russian exports to China grew from 5.4 percent of its total in 2005 to 6.8 percent in 2012. Russian exports to the United States in 2012 were only 36 percent of exports to China. Russian imports from China grew more than fivefold from 2005 to 2011, rising from 5.2 percent of the total in 2005 to 14 percent of the total in 2012.[27] Thus, Russia is more dependent on mutual trade than China. In 2013, total trade rose only 2 percent from the previous year to $90 billion.

While increasing trade is beneficial for both states, the nature of trade is of concern to Russia. Russia fears becoming a provider of natural resources to China and little else, and in 2006 Putin made a political issue of unbalanced trade. Chinese observers tend to complain of structural issues. For example, writer Qiu Huafei notes that Sino-Russian trade is largely focused on the needs of border communities, involving too few advanced technological goods. Qiu also points out that trade is hindered by contract violations, lack of institutionalized channels for resolving disputes, poor treatment of Chinese business personnel in Russia, the prevalence of a "China threat" mentality in Russia, and unsettled Russian debts. Other Chinese analysts, however, are more optimistic, pointing to the potential for Russian high-technology exports to China and foreseeing a Chinese move toward more of a domestic consumption-based economy that will provide greater export opportunities for Russia.

Security

Following armed clashes in 1969,[31] both sides' desire for border security became a major factor leading to rapprochement in the late 1980s and early 1990s and continues to be a key issue. Russia looks defensively at the United States and NATO and also sees a major contemporary threat in terrorism coming from its south. At the same time, China is embroiled in disputes with Japan and Southeast Asia and seeks to suppress minority unrest within its borders. Each side needs assurance that their joint border will not create problems.

One fascinating aspect of the security relationship is the recent change in relative power positions. During the Cold War, the Soviet Union was the dominant power in the political, economic, and military arenas. Today, apart from nuclear forces and the technological sophistication of some major weapons systems, China is ascendant in the relationship. In fact, the rapid buildup of the PLA might lead one to expect that Russia would shift to a more defensive posture toward China.

There is some evidence that this is occurring, although for the most part, Russia does not see China as a major security threat at this point. China's rise makes the world more multipolar, giving space to Russia. Moreover, Russia sees China as focused on its east and south and understands that China has many domestic problems that take up resources and the attention of its leaders. For Russia, good ties with China are important for Russian security. From China's perspective, strong ties with Russia help prevent closer Russian ties with NATO in a manner that would isolate China. Likewise, Russia's annexation of Crimea was seen by many in China as a welcome defeat of the West. Taking various factors into consideration, one Chinese analyst suggests that the United States, Russia, and China are all hedging against each other.

Arms sales are one important component in the Sino-Russian security relationship. China has been engaged in a sustained, long-term buildup of high-tech arms since the 1990s. With the United States and Europe refusing to sell China most types of military equipment since 1989, Russia has been China's most important source of foreign weapons. From 2006 to 2010, 84 percent of Chinese arms imports came from Russia.

From the Russian perspective, the period since the collapse of the Soviet Union has been marked by severe economic difficulties, moderated now by energy exports. As a result, military sales to China have been a welcome and at times industry-saving source of funds, and Russia has sold China a large variety of weapons. These include Su-27 and Su-30 fighter aircraft, surface to air missile (SAM) systems, *Sovremenny*-class destroyers, helicopters, transport aircraft, antiship missiles, torpedoes, radars, and jet engines. Nevertheless, Russian arms sales to China peaked in 2005 and have declined since then. Sales have dropped from $3.13 billion in 2005 (in constant 1990 prices) to $679 million in 2012. While sales to China comprised 60 percent of Russian arms exports in 2005, by 2012 the figure had fallen to only 8 percent. Most major weapon system deliveries from Russia to China were completed by 2009, and since 2006, major arms exports have been limited to jet engines, fire control radars, transport aircraft, and helicopters.

There are a variety of explanations for this drop in arms sales. From China's perspective, its own defence industries are capable of producing many of the weapons previously purchased from Russia. Additionally, there was some dissatisfaction with Russian arms sales. Russia often refused to sell China its highest-technology equipment, even though it was willing to sell more-advanced items to India. This has been an irritant to China. China hoped for more licensed production of systems within China and technology transfers, and was unhappy with delivery delays and the quality of Russian arms.

The Russian perspective is more complex. On the one hand, there is consternation about China reverse-engineering Russian technology and then using it in its own weapons exports, beating Russia on price in the process. Russians claim the Chinese J-11B fighter plane is a copy of the Su-27, while China is heavily marketing the JF-17 fighter, developed with Pakistan. In 2011, the Russian government commissioned a report entitled "The Strategies and Tactics of Chinese Exporters of Arms and Military Equipment," and the head of the Mikoyan (MiG) and Sukhoi design bureau sent a letter to Roxoboronexport asking that it not sell large numbers of RD-93 engines to China because the MiG-29 competes against the JF-17 for export sales and the JF-

17 uses that engine. Various Russian officials are also concerned about the strategic implications of China's growing military power. In this regard, there are differing opinions among Russian elites. Kevin Ryan notes that "the view from Moscow of military relations with China varies depending on the organizational viewpoint of the individual." Arms manufacturers have a different perspective from strategic planners. Russia faces the conundrum that China wants more and more sophisticated weapons, which might decisively affect the balance of power in the Asia-Pacific region (alienating the United States), as well as the balance of power between China and Russia itself.

The arms sales relationship between Beijing and Moscow will require careful observation as a barometer of their defence cooperation. Recently, there has been discussion of renewed Russian arms sales to China, especially the 400-kilometer-range S-400 SAM system and the Su-35S fighter, Russia's most advanced weapons. In December 2012, *Jane's 360* reported that Russia will also sell four *Lada*-class diesel submarines to China. Nevertheless, these deals are not firm. Another indicator of Sino-Russian defence ties is joint military exercises. The first military exercises were Peace Mission 2005, held under the auspices of the SCO with the publicly stated aim of combating terrorism. This exercise was conducted in the RFE and China's Shandong province and involved naval and amphibious operations. Ten thousand troops participated, as well as submarines and strategic bombers. This led to speculation that the exercises were about much more than terrorism, with China hoping that they would be seen as simulating an invasion of Taiwan. Various other Peace Mission exercises have been held as well. However, the level of actual coordination in such exercises is usually low.

Recent naval manoeuvres demonstrated greater coordination in military cooperation. From 5 to 12 July 2013, Russia and China conducted joint naval exercises of unprecedented size, named Joint Sea 2013. China sent seven naval vessels, including a guided-missile destroyer and frigates, while Russia provided 11 warships, including the Pacific fleet's flagship *Varyag*, a guided-missile cruiser, and a Kilo-class submarine. The exercises focused on surface warfare, antisubmarine warfare, air defence, and the rescue of a kidnapped vessel. Apart from the military aspects of the drills, the political message was also important. China would like the exercises to be seen as a warning to the United States and Japan, with an implication that Russia stands beside China in its various maritime disputes, especially the Diaoyu/Senkaku Islands. Russia, however, has taken a neutral position in these disputes, thus the exercises may misrepresent Russia's actual position.

As if to balance these exercises, shortly after the Chinese departed, Russia began its own unilateral military drills. In the largest military exercise since the fall of the Soviet Union, it reportedly conducted manoeuvres involving 160,000 troops, 500 tanks, 130 combat aircraft, and ships from the Pacific fleet. The exercise involved the rapid reaction of Russian forces deployed to the RFE. It was designed to demonstrate the power of the Russian military to its Asian neighbours and its ability to quickly move forces to defend its eastern domains. Thus, while the naval exercises in early July showed tight cooperation with the Chinese military, the exercises later in the month demonstrated Russian independence and the ability of Russia to defend itself against any potential Chinese encroachment.

Central Asia

Central Asia (defined here as Kazakhstan, Kyrgyzstan, Tajikistan, Uzbekistan, and Turkmenistan) is an arena of relatively weak states with small populations attempting to govern vast areas. The region has large energy reserves and is strategically located between China, Russia, and the Middle East. Moreover, it can contribute to stability in Afghanistan but is also vulnerable to radical ideology and violence spilling over Afghanistan's borders. Thus, it is a region where Russia, China, the United States, India, Pakistan, Iran, and Turkey all seek influence. The Central Asians themselves, of course, strive for autonomy and room to maneuver, playing the various powers against each other. They also have squabbles with each other.

In this setting, Russia and China engage in both conflict and cooperation. So far, their common interest in regional stability and keeping US influence out of the area has led the cooperative element of the relationship to dominate. Charles Ziegler notes, "Surprisingly, these two powers have found their interests coincide remarkably well in Central Asia, at least in the short term."

Zbigniew Brzezinski noted in 1997 that Russia's dilemma in Central Asia is that it is too weak to dominate the area politically and too weak economically to develop the region. This still holds true today. Central Asia is part of Russia's "near abroad," a strategic part of the former Soviet Union. Russia sees Central Asia as being within its sphere of influence. The security of Central Asian states, and the form of government they adopt, is particularly important to Russia. However, it also has economic interests. Russia has attempted to control the energy infrastructure of Central Asia, purchasing energy at cheap prices and then reexporting it to Europe at a profit. It further uses its influence to protect ethnic Russians left in the area after the disintegration of the Soviet Union.

China has three major interrelated goals in Central Asia. The first is to ensure stability in its northwestern Xinjiang Uyghur Autonomous Region. China does not want Central Asia to be used as a base for promoting separatism in Xinjiang. Second, China desires closer overall economic and infrastructure linkages with Central Asia. This will further its overall goal of rapid economic development and, in Beijing's view, stabilize Xinjiang. Third, China strives to increase energy imports from

Central Asia by winning energy contracts and developing the infrastructure to deliver oil and gas to China. China sees this as an essential part of an energy diversification strategy. Moreover, it sees pipeline routes across Central Asia as more secure than sea lanes from the Middle East that are susceptible to disruption by the US Navy.

Russia and China both want to eliminate the "three evils" of "terrorism, separatism, and religious extremism" from the region. They work to reduce as much as possible the influence of the United States in Central Asia by seeking to limit US military basing in the region and preventing new "colour revolutions" that might bring stronger democratic governance to the states of the area.

China has been active in developing infrastructure in Central Asia. For example, the China Road and Bridge Company won a contract to build a road from Osh in Kyrgyzstan to the Irkeshtam Pass with China, funded in part by the Chinese government. China is developing rail links to connect Xinjiang with Afghanistan via Tajikistan, while Chinese telecom and internet companies are tying the region together electronically. China has been active in the Asian Development Bank's (ADB) Central Asia Regional Economic Cooperation (CAREC) program, designed to accelerate economic growth and reduce poverty. Moreover, China is systematically attempting to increase its soft power and "people to people" understanding in Central Asia through Confucius Institutes, government-funded organizations that promote Chinese language and culture outside China. Russia has lost ground to China here, although there is still suspicion of the latter among residents of the region due to China's size and potential influence.

Chinese president Xi Jinping's visit to Central Asian states in September 2013 illustrated the success of China's strategy when he sealed economic deals in what he called the "Silk Road Economic Zone." President Xi visited Turkmenistan, Uzbekistan, Kyrgyzstan, and Kazakhstan. In Kazakhstan, Xi and Kazakh president Nursultan Nazarbayev signed $30 billion worth of agreements and symbolically opened a 700-mile gas pipeline that, in conjunction with other pipelines, will take gas from the Caspian Sea to the Chinese coast. China, through CNPC, also purchased an 8.4 percent stake in Kazakhstan's Kashagan oil field in the Caspian Sea, joining a consortium of international oil companies. In Turkmenistan, Xi opened the world's second biggest gas field, Galkynysh, which will lead to a tripling of Chinese gas imports from that country. In Uzbekistan, he signed $15 billion in energy deals.

With China's major economic investments in the region and establishment of new "strategic partnerships," Russian deputy foreign minister Igor Morgulov felt it necessary to assert, in a not entirely convincing manner, "Our Chinese friends recognize the traditional role our country continues to play in this region, so we do not see any regional rivalry problems."

The institutional body that ties Russia and China together on Central Asian issues is the SCO. The SCO consists of China, Russia, Kazakhstan, Kyrgyzstan, Tajikistan, and Uzbekistan.

Established in 2001 with a history rooted in successful border negotiations, the SCO provides a mechanism for Russia and China to cooperate on issues relevant to Central Asia, and, as mentioned earlier, is the institution through which China and Russia conduct military exercises. The SCO is a unique organization for China in that China took the initiative in its founding and considers itself a leader of the organization. Chinese analysts proudly point to the SCO as a key example of China's "new diplomacy" based on trust, equality, respect for diversity, and an emphasis on development.

In some ways, the SCO has been very successful from the perspective of its founders. One Chinese analyst notes that the SCO has been able to maintain stability through the world economic crisis that began in 2008, and there was no "Arab Spring" in the region. There have been no major terrorist attacks in the area, Chinese and Russian relations are good, and the Central Asian states are cooperating. Moreover, other regional actors have been eager to join the SCO as observers.

However, Russia and China do have differences over the SCO. Russia demonstrates some ambiguity toward the organization. It would prefer that the Collective Security Treaty Organization or the Eurasian Economic Community, both of which Russia dominates and do not include China, take the lead security and economic roles in Central Asia.

Moreover, Russia prefers that the SCO primarily focus on security cooperation and strategic issues, while China's emphasis is on economic cooperation. From a Chinese perspective, Russia is not very active in cooperating with China in the SCO but does not block Chinese initiatives. There has been disagreement on additional members, too. One Chinese analyst claims that while Moscow has reportedly supported the membership of Iran, India, and Pakistan, China believes that this would move the focus away from Central Asia and give the SCO an anti-Western character, which China does not want. Furthermore, the SCO has challenges in actually implementing its cooperative agreements, due in part to the lack of capacity in Central Asian member states. Yet, in spite of these differences, the SCO remains a relevant organization in structuring ties between Beijing and Moscow.

Implications for the United States

The United States does not and should not oppose good relations between Russia and China. A peaceful relationship between these two nuclear powers leads to stability in Eurasia. The time period in the 1960s and 1970s when China and the Soviet Union were close to war was very dangerous. Washington also views closer ties between Russia and China as helpful to US interests in a variety of areas. For example, energy cooperation between Russia and China can, in the long run, make China less dependent on Iranian oil supplies, possibly loosening China's ties with Iran's government. Chinese and Russian cooperation is useful in developing Central Asia while preventing any one power from dominating the region, while greater coordination between Russia and China may help in efforts to stabilize Afghanistan after the US withdrawal.

Nevertheless, the relationship between the United States, Russia, and China also has a competitive, triangular aspect to it, with each side adapting hedging strategies. One analyst in Beijing explicitly stated that, despite much of the rhetoric coming out of Beijing to the contrary, the US pivot to China is a hedging strategy rather than a containment strategy. China, similarly, is hedging against the United States through its relationship with Russia. Russia hedges against both China and the West. Each state worries about the other two countries getting too close, although arguably the United States is less susceptible to this worry than China or Russia. For example, Russia strongly objects to the concept of a G2 between the United States and China, as this would deny Russia a seat at the table in making decisions on world order. In fact, Russia is overshadowed by more powerful states in most multilateral forums, including the G8 and BRICS gatherings. Similarly, China is worried about the potential for closer Russian ties with NATO, and in particular does not want to see joint missile defence cooperation between the two sides. At the same time, China does not want the United States to believe that it has entered an alliance with Russia that would threaten US interests. Similarly, Russia looks to the West for modernization and development and does not want a relationship with China that would isolate it from Europe or the United States.

How can the United States best manage this foreign policy triangle? First, it needs to understand the dynamics of this triangle and consider how policy decisions on issues important to Russia or China affect the triangle. When the United States supports policies that Russia and China oppose or commits to policies targeted at China or Russia, it drives those two states closer together. This does not mean the United States cannot oppose Russia and China on any given issue, but it must understand that closer Russian-Chinese cooperation on world order issues will result. One example is Syria. We can debate whether the US decision to back away from a military strike on Syria was correct in terms of Middle East policy. However, the decision to compromise with Russia did defuse a world order question that was pushing Russia and China closer to each other and further from the United States. Another example is the Ukraine conflict. Recent Western economic sanctions on Russia have created stronger economic links between China and Russia. Policymakers should assess regional policies both in light of their regional impact and a broader strategic perspective.

Second, Russia wants to again be an important player in the Asia-Pacific region. The historic US interest has been to ensure that no single country dominates the region. A stronger

Russian role in Pacific affairs, bolstered by a more prosperous RFE, can be good for the United States once the Ukrainian crisis is resolved. Therefore, the United States should in the long run encourage better relations between Japan and Russia and between South Korea and Russia. This means encouraging energy exports from Russia to South Korea and Japan and encouraging a resolution of the dispute between Japan and Russia over the Kurile Islands.

The United States should provide incentives for US companies to invest in the RFE to the extent it is profitable. The US Pacific Command has engaged Russia through port calls and Russian participation in RIM-PAC exercises, but more might be done to develop military-to-military cooperation.

Third, the time may soon come to press for three-way nuclear negotiations. China's historic policy has been to maintain a small nuclear deterrent whose numbers are a tightly controlled secret, claiming that the United States and Russia must substantially reduce their forces before China will enter into arms control negotiations. However, the United States and Russia have reduced their deployed nuclear weapons, while China has been presumably increasing its weapons. Thus, Alexi Arbatov and Vladimir Dvorkin assert that "it can be speculated that the real motives behind China's complete secrecy about its nuclear forces lie not in their 'weakness' and 'small size' but in the much larger strength of China's actual nuclear arsenal than can be construed from observing the weapons deployed on its surface. In addition, China's economic and technical potential would allow it to build up its nuclear arms rapidly."

This is more threatening to Russia than the United States because of Russia's greater reliance on nuclear weapons for defence. Thus, it may finally be time to push for trilateral arms control negotiations, although at this point there are still serious obstacles to such negotiations. These include new strains in US-Russian ties, continued Chinese secrecy over the size of its arsenal and its nuclear doctrine, as well as Chinese insistence that Russia and the United States further disarm before China engages in meaningful nuclear reduction talks.

Fourth, the US withdrawal from Afghanistan opens new possibilities for three-way cooperation to work for stability in Afghanistan and all of Central Asia. While the United States was criticized by both Russia and China for having troops in Afghanistan, they now fear the results of a US withdrawal.

China feels it lacks the resources to deal with Afghanistan, and many Chinese analysts feel the Afghan government will fall after 2014 when Washington withdraws combat troops. China, which is heavily concerned with its own domestic stability, is worried about the implications of potential chaos in Afghanistan for what it sees as its Uyghur problem.

Thus, it is clearly in the interest of all three states to have a strong Afghan government after 2014 that can minimize the level of violence within Afghanistan and prevent the spread of extremism and terror outside its borders. The United States, Russia, China, and perhaps the SCO can coordinate policies to produce an outcome that will be in the interest of every state. In other words, the struggle in Afghanistan and its environs is one of organized states against nonstate actors, and the states have incentives to cooperate.

In conclusion, the Chinese-Russian relationship is strong and has been building momentum for close to two decades. Russia and China are bound together by a desire to bring about a world order that is marked more by a concert of great powers than US hegemony, an order that is defined by classical Westphalian values as opposed to liberal concepts that degrade the sanctity of state sovereignty.

The relationship is also built on practical cooperation in the realm of economics, energy, security, Central Asian issues, and the SCO. Nevertheless, this is not an anti-US alliance. For their own development goals, Russia and China need the United States and Europe. China feels that its developmental accomplishments are fragile and domestic unrest is a threat, while Russia has failed to substantially expand its economic base beyond energy production.

A certain degree of cooperation between Russia and China can be in US interests. Moreover, each of the issue areas discussed in this article has arenas of conflict. If in the long run Chinese power continues to grow relative to that of Russia, these conflicts will become more intense as Moscow resists being identified as a junior partner of Beijing. With smart policies, Washington can work the strategic triangle to ensure that its core interests are maintained.

INDIA'S CHINA POLICY SINCE THE END OF THE COLD WAR

Certain scholars believe that India's China policy has undergone three major phases of adjustment since the end of the Cold War: the pre-1998 phase policy of reconciliation; the 1998–2000 phase policy of hostility; and the 2000 to present phase policy of engagement. The second phase around the time of the 1998 nuclear tests featured harangues from the Indian government regarding the 'China threat' and a brief deadlock in Sino–Indian relations. The author, however, believes that two, rather than three, phases of adjustment are applicable to an explanation of the state of bilateral relations between China and India in the post-Cold War era.

When considering India's overall strategic aims at the time of the 1998 nuclear tests and the implications and specific actions of its subsequent China policy, it is difficult to pinpoint two 180 degree-policy shifts in the course of just two years. Facts demonstrate that India named China as a threat at the time of the 1998 tests as a matter of expedience to acquiesce in the anti-China stance of certain parties in the United States and other Western nations; it was a ploy whose purpose was to divert attention from and rationalize the nuclear tests, thereby dispelling any notion of sanctions.

It should be borne in mind, however, that India's understanding of comprehensive national strength deepened after the Cold War, as did its leaders' belief that nuclear arms and credible nuclear deterrence were hallmarks of a superpower. Entering the nuclear club was consequently a stride towards achieving one of the sub-continent's greatest national aspirations. The Rao government, which pursued a China policy of reconciliation and engagement, had made preparations for nuclear tests but stopped short of carrying them out for fear of the potential burden on the newly recovered economy of international sanctions.

Prime Minister Vajpayee and other political leaders repeatedly and publicly expressed soon after the 1998 tests that India had no wish to hold China as an enemy or a threat, stating, to the contrary, their desire for reinforced friendly relations. At no point during this period did diplomatic engagement between India and China cease. Indian External Affairs Minister Jaswant Singh's visit to China in June 1999 demonstrated that the Sino–Indian relationship had recovered in the space of a year from any damage that the nuclear tests had inflicted upon it. That becoming a nuclear power while maintaining stable relations with China were post-Cold War India's strategic goals was also implied by the sub-continent's explicit moves towards repairing its relationship with China. The 1998 nuclear tests constituted no fundamental change to India's China policy and should, within the scope of Sino–Indian relations, be regarded as a minor episode. Moreover, the shift of India's China policy in 1988 was not prompted by any change of security concept; Prime Minister Rajiv Gandhi's trip to China that year was motivated by the fact of Sino–Soviet reconciliation. Changes in security concept explicitly propelled India's; post-Cold War China policy adjustments. This book, therefore, primarily examines developments and changes in India's China policy after the Cold War. It holds that a substantive change indeed occurred; specifically from one of hostility and antagonism during the Cold War (especially 1962–1988) to reconciliation and engagement thereafter. This policy change, however, was by no means instantaneous but characterized by gradual, phased development. Two, rather than three, phases of adjustment tally with changes in India's post-Cold War security concept.

India's China Policy from the End of the Cold War to 1998

Indian leaders believed after 1962 that hostilities between China and India were inevitable, and viewed China as a major enemy. Prime Minister Indira Gandhi considered Sino–Indian antagonism as going far beyond border disputes, and that China was pursuing the more 'complex' policy of pressing India on all fronts and, moreover, displacing the sub-continent by establishing its own dominant position in the Asian power hierarchy.

The goal of India's China policy during this period, therefore, was to ensure its supremacy over China in Asia and, in the event of armed conflict, to avoid repeating mistakes that had led to its defeat in the 1962 Sino–Indian conflict. India's policy at the time can be so summarized: strengthen military capability and deployment; seek aid from major powers, respectively, the United States, United Kingdom and USSR; and support Chinese separatist forces. After the Cold War ended, however, changes in India's domestic and international situation brought tremendous challenges, and its position as regards China and its related policy goals showed clear adjustments. India considered China as a nation going through a reflective, 'inward looking' period and, as such, had no intention of attacking the sub-continent. In the short-term, therefore, it constituted no threat. The goal of India's new China policy was to maintain stability in Sino–Indian relations, ensure peaceful borders and create conditions suitable for India to gather its resources and restore economic and military strength. The specific policy adjustments were as follows.

Achieve Simultaneous Progress in Solving Border Disputes

For almost two decades after 1962, India made resolution of border disputes a pre-condition for normalizing relations with China. Its insistence in this regard was the main reason for the longstanding chill in Sino–Indian relations. Although the two nations restored ambassadorial-level diplomatic relations in 1976, and in 1981 agreed to begin talks on the border issue, this principled standpoint did not change. Upon meeting with visiting then-External Affairs Minister Vajpayee early in 1979, Comrade Deng Xiaoping proposed an agreement that would provide 'a package solution' for relevant border disputes.

He said that if it were not possible completely to resolve border disputes at an early date, he would consider cooperation in other areas. But it was not until 1988 during Rajiv Gandhi's trip to China that the Indian government accepted this suggestion and formally initiated the process of normalizing bilateral relations which the successive Indian governments pursued and implemented after the Cold War ended. It is notable that during the time the two sides promoted negotiations on border issues they also exchanged high-level visits in which the two nations signed cooperative agreements in such areas as trade, technology, education and culture, and that cooperation between them grew ever greater in depth and breadth.

Shift Strategies on Border Talks

As India needed a peaceful, stable environment in which to concentrate on economic recovery, securing Sino–Indian borders was its primary goal in the early 1990s. Because of India's; pre-1988 insistence on not normalizing Sino–Indian relations until the border issues were settled, there were suspicions that the sub-continent was 'taking improvements in bilateral relations as a bargaining chip through which to force China to yield in border disputes'. India consequently insisted in the talks that began in 1981 on its own position as regards a segmented solution to the issue. India's objective understanding of the complexity of the Sino–Indian border dispute after the Cold War and of realistic strategic considerations and needs prompted an adjusted strategy for these talks. This was manifest in its suggestion of a gradual solution to border disputes: the first step would be to stabilize the Line of Actual Control (LAC) situation and eliminate disagreements over its demarcation; the second to reach agreement on preserving peace and tranquillity along the LAC; and the third to take measures to establish mutual trust along the LAC.

This accomplished, the two nations could then address substantive problems in their border dispute. This tentative plan enabled India and China to approach a consistent position whereby the two sides worked to achieve a solution to Sino–

Indian border disputes and create an atmosphere of reasonableness and peace. The two nations made progress, signing in 1993 the Agreement on Maintenance of Peace and Tranquillity along the Line of Actual Control in the Sino– Indian Border Areas, and in 1996 the Agreement Between the Government of the Republic of India and the Government of the People's Republic of China on Confidence-Building Measures in the Military Field Along the Line of Actual Control in the India–China Border Areas. India saw these two agreements as on the one hand ensuring the two sides could resolve border disputes peacefully without resorting to violence, and on the other that border disputes would not inhibit the development of their bilateral relations.

Tibetan Issue and do not Provoke China

Leaders of India's independence movement had at the time of the British Raj followed the British colonialist concept of Tibet as a 'buffer region' between India and China. After winning independence, therefore, the Indian government supported from the very beginning the so-called 'Tibetan independence movement'. At around the time of the founding of the People's Republic of China, India seized the opportunity offered by China's political upheaval to promote the international standing of the local Tibetan government and thwart China's liberation of Tibet. New Delhi continued unremittingly in its efforts to convince China's central government, even during the 1950s heyday of Sino–Indian amity, to give Tibet substantial autonomy and to reduce to the greatest extent possible the size of its garrison there. After the insurrection of 1959 the Indian government was more overt in its support of Tibet, giving asylum to fugitive rebels and propping up the so-called 'Tibetan Government in Exile' established by the Dalai Lama in 1960 in the Indian city of Dharamsala. India further incited and encouraged Tibetan independence activities after the Sino–Indian conflict of 1962.

In truth, Indian leaders considered their support for exiled Tibetans' separatist activities as an effective containment against

China. But when Prime Minister Rajiv Gandhi visited China in 1988 he issued the statement: 'The Indian side reiterates the long-standing and consistent policy of the Government of India that Tibet is an autonomous region of China and that anti-China political activities by Tibetan elements are not permitted on Indian soil,' which implied India's change of approach from that of support for Tibetan independence. Indian leaders reiterated this pledge after the Cold War ended and imposed limits on Tibetan fugitives' anti-China political activities. For instance, Indian officials would generally contact the Dalai Lama and leaders of the so-called Tibetan government in exile before a visit by Chinese leaders to India, requesting that they refrain from Tibetan protests, demonstrations or other anti-Chinese behaviour.

Yet, differences still exist between China and India on the issue of Tibetan autonomy. Although, proceeding from the requirement of preserving stable Sino–Indian relations, the post-Cold War Indian government has been low-key in its support of the Dalai Lama and other Tibetan fugitives, this does not signify a substantial change in its strategic treatment of the Tibetan issue.

Changes in India's China Policy from 1999 to Present

Achieving recovery, contending for the status of global power had been India's ambition for decades. The growth of the sub-continent's comprehensive strength and improvements in the international environment in the late 1990s presented to it a real possibility of realizing this ambition, as well as a number of other unprecedented strategic opportunities. Against this backdrop, reconciliation with China and the unchanged overall direction of the relationship produced several new adjustments to the positions and goals of India's China policy. At this stage, India saw China neither as enemy nor friend, believing that cooperation could coexist with competition between the two nations. India still considered China as constituting no threat in the short term, but began focusing on long-term trends in the balance of power. The emphasis of the goals of its new China policy are on ensuring that future Sino–Indian relations are of benefit to India by making China a positive factor in the process of its rise. Maintaining the stability of Sino–Indian relations remains fundamental. The new policy adjustments are as follows.

Expand Economic Cooperation with China

Trade between the two nations ceased after the 1962 Sino–Indian Border Conflict, and did not resume until 1977. The volume of trade between the two sides in the 1980s wavered at around roughly Us." million. But after the Cold War ended, Sino–Indian trade experienced a seemingly spontaneous phase of rapid development. The trade volume between China and India increased from $264 million in 1991 to $1.988 billion in 1999—a yearly average of 31.2%—or an increase factor of 6.5 over eight years. Indian leaders' concerns about India's economic recovery nonetheless maintained at this point the China policy focus on stabilizing political relations and establishing tranquil borders. Indian leaders' understanding of economic strength and security having becoming more profound since 1999, their enthusiasm for developing bilateral trade soared.

As China and India were the world's two most rapidly developing nations, Indian leaders could see the obvious potential for trade between them and that strengthening bilateral trade would be of great mutual benefit. Also that close economic ties could have a stabilizing influence on their political relationship. Statistics show that bilateral trade since 1999 has entered into a new period of growth. The average yearly growth to 2006 was 44.4%—a rate which exceeded that of the preceeding period and which is being achieved on an ever-stronger numerical foundation. The volume of Sino–Indian trade reached US$24.8 billion in 2006, having increased by a factor of 11.5 over 1999 and one of 93 over 1991. China became India's second largest trading partner in 2006, and India China's tenth largest. It may be said that the role of Sino–Indian trade has grown from one unworthy of mention to a decisive aspect of the overall bilateral relationship.

RUSSIA-PAKISTAN RELATIONS IN THE POST-COLD WAR ERA

Russia-Pakistan relations in the post cold war era have improved reasonably. It is known that friends and enemies changes in international politics as per the circumstances depending upon the national interest of the country. Keeping this in mind, one could see how the strong US-Pakistan relationship deteriorated after maintaining almost 60 years of a strong bond between each other. Today a shift has occurred between the Pakistan-US ties, between US-India ties and also between Russia-Pakistan ties. A new era of friendship and cooperation started between these nations. While it is important to diversify the relationship for the development of the country at the same time, it is also important to maintain the old trusted ties.

Whenever a talk on the growing Russia-Pakistan partnership comes-up, a question is raised about whether this relationship will have any adverse impact on Indo-Russian relations. In particular, whether Russia will sell arms to Pakistan, which might be a worrying factor for India. As far as India-Russia relations are concerned, they are time-tested and cannot be easily disturbed and will not be affected anyway due to Russia's growing engagement with Pakistan. Looking into Russia's historic relationship with India, it appears unlikely that Russia will permit allow its ties with Islamabad to have any negative impact on New Delhi. Similarly if the India-US relationship improves then Russia need not worry on this growing proximity either, as for India, Russia's friendship and strategic partnership is extremely valuable.

Russian President Vladimir Putin is set to visit Islamabad on 26th September for a quadrilateral meeting with Tajikistan, Pakistan and Afghanistan, mainly to discuss the future of Afghanistan. Russia-Pakistan relations took a new start in 2002, when the then Pakistan President Parvez Musharraf paid a visit to Moscow after a gap of almost 30 years since President Zulfikar Ali Bhutto visited Russia. Of course, during the Cold War period Pakistan and the USSR did cooperate with each other on a number of occasions and some exchange of visits and dialogue also took place.

A steel plant was also built in Karachi with Soviet technical assistance. However, Russia-Pakistan relations could not reach the same height as Russia-India relations during the Cold War era. One of the main reasons for this was mainly due to Pakistan's growing proximity towards the USA Also the USSR-Pakistan relationship deteriorated sharply during 1979-1989 Soviet-Afghan war, due to mistrust and suspicions that developed because of the Soviet invasion of Afghanistan.

However, in the post-Cold War period things have changed reasonably. Today, Pakistan and Russia agree to promote trade, investment and joint projects particularly in energy, infrastructure development, metal industry and agriculture sectors.

Expanding defence ties by holding joint military exercises are also under consideration. Moscow has offered to sell Pakistan the Sukhoi Superjet 100, a new aircraft with a capacity of up to 95 passengers, while Pakistan and Russia jointly agreed to upgrade the steel plant built in Karachi during the Soviet period.

Russia has offered Pakistan counter-terrorism equipments and to cooperate in fighting terrorism and radicalism. Russia has also promised to explore the possibilities of developing the CASA (Central Asia-South Asia) 100 electric transmission project from Tajikistan and improve the heavy mechanical complex in Taxilla. Russia has expressed its support for the Turkmenistan-Afghanistan-Pakistan-India pipeline project.

Both the countries are showing interest to enhance the cooperation, which would help in developing a strong bilateral relationship based on mutual interests. Today, Pakistan is an observer in the Sanghai Cooperation Organisation (SCO) and is hoping to get full membership. In 2011, Prime Minister Putin publicly approved Pakistan's proposal to join the SCO as a full member along with India and emphasised on improving relations with Pakistan. Today, Russia wants to get more involved in the regional affairs mainly in stabilising Afghanistan before the withdrawal of US troops by 2014 from the country.

Instability in Afghanistan and its consequence which can easily spill over to the neighbouring Central Asian region as well as to the North Caucasus is a concern for Russia. Apart from the threat of radicalism, Russia is also concerned about the drug-trafficking that flows from Afghanistan to Russia through Central Asia. Almost one fourth of the drugs produced in Afghanistan flows to Russia. With a drastic demographic fall and with nearly 3 million drug addicts, Russia today cannot afford to continue this situation for long. Russia understands Pakistan's importance as the key player in Afghanistan and its geopolitical significance.

Increasing ties between Russia and Pakistan is also a reflection of US's deteriorating clout in the region. Russia feels that Pakistan can play vital role in bringing stability in Afghanistan. Probably this is one of the major reasons for Russia to develop closer contacts with Pakistan. While the end of the Cold war saw Indo-US growing engagement, Russia-Pakistan closeness was quite an expected move. Both countries are now trying to develop ties looking into their national interest.

Today Russia and Pakistan are trying to forget their past mistrust and suspicions. President Putin in his third term is trying to improve the relationship with Pakistan as part of Russia's Asia policy. President Putin's forthcoming visit to Pakistan after a long gap going to be first ever visit by a Russian President to Pakistan. This visit would create an environment for a new perspective for moving forward with optimism in growing the relationship. Though it is very early now to predict the strength of the relationship, however, as a first step, both are trying to establish regular contact, which is noteworthy. However, continuity in the relationship will definitely depend on both sides' efforts and interest and on how much value and dependency the two countries show towards each other.

INDIA, RUSSIA SIGN 'MILITARY COOPERATION ROADMAP'

Indian Defense Minister Arun Jaitley and his Russian counterpart Sergei Shoigu signed a military cooperation roadmap during the 17th meeting of the Russian-Indian intergovernmental commission for military-technical cooperation, which took place in Moscow, Russia on June 23, according to Russian media reports.

"We are determined to go ahead with building up cooperation in order to enhance the combat readiness of both countries' armed forces and to exchange experience in various defense-related matters," the Russian defense minister said following the conclusion of the agreement, *TASS* news agency reports.

The roadmap is to become the basic document in planning bilateral contacts, but Shoigu did not provide details on the contents. Shoigu also emphasized that with India's accession to the Shanghai Cooperation Organization, new venues for cooperation will be possible. "We welcome India's accession to the Shanghai Cooperation Organization as it opens up new prospects for cooperation," he said.

"Over the past years, Russia and India have been able to develop particularly close friendly relations, consistent and trust based," the Russian defense minister added. "It was once again confirmed at the recent meeting between Russian President Vladimir Putin and Indian Prime Minister Narendra Modi, which took place in St. Petersburg on June 1."

During their June 1 meeting, the Indian and Russian heads of government agreed to push for "qualitatively higher level of military-to-military cooperation" within the framework of the Special and Privileged Strategic Partnership between the two countries, according to a joint statement issued by Modi and Putin following the annual India-Russia summit in June.

India and Russia are also set to upgrade joint military exercises. "Military cooperation is a major component and platform of Russian-Indian strategic interaction. Joint military exercises are the most important aspect of this," Shoigu said on Wednesday.

As I explained last month, this year's iteration of the Indo-Russian Indra bilateral military exercise will for the first time involve personnel from all three service branches from both countries. Russia and India have held the Indra exercise since 2003.

One of the major recent stumbling blocks to deeper Indo-Russian military ties remains defense industry cooperation, as I pointed out in May:

India-Russia defense relations have somewhat cooled over the last months with the cancellation of an aircraft deal and continuing disagreements over one of their most prestigious defense projects — the co-development and production of the Sukhoi/HAL Fifth Generation Fighter Aircraft (FGFA), known in India as the Perspective Multi-role Fighter (PMF).

On Wednesday, the Indian defense minister made an effort to mend fences by encouraging Russian defense firms to continue to continue their engagement in India. "I invite Russian companies to come forward with proposals for technology transfer to Indian companies and facilitate manufacturing of more advanced components/parts and subsystems. This can start with platforms of Russian origin where the requirement is in large numbers and is recurring in nature," Jaitley said.

Last month, India issued a new policy that will allow private firms to enter into agreements as "strategic partners" with non-Indian original equipment manufacturers (OEMs) for certain types of military systems including tanks, aircraft, and submarines as part of the Indian government's "Make in India" initiative.

"Here again, Russia as India's largest, oldest and most trusted partner in defense hardware and equipment, would have a comparative advantage in partnering with Indian companies for realizing 'Make in India' potential in defense production," Jaitley said, according to the Press Trust of India.

Among other things, Russia and India are in the final stages of negotiations over the delivery date of new missile air defense systems and four *Admiral Grigorovich*-class frigates. Both sides also signed an agreement for India to lease an inactive *Akula*-class multi-purpose nuclear submarine last year. Rosoboronexport, Russian Helicopters, and India's Hindustan Aeronautics Limited (HAL) have also agreed to create a joint venture for the production of 140 Ka-226T helicopters in October 2016. (60 additional helicopters will be received in fly-away condition from Russia.)

CONCLUSIONS

The strategic triangle among the United States, China, and the Soviet union has undergone a host of vicissitudes throughout the last four decades of the Cold War, culminating in a unipolar world order based on U.S. dominance in international relations. The collapse of the power balance within the triangular system in 1991 had a consequential impact on Sino-Russian relations and U.S.-Chinese relations alike. As regards the U.S.-Russian relationship in the new millennium, both powers attempted to forge closer ties with China, albeit not simultaneously, when relations between Washington in Moscow deteriorated. By the end of the 1990s China and Russia began to express their dissatisfaction with U.S. unilateralism, and such a stance was reflected in the countries' shared vision of a multipolar world and the concept of the "strategic relationship directed towards the 21st century." Despite grandiose proclamations of the "strategic partnership," shared vision of a multipolar world, and increased diplomatic cooperation, Sino-Russian relations are utterly lacking in substance. Much like during the Cold War, the relationship between Moscow and Beijing is based upon counterbalancing the United States in global politics, for cleavages within the strategic triangle among the three powers have generally led to the reorientation of China and Russia's foreign policies in the 1990s and late 2000s.

In so far as economic relations between Moscow and Beijing are concerned, notwithstanding increased economic interaction, neither country truly regards another as a strategic partner. Russia still considers its relations with the European Union indispensable, while the United States remains priority for China (Kotkin, 2009). This configuration is unlikely to change in the future: besides military hardware and natural resources, there is little Russia can offer to its "strategic partner." Likewise, most joint projects between Russia and China are aimed at enhancing energy cooperation through building oil and gas pipelines in Central Asia. Given the resource-oriented model of Russia's economy, Moscow will likely remain China's resource and weapons supplier for decades to come. China, for its part, has been using its "strategic" alliance with Russia as "strategic" leverage vis-à-vis Washington. Diplomatic cooperation with Moscow has helped China promote the idea of multipolarity as it relates to Beijing's national interests. It can be assumed that China's relationship with Russia will become irrelevant as soon as China becomes an independent power in global affairs.

This, in all likelihood, will mark the end of the "strategic" partnership between the two powers, paving the way for U.S.-China rivalry.

7

Russia's Strategic Partnerships with China and India

The Sino-Russian strategic partnership predates the Indo-Russian strategic partnership, which was finally realized with President Vladimir Putin's trip to India in October 2000. In the first half of the 1990s, the United States and the Russian Federation described their relationship as a strategic partnership, but by the end of the decade this term was discredited in both Washington and Moscow. Since coming to power in January 2000, President Putin and his administration have increasingly referred to the European Union and/or Europe as a strategic partner, but that relationship has not been endorsed in official documents in the same way as Russia's relationships with China and India.

The Sino-Russian and Indo-Russian relationships share a number of common features, but there are some important differences as well. In each case there is strong rhetorical support for a multipolar world order not dominated by the United States. As a declining power—experiencing, in fact, the most rapid and precipitous decline in peacetime in modern history-Russia is coming from a very different place in supporting multipolarity than are rising powers like China and India. Russia has witnessed its power and significance erode tremendously in the last decade, while the United States has enjoyed nearly a decade of unprecedented economic growth. Russia warily regards globalization as a fig leaf for the extension of U.S. hegemony throughout the world. U.S. economic strength is outstripped only by its military advantages, and the Russians can find no comfort in comparing the performance of U.S. forces in Iraq and Kosovo with that of Russian forces in Chechnya in the 1990s. After the hopes of a U.S.-Russian partnership dissipated with a series of disappointments in the last decade, former foreign minister Yevgeny Primakov and the majority of the Russian foreign and security policy elite increasingly supported Russia's strengthening its relations with China, India, Iran, and major European powers to stem what Moscow views as the overbearing dominance of the United States in international affairs.

Russia, China, and India all support an enhanced role for the United Nations, and Russia has specifically endorsed India's candidacy to join the UN Security Council. All three denounced the NATO action in Kosovo as a violation of international law since it did not receive a UN mandate. All three are also very sensitive to violations of national sovereignty and are reluctant to support international mediation of civil conflicts because of challenges to their own territorial integrity in Taiwan, Kashmir, and Chechnya. Both Russia and China share a strong aversion to U.S.-led alliances' taking such action, because to a greater or lesser extent they fear the prospect of U.S. intervention in their own territory. During the Kosovo war, the sense grew among Russians that today NATO was taking action in Yugoslavia, but tomorrow it could be in Chechnya or elsewhere in Russia. Although that seems quite unrealistic, the growing relationships of former Soviet republics such as Georgia, Ukraine, Azerbaijan, and others with NATO are viewed nearly unanimously by the Russian foreign and security policy elite as contradictory to Russian national interests.

For China, recovering Taiwan is about as high a policy priority as promoting economic development. The prospect of U.S. intervention to support Taiwan in the event of a conflict is the most likely scenario for great power conflict in the early twenty-first century. China has regarded the broadening of the geographical scope of the U.S.-Japanese security alliance at the end of the 1990s with the same trepidation with which Russia has viewed the expansion of the NATO mission to include out-of-area activities. The most recent Chinese white paper on national defence, issued in fall *:woo,* views the United States in very threatening terms, and Chinese defence thinkers now talk more openly about the increasing likelihood of conflict with the United States. The Indian/Pakistani conflict over Kashmir may present the world's most imminent danger of nuclear conflict.

China, Russia, and India share sensitivities about Islamic threats, as each country has large Muslim populations and each shares borders with states containing Muslim majorities. India has cause for the greatest concern because the Kashmir problem has the potential to escalate into a nuclear conflict with archrival Pakistan. In a little over fifty years since independence, India and Pakistan have already fought three major wars against one another, and there has been continual fighting in Kashmir during at least the last decade. In the last two decades, Russia has fought only Muslim foes.

In Afghanistan in the 1980s and Chechnya in the 1990s, Russian forces have performed poorly, and each war has sent shock waves through Russian society. With large Muslim populations reaching into the heart of the Russian Federation in the Volga region, Russian sensitivities about Islamic threats focus more on the potential for state disintegration than interstate conflict.

As China is the most ethnically homogeneous of the three states and its Muslim population is more isolated in the west of China in Xinjiang Province, China's concern about Islamic separatism is more muted than that of Russia and India, but it is real nonetheless. In particular, all three governments fear that the increasingly weak and failing states of Central Asia will serve as conduits for more radical Muslim groups, terrorist activities, and drug trafficking, which will erode their authority in peripheral territories. Each country also views Afghanistan under the Taliban as the dangerous hub of these activities.

India and China have increasingly relied on Russia as a source of conventional weapons and possibly other weapons technologies. They are the two biggest clients of the struggling

Russian military-industrial complex—each now purchases about $1 billion worth of arms a year-and the relationships are growing. Since domestic Russian procurement virtually dried up in the 1990s, arms sales to China and India are a vital, if controversial, national security interest for Moscow. Three basic rationales explain much of the Russian enthusiasm for arms sales to China, India, and others-notably Iran, since Moscow's announcement in December 2000 of the decision to resume sales of conventional weapons to Tehran.

The first reason is simply economic. The Russian economy has floundered badly since the Soviet collapse (and before the collapse, for that matter), and aside from natural resources, weapons systems are one of the few areas in which Russia can compete with some success in the global marketplace. The Russian military-industrial complex also benefits from U.S. sanctions against sales to China after the massacres at Tiananmen, to Iran for more than two decades after the hostage crisis, and to India after its nuclear tests in 1998. In 2000, Russian arms sales amounted to about $4 billion, which represents a modest increase over the previous five years, when arms deliveries averaged a bit over $3 billion. Even at $4 billion, Russian arms sales amount to only about 15 percent of U.S. arms transfers, and they run considerably behind France's and Great Britain's. This is a far cry from the height of Soviet arms sales in the 1980s, but much of that income existed only on paper, as many Soviet clients were unable or unwilling to pay in hard currency or the equivalent. Still, the basic story for Russian arms sales after the collapse of the USSR is one of massive market loss. Powerful domestic industrial and institutional lobbies, including the Ministry of Atomic Energy, strongly promote Russian weapons systems and related technologies sales.

The second reason is also economic, but with a national security slant. Because Russian procurement nearly came to a standstill in the last decade, without sales abroad the struggling Russian military-industrial complex would have collapsed entire!y. In 1999 and 2000, Russian arms sales averaged about four times the level of domestic procurement. For Russia, losing all of the human and industrial capital invested over many decades in the Soviet weapons complex would have catastrophic implications for future Russian national security. No doubt excessive allocations to the military during the Soviet period were a major factor in Soviet economic decline and consequently detrimental for long-term national security. But even the most liberally inclined Russians understand that Russia must maintain a military-industrial complex, albeit one that commands a far smaller portion of the national product than in Soviet days. Already the erosion of their military-industrial complex raises serious questions about Russia's ability to deliver on arms sales agreements, as increasingly Moscow is offering to sell new systems, such as the Su-30MKI superfighter, that have not gone into serial production before. 16 Most of the conventional arms transfers in the 1990s consisted of off the-shelf systems that had been in production for years. Although Russian enterprises can still build impressive prototypes, the subcontracting networks of the Soviet military-industrial complex have deteriorated to the extent that serial production is very difficult.

The third rationale is directly tied to Russian perceptions of its medium-and long-term security interests, which must be defined to some extent by geography. Although international security may not fully subscribe to the first three rules of real estate, "location, location, location," Russians have historically and culturally attached great importance to the role of geography, and after the ideologically imposed hiatus of the cold war, the study of geopolitics has once again become quite popular in Russia. Russia is surrounded by a belt of weak, and in many cases failing, states to the west and south (former Soviet republics), and just beyond the territory of the former Soviet Union are rising powers China and India and other states with regional aspirations such as Pakistan, Iran, and Iraq; these states have varying interests in international stability and the international system as currently construed. Russia has chosen to use its role as a supplier of weaponry as a means to maintain some leverage and influence on the rise to power of many of these states. In an ideal world Russia would probably prefer to be surrounded by countries that did not seek to develop weapons of mass destruction and their means of delivery, and the official Russian position supporting the nonproliferation regime is not exactly disingenuous. But the reality is that Russia is not surrounded by, let's say, Canada, Mexico, and two huge oceans, but rather by a number of countries that have developed or likely will develop weapons of mass destruction and their means of delivery. By maintaining a shadowy role on the periphery of those weapons programs, Russia maintains some control over their development as well as knowledge about their status. Thinking hypothetically, if you are in Moscow and you have concluded that Iran will eventually, with or without your involvement, develop weapons of mass destruction, the rationale for some degree of involvement becomes more understandable. Determining precisely what that role is without access to classified intelligence reports is virtually impossible, and even with such access, reaching clear conclusions must not be an easy task. 18

The combination of the economic and national security factors driving Russian weapons and weapons technology sales to China, India, and other states suggests that this will be an enduring feature of Russian foreign policy, and there are a number of indications that the Putin administration has made a strategic decision to promote Russian arms sales more aggressively despite the objections of the United States and others. However, there is a competitive aspect to Chinese and Indian conventional purchases from Russia, since Beijing and New Delhi to some extent regard each other as security threats.

INDIA'S RELATIONS WITH RUSSIA

During the March 2010 visit of the Russian Prime Minister Vladimir Putin to New Delhi, the Indian Prime Minister Manmohan Singh described Russia in fulsome terms:

Relations with Russia are a key pillar of our foreign policy, and we regard Russia as a trusted and reliable strategic partner.

Ours is a relationship that not only stands independent of any other, but whose significance has grown over time. Our partnership covers areas such as defence, civil nuclear energy, space, science and technology, hydrocarbons and trade and investment.

During discussions, bilateral economic as well as regional security issues were top of the agenda. Putin's India visit was also watched very carefully in many Western capitals as this was happening immediately after the London Conference, where the Western alliance had been working on exit strategies in Afghanistan. The Putin visit was seen by many in India as a precursor to any hedging strategy involving Russia, India, Iran and the Central Asian republics against the possibility of a Taliban return in Afghanistan. Since the signing of their Declaration on Strategic Partnership in October 2000, this had been the subsequent 11th summit meeting. Similar to earlier meetings, five more agreements were signed in March 2010. Apart from multi-billion dollar arms deals, an inter-governmental agreement on broad-based co-operation in atomic energy and a 'road map' for future co-operation were also signed. Similar to the last few summits, strategic congruence, defence purchases, hydrocarbons and nuclear power dominated the agenda. The visit obviously gained more significance because of a changing strategic scenario in India's neighbourhood. This chapter aims to analyse how and if, to use Manmohan Singh's phrase, its 'significance has grown over time', in a relationship that first took shape in the days of the old USSR.

Historical background

Historically, the USSR under Stalin (Iosif Dzhugashvili), was suspicious of the genuineness of India's independence and non-alignment. However, Indo-Soviet bonhomie started with Jawaharlal Nehru's visit to the USSR in June 1955 and the Nikita Khrushchev/Nikolai Bulganin visit to India in December 1955. This was also the time when the Congress party in India was afirming its belief in state planning and a 'socialistic pattern of society', and Nehru was playing a leading role in the Bandung

Conference (1955) of 29 Afro-Asian nations. During the same period, the USSR began to use the instruments of aid, trade and diplomacy in developing countries, to limit Western influence. Subsequently, Indo-Soviet relations flourished over the decades in the metallurgy, defence, energy and trade sectors. During the India–China war in 1962, the USSR tried to be neutral between what it called 'brother China' and 'friend India', with the People's Republic of China seeing this as a betrayal of international communist solidarity on the part of the USSR, and a factor that reflected and further exacerbated the growing Sino–Soviet split. In the early 1970s both Indian and Soviet leaders looked on the emerging US-Chinese rapprochement as a serious threat to their security. Their response had been in 1971 with the Indo-Soviet Treaty of Peace, Friendship and Cooperation, which provided immediate consultation in case of military action against parties to the Treaty. During the India–Pakistan war in 1971, the USSR took a firm position in favour of India and sent ships to the Indian Ocean to counter any move by the USA, which had already sent its 7th Fleet ships into the Bay of Bengal. The results of the 1971 Indo–Pakistani war and emergence of Bangladesh established a trusted partnership between India and the USSR. During the 1980s both Rajiv Gandhi and Mikhail Gorbachev advocated a nuclear-free world. However, after the Soviet invasion of Afghanistan in 1979, India was also confronted with a dilemma of how to preserve its non-aligned credibility without jeopardizing its relations with the USSR.

In the initial post-Soviet period, bilateral relations in the 1990s went through a period of uncertainty when Russia was preoccupied with domestic economic and political issues, and with its relations with the USA and Europe. Now India had to deal with a new Russia which was Eurocentric, economically dependent on the West, and neither had the interest nor the resources for Third World regimes. President Boris Yeltsin, during his visit to Delhi in 1993, tried to recreate the spirit of old friendship with a new Treaty of Friendship to replace the old India-Soviet 1971 treaty. However, the fundamental character of the Treaty was transformed and in case of any threat to peace, the new Treaty vaguely called for regular consultations and co-ordination. Although Yeltsin described India and Russia as 'natural partners', he was careful not to give the impression of a 'special relationship'. Although relations were restored to respectable levels, the early years (1991–96) of 'benign neglect' of India by Russia left a deep mark on Indian policy-makers.

The situation changed when the new Russian Prime Minister Yevgeny Primakov (1998–99) started shifting from the previous pro-Western Russian foreign policy. To strengthen his country's relations with old allies, Primakov visited India in 1998 and pushed proposals for creating a Russia-India-China (RIC) strategic triangle, although RIC coherence remains questionable for some Indian commentators like Abanti Bhattacharya: 'the development of a strategic triangle would be unrealistic. The reasons can be easily found in the mutual suspicion between India and China'. The new Russian leadership under Vladimir Putin (president, 2000–08) reversed the Yeltsinera drift in India-Russia bilateral relations, signed the Declaration on Strategic Partnership with India in 2000 and established the institution of annual summit meetings. Moscow realized that as a Eurasian power, an active Russian role and influence in dynamic Asia would be limited without a solid partnership with old friends like India.

Indian commentators welcomed Putin's comment in his 2004 visit, that 'India is our strategic privileged partner [...] And speaking from the point of view of geographical representation [...] India is number one', as recognition of India's own rise:

> The emphasis is to be interpreted both in the geopolitical context and also in the military context. In terms of geo-political interpretation one could say that Russia accords primacy to India in the Indian sub-continent and all that it implies. In the military context it stresses that Russia recognizes India not only as a strategic partner but also as a 'privileged strategic partner'. If this is Russia's emphasis truly, then the long range prospect of Russia-India strategic cooperation is pregnant with exciting prospects.

Despite its improving relations with the USA, China and Europe, India also did not want to abandon its time-tested relationship with Russia. In a world dominated by a single power (the USA), both the Indian and Russian vision of a multi-polar world coincided. The issue of terrorism has also brought the countries together. Within South Asia, Russia has consistently supported India on the issue of Kashmir unconditionally over time or regime change and opposed its internationalization. These issues continue to be reiterated at their Summit Declarations. Another point which both the partners have been emphasizing after every important meeting is that their partnership is neither against any third country nor at the expense of their relations with other major powers, understandable given Russia's strategic links with China and India's with the USA.

State Linkages

Since 1992 about 15 summit meetings have taken place and about 135 agreements have been signed between the two countries. To improve their economic relationship, an Indo-Russian Inter-Governmental Commission on Trade, Economic, Scientific, Technological and Cultural Cooperation (IRIGC-TEC) has been working towards promoting bilateral co-operation. The Commission covers 11 joint working groups, namely: trade and economic co-operation; phar-maceuticals; petroleum; the coal industry; metallurgy; science and technology; cultural co-operation; information technology; power and energy; the environment and natural resources; and co-operation with the regions. In the 15th meeting of IRIGC-TEC, held in Moscow in October 2009, a new trade target of US $20,000m. by 2015 was agreed.

As already mentioned, a major turning point in their bilateral relationship was their formal Declaration on Strategic Partnership between Republic of India and the Russian Federation, signed during Putin's visit to India in October 2000.15 Broadly, this agreement meant enhanced co-operation in the political, economic, defence and cultural fields. It talked of 'deepening and diversifying cooperation in sectors such as metallurgy, fuel and energy, information technology, communications and transport, including merchant shipping and civil aviation', and of 'further development of cooperation in banking and finance, and improving credit and insurance facilities'. There was mention of simplifying rules and procedures for travel by entrepreneurs and businessmen of both countries. It was also agreed to jointly explore the possibilities of regional trading arrangements with third countries. Since then, summit meetings are taking place almost every year with many more agreements signed every year. The crux of all these summit meetings and accompanying declarations has been common positions on major global issues like international terrorism and desire for a multipolar world and close bilateral relations. These summits have been a very useful platform for formulating common positions and responses to emerging global political and economic issues.

However, what do these Summit declarations actually mean in real terms? There are many ways of looking at these developments. Every time the summit meeting takes place, the diehard proponents of old Indo-Soviet/Russian friendship emphasize the need to look at these agreements and declarations as a testimony of a time-tested, mutually beneficial friendship. They even go one step further and suggest that along with Russia, India should forge solid friendships with other like-minded countries including China to soft balance some of the negative trends of a unipolar world, dominated by a single economic and military power.

However, many people in the new generation of Indians, who have entered the business or academic professions in the post-Soviet period, have somewhat different impressions about these summit meetings and declarations. They argue that countless bilateral meetings have taken place since 1992, and a plethora of agreements have been signed between the two countries. Various inter-governmental commissions and committees are also working to improve bilateral relations. In addition, both the countries are in an avowedly 'Strategic

Partnership'. Yet, despite all this rhetoric, India's exports to Russia have remained lower than countries like Bangladesh, Nigeria, Kenya, Thailand, Israel and Viet Nam. In today's Russia about 70% of the economy is in the private sector, yet India has not moved beyond public sector and government declarations. So it is argued that India needs to strengthen the commercial component of its relationship through the linkages between the dynamic sectors of Indian industry, commerce and services and the newly emerging Russian private sector. In the absence of this relationship, it is argued that 'strategic partnership' may soon start losing its charm.

There is truth in both arguments. Even 20 years after the Soviet collapse, India's relations with Russia were still in transition, particularly in the commercial field. After some disruption, both have been able to restore and improve their political linkages. In the economic and academic fields, however, most old India-Soviet linkages have broken and new India-Russia links have not developed to the same extent. Both governments have recognized this fact. Still, these summit meetings have been able to tackle the issue in a significant manner.

It could be argued that under new circumstances, business in both countries is no more the business of the governments. Therefore, it is up to the private sector to take advantage of conditions created by these agreements. Despite this, these high-level visits could have been used more effectively to promote Indian economic interests in Russia. Compared with India, Russians have done good business during these visits. Russia has a comparative advantage in the arms industry and India has purchased arms worth billions of dollars during these visits. Nine annual summit meetings over nine years were good opportunities for special bilateral economic relationships to have been created, even under entirely different circumstances. In 2005/06 trade still stood at a relatively modest $2,760m. In 2006 a Joint Study Group was set up to work out a programme for increasing bilateral trade to $10,000m. by 2010, and to explore the possibilities of a Comprehensive Economic Cooperation

Agreement (CECA) between the two countries. The group submitted its lacklustre report in July 2007.17 Except for the recommendation of a CECA, there were few specific recommendations. Subsequently, a Joint Task Force between the Indian Ministry of Commerce and Industry and the Russian Ministry of Economic Development was set up in February 2008 to monitor progress on a CECA, but with few concrete results emerging from the exercise. Trade by 2008/09 had increased to $5,420m., but fell back to $4,550m. in 2009/10, some way off the earlier target set for $10,000m. by 2010.

Defence linkages

There are estimates that about 800 Russian defence production facilities are kept in operation by Indian defence contracts. Although China used to be the number one arms importer from Russia, India has emerged as number one since 2007. Some analysts have argued that in arms exports, geopolitical and economic factors will eventually force Russia to make a choice between China and India, a contest that India will probably win.

India's major purchases from Russia over the last 18 years have been varied and extensive, including aircraft (MIG 29, MIG 29 SMT, SU 30K, SU MK1), helicopters (Mi-17, Mi-18, etc.) and air-defence systems (AK 630 30mm, etc.). In June 2010 the Cabinet Committee on Security cleared another deal of more than $3,000m. to buy an additional 42 Sukhoi-30 MKI fighters from Russia. The deal came on top of the 230 aircrafts already contracted from Russia in three deals worth a total of $8,500m. The initial contract was for 50 fighters, at $1,460m. In 2000 the Government contracted the licensed production of 140 fighters by Hindustan Aeronautics Limited. Then another 40 were added to the contract. Some purchases have been of artillery and armoured vehicles (256M Tunguska), engines, sensors and a variety of missiles. Maritime purchases have been noticeable, including frigates (Talwar stealth class), submarines (Kilo/Sindhughosh), nuclear submarines (Akula-2 lease) and an aircraft carrier (the delayed Gorshkov purchase originally due for handover in 2008–09, now scheduled for handover at the end of 2012). Joint production has seen India also starting to producing significant portion of armaments at home, including Brahmos missiles, T72M1 tanks, radars, anti-ship and anti-tank missiles, etc. Most tanks and aircraft are also being assembled in India. In 2009 both countries agreed on a new military technical co-operation agreement for the period 2011–20. The new programme covers both ongoing projects, such as the Su-30 MKI fighter plane and the T-90 tank production in India, and 31 new projects, which include a fifth-generation fighter aircraft, the multi-role transport aircraft and a new multi-role helicopter. Under this programme India hopes to further shift from the buyer-seller relationship to joint design, development and production.

India also has a long tradition of collaboration in space with the USSR/Russia. Thumba Equatorial Rocket Launching Station was set up with Soviet help and many Indian experimental and remote sensing satellites were launched with Soviet co-operation. In 1990 India entered into a $350m. contract agreement with Russia to supply the cryogenic engines and technology for their manufacture within the country. Russia earlier agreed to provide India with the technology, but then reversed the decision after it signed the Missile Technology Control Regime agreement with the USA. The USA objected to giving India the technology because of its potential use for nuclear missiles. Commercial and political factors later compelled Russia to sell the rocket engines while withholding the technology. Soon afterwards Indian scientists were able to develop Indian engines. Currently, both countries collaborate on many space projects, which include India's unmanned lunar space fight project (Chandrayaan-2), the human space flight project and the development of the Indo-Russian Student Satellite, Youthsat. Russia has also agreed to provide India with access to signals from its Global Navigation Satellite System (GLONASS).

Commercial linkages

One important point of the old Indo-Soviet friendship was a special bilateral trade and economic relationship. Although this arrangement had many of the usual weaknesses, like corruption and patronage transactions in low-quality products, it helped many small and medium-sized private Indian companies to become exporters. After the disintegration of the USSR, this relationship was badly damaged. Economic transformation in Russia from a centrally planned economy to a market economy in 1992 coincided with the policies of economic liberalization in India. These developments changed the nature and character of foreign economic relations in both countries. Therefore, despite having solid economic and trade relations in the past, most Russian and Indian companies are still struggling to adjust in each other's markets. Economic relations are still surviving mainly because of defence purchases and some public sector investments by India. Commercial initiatives are slow to take advantage of Russian economic transformation. Despite good intentions, both governments have been unable to facilitate any major economic initiative which could have given a new direction to bilateral commercial ties.

Background of trading linkages

Since 1953, when the first trade agreement took place, seven long-term agreements have been signed between the two countries up to the collapse of the USSR. This bilateral trade was conducted through a specific system of trade and payment called the Rupee Trade System, based on annual plans. The important point of the system was payments in non-convertible currency. The trade turnover between the two countries increased from less than 2 crores in 1953 to about 8,000 crores in 1990–91. In 1990–91 more than 16% of Indian exports went to the USSR and about 6% of imports came from there.

One of the most striking characteristics of the Soviet centrally planned economy was that it had created a system of exchange in non-convertible currencies with many of its trading partners. This trade behaviour existed not only with the Council for Mutual Economic Assistance (CMEA) countries, but also with some other friendly countries like India. The value of exchange between the Russian rouble and Indian rupee currencies was arrived at through periodic bureaucratic negotiations.

Most of the ideologically-motivated scholars in India regarded this arrangement as a Soviet version of bilateral aid. The mainstream academia in India also declared that India had 'derived substantial benefits from its trade with the socialist world'. In the late 1970s and early 1980s a few scholars in India had already warned that despite short-term gains, this type of arrangement would harm long-term requirements of efficiency and growth. After initial industrialization, India had problems of importing further machinery either for joint production for third countries or for the exclusive production for the socialist bloc. India did not want Soviet participation in those areas where it could get markets of its own. It also did not want 'captive units', the production of which could not be exported anywhere else but to the Soviet bloc and could give the Soviets the possibility of dictating terms. Except for a few works, academia in India by and large did not bother to critically examine this pattern. The whole arrangement reflected political imperatives rather than economic rationality. After the Soviet break-up, the new policy elite in Russia also found these 'irrational' arrangements with developing countries unaffordable.

The haste with which bilateral payment arrangements were scrapped in favour of payments in convertible currencies indicated that Russian and Indian policy-makers considered such bilateral arrangements undesirable under the new economic policy regimes in both countries.

After the collapse of the USSR, the Indian and Russian Governments renegotiated the entire trade regime. The 1993 agreement terminated the traditional rupee trade arrangement and mandated all bilateral trade transactions to be conducted on a hard currency basis. However, with this agreement the issue of repayment of civilian and military loans taken by India from the former USSR also came up. Finally, after prolonged negotiations, the rouble credit was denominated in rupees and a repayment schedule was drawn up. The agreement provided for an annual repayment of about the equivalent of $1,000m. in rupees to Russia over a period of 12 years starting from 1994, with smaller amounts for a further period of 33 years. The rupee debt funds were to be used by the Russian side for import of goods and trade-related services from India. The rupee debt funds are maintained in a central account with the Reserve Bank of India. Under a three-year perspective plan, which came to an end in 1997, a part of the rupee debt funds was allocated for the import of tea, tobacco, soya meal and pharmaceuticals to designated Russian agencies. The balance was either auctioned or allocated to various states or importing organizations in Russia. In January 1998 this mechanism was replaced with a weekly auction of rupee debt funds conducted by the Vnesheconombank (Bank for Foreign Economic Affairs). During 1999 allocations made for the import of pharmaceuticals and medical equipment from India were utilized by several ministries in Russia. Between 2000 and 2006 the utilization of rupee funds continued through the auctions. In 2007 it was agreed that India's restructured rupee debt would be invested in Russian projects in India. According to Indian finance ministry sources, in December 2007 India still owed $1,970m. in debt to Russia under this category.

Contemporary trading ties

As a result of these changes, contemporary trade between India and Russia is based on payments in freely convertible currencies. All Russian exports to India follow the new system. However, in the 1990s about two-thirds of Indian exports were financed through the renegotiated rupee debt-repayment mechanism. As a result of all these economic policy changes, traditional actors in Indo-Russian trade and other economic relations like the public sector units and state trading corporations are no longer as relevant as they used to be in the Soviet era. Sections of the Indian private sector, which used to get away with selling many products of questionable quality under the bilateral system, also found it difficult to adjust to the radically changed economic and commercial environment in Russia, driven by market forces.

Although Indo-Russian trade has improved in the last few years, it has hovered around a 1% share during the first decade of the century. In quantity terms, although its volume has gone up from $905m. in 1995/96 to $4,547m. in 2009/10, it is still a very small sliver of India's trade; indeed, a 1.98% share in 1995/96 down to a 0.97% share in 2009/10. Of course, statistics may not reveal the full story. Some imports from Russia, particularly metal, metal scrap, fertilizers, paper and paper products, may be sourced through international suppliers and are not reflected in these official figures. Similarly, many Indian goods enter Russia via 'shuttle trade' or through third countries. Still, this will not significantly change the broader picture. Russian trade figures have also included some of the arms exports in commercial trade figures in the last few years.

Main items of traditional exports from India are pharmaceuticals, tea, coffee, ready-made garments, cotton, tobacco, edible preparations, iron and steel, etc. Recently, some non-traditional items like machinery have also shown some growth. Imports from Russia include iron and steel, fertilizer, wheat, minerals, chemicals, paper, rubber, copper, nickel, nuclear machinery, project goods, etc. Apart from goods, services trade may also become more significant in coming years.

According to the Russian Central Bank, India and Russia had about $680m. in services trade in 2008. Russian services exports are mainly associated with construction and maintenance of equipment. In the last two years, services trade has moved in favour of India, with Indian exports in this category increasing from $90m. in 2003 to about $500m. in 2008.

Investment linkages

In the energy sector India's state public sector Oil and Natural Gas Corporation (ONGC) is active in Russia. In 2001 ONGC Videsh Limited (OVL) acquired a combined 20% interest in the Sakhalin-1 project. From 2006 this project started to generate positive cash flow. During 2008/09 ONGC's share of production was 1.853m. metric tons of oil and 0.372 billion cubic metres of gas. In 2009, at a total cost of $2,100m., OVL also completed the acquisition of seven blocks in the Tomsk region of western Siberia, previously held by a United Kingdom-listed company, Imperial Energy. At present, this Tomsk acquisition produces oil mainly from two fields and has its own infrastructure including pipeline network, field processing facilities and connections to the Transneft pipeline system.

The Indian ICICI Bank has opened its subsidiary ICICI Bank Eurasia in Russia, with branches in Moscow and St. Petersburg. TATA Motors launched a project to assemble its light-duty trucks at Russia's Urals Automobile and Motors plant and assembling plant for buses at Volz-hanin and Samotlor. The SUN group has also invested in Russia's food and real estate industries. Similarly, pharmaceutical companies like Dr. Reddy's Laboratories Ltd. and Lupin Ltd. have investments in Russia. Berger Paints has also started operations in Russia. Carborundum Universal has purchased an 84% share in Russia's Volzhsky Abrasive Plant in the Volgograd region. The GMR Infrastructure has participated in a tender for the reconstruction and maintenance of St. Petersburg's Pulkovo Airport. Other companies that are exploring possibilities for investment in Russia include GAIL, Indian Oil, Coal India, Reliance and Tata Tea.

Similarly, a few Russian companies are active in the Indian market. Silovyie Mashiny and Tekhnopromeksport are providing equipment and technical assistance for the construction of the Sipat thermal power plant in Chhattisgarh, Bihar and Uttar Pradesh. Two 1,000-megawatt nuclear power plants in Kudankulam, Tamil Nadu, are being constructed with the help of Russian Atomstroiekspor. In March 2010 both agreed on the construction of two more reactors (units five and six) at Kudankulam and two reactors at Haripur in West Bengal during India's 12th Five-Year Plan period, 2012–17. Their agreement also outlined the timeline for the steps to be taken for the construction of Kudankulam units three and four, and called for progressive indigenization of supplies for units five and six at Kudankulam. For all six reactors at Kudankulam, Russia will provide the equipment and components, while Nuclear Power Corporation of India will build them.

The Russian AFK Sistema owns a 73% share in the Indian telecom operator Shyam Telelink. It is constructing a pan-Indian transmitting network, Shyam. The Russian VTB bank has also started operations in India. Sberbank also intends to enter the Indian market. The numerous other infrastructure companies that are already operating in India include Transstroi and Tsentrdorstroi (road construction), Elektrostal and Tyazhpromeksport (metallurgical industry) and Stroitransgaz (gas pipeline). A joint venture between Russian truck-maker Kamaz and India's Tatra Vectra Motors is nearing completion. The unit will produce Kamaz-6540 dump trucks of over 25 metric tons and Kamaz-5460 prime movers. Zarubezhneftegaz is doing exploration work along with GAIL in the Bay of Bengal. Russia's Gidro OGK and India's SUN Group launched a joint venture called RusSUNHydro in 2009, with the newly formed company planning to participate in hydro-electric projects in India. At the India-Russia Summit in 2007 a decision was made to establish a joint India-Russia titanium product facility. In February 2008 Russia's State Property Committee, the St. Petersburg-based engineering company Tekh-nokhim Holding and India's Saraf Group agreed to set up a plant in Orissa. The Russian share in the project is 55%, which is expected to be financed through Indian outstanding debts to Russia. Overall, however, Russian investment in India remains minuscule. According to the Indian Ministry of Commerce and Industry, total foreign direct investment (FDI) from Russia during the period between April 2000 and March 2010 was about $373m., which was 0.34% of total FDI inflows to India during that period.

Conclusions

Except for a very brief period in the early 1990s, India's relations with Russia have been based on mutual trust and confidence. In the mid-1990s relations were restored to respectable levels which have been further strengthened since the signing of their 'strategic partnership' in 2000. Currently, the main pillars of this relationship are strategic congruence, defence ties, nuclear power and hydrocarbons. The trouble for

Indian policy-makers is that these areas still remain skewed in favour of Russia.

The major challenge for both India and Russia is how to sustain this relationship in the absence of dynamic commercial ties. Future bilateral economic relations will depend on Russia's importance to India's developmental needs and vice versa. In the past, the USSR played an important role in India's industrialization process. It had a comparative advantage in sectors like steel, which was central to its needs. India now has to assess where Russia has a comparative advantage. So far, India has been able to develop linkages in defence production, the oil and gas sector and in nuclear energy. Indian industry has already identified areas of mutual interest, namely information technology, pharmaceuticals, telecommunications, financial services, hydrocarbons, energy and power, oil and gas, food processing, financial consultancy, management services, textiles and diamond processing. The problems are well known, however, including lack of information, visa problems and logistical issues. Still, very little attempt has been made to address these issues. There was a lot of hope that a Eurasian north–south trade corridor would be able to tackle some of the transportation problems. Owing to low trade volumes, however, the trading community has not yet developed this route. The strong political will in both countries to improve bilateral economic relations could have been converted into real economic gains if some imaginative initiatives had been taken, particularly when the Russian economy was booming between 2000 and 2007. With the global economic slowdown impacting in 2008/09, things have become more complicated for increasing India-Russia economic links, with trade declining from $5,420m. in 2008/09 to $4,550m. in 2009/10.

Current Indo-Russian commercial relations are certainly not commensurate with existing potential. In the last few years India has signed bilateral trade deals with many partners and many are under negotiation. However, until Russia joins the World Trade Organization (WTO), it is highly unlikely that India and Russia will be able to sign any significant bilateral trade and economic co-operation agreements. In the last two decades the Indian and Russian economies have moved far from each other. With no major breakthrough, Indian and Russian economic ties will continue to depend on the arms trade, and nuclear and energy industry linkages. Russian exports to India are likely to be from the extraction industries and limited Indian exports will continue to be from low-volume, high-value and high-profit sectors.

It is clear now that defence ties constitute the core of bilateral relations. Russia has provided the most advanced aircrafts, tanks, rocket launchers, missiles, frigates and submarines to India. Through licensed production of arms, missiles and aircraft, India is slowly developing its own defence industry. There have been problems in defence supplies concerning product support, cost escalations, delays in delivery and incomplete transfers of technology. Still, substantial arms imports continue to come from Russia. With a changing foreign policy orientation in India, the importance of arms imports from Russia may see a declining trend in coming years. There was some uneasiness in Russia when India signed a Strategic Partnership with the USA in 2006, and there was talk of Russia being elbowed out as India's main arms supplier, particularly in the midst of troubled negotiations during 2008–10 over the sale of the Admiral Gorshkov aircraft carrier. Nevertheless, overall Russia remains an important factor in Indian foreign policy debates. Moreover, at the broadest level, the Indian elite believes that a strong Russia is important for maintaining a desired international equilibrium, both supporting the idea of multi-polarity and a rule-based international system, within which India can continue its rise. This remains India's basic 'strategic synergy'.

RUSSIA'S STRATEGIC SWITCH: CHINA FAVOURED OVER INDIA

The mainstay of India-Russia strategic partnership and the Indo-Soviet Peace and Friendship Treaty of 1971 was to make India secure against threats from China and Pakistan. Russia in acceding to the 1971 Treaty had made a conscious strategic choice between India and China. Gorbachev set in motion the paradigm switch towards China. It is unclear whether the Indian authorities sensed it. His successor Yeltsin followed this switch more vigorously. Following Yeltsin, President Putin seems to be continuing the policies set by his two predecessors in giving China overriding priority in Russia's foreign policy relationship.

"By the middle of 1989, Indo-Soviet relations drifted into a situation, presaging the need for their complete re-casting which had to come about with Gorbachev's removal ....." so writes an eminent Indian Foreign Secretary. In fact it can be maintained that India's Russia policy needed rehashing soon after Gorbachev's Vladivostok speech in 1986 when he initiated the Russian switch towards China.

It was Gorbachev who "called for a new China Policy" and it was he "who called for an end to a China encirclement policy" and it was Gorbachev who conceded China's "basic demands for normalisation of relations: Soviet withdrawal from Afghanistan, Soviet pressure to get Vietnamese withdrawal from Cambodia and the reduction of Soviet military presence along its borders with China."

The decade of the 1990s witnessed a rapidly galloping Russia-China relationship especially in strategic spheres. Concurrent with this was the growing cold-shouldering of India especially between 1989 and 1996 when some corrections were applied, Primakov became the Prime Minister.

Yeltsin while adopting a policy of building up a strategic relationship of coalition with China, "emphasised a need for de-ideologisation of its (Russia's) foreign policy" which "resulted in Russia adopting a 'wait and see' policy towards India " led to" in the new Russia placing the Indo-Russia relations in a precarious position." President Putin's Government documents 'Foreign Policy of the Russian Federation issued on July 10, 2000 continues to reflect the Russian switch to China. This document states the following objectives on China and India:

China

"The concurrence of the fundamental approaches of Russia and People's Republic of China to the key issues of world problems is one of the mainstays of regional and global stability. Russia seeks to develop mutually advantageous cooperation with China in all areas."

India

"Russia intends to strengthen its traditional friendship with India, including in the international affairs and to aid overcome problems persisting in South Asia and strengthen stability in the region."

An analytical observer would be able to grasp the subtle Russian nuances in terms of Russian priorities vis-à-vis China and India. This would indicate that what remains of the Russia-India strategic cooperation now is only 'traditional friendship'. Russia's switch towards China, and which is likely to grow further into an intensified 'strategic coalition' (they may both shy away from terming it a 'strategic alliance') necessitates examination of two other topics, namely:

India's military dependence on Russia

Russia's advocacy of establishment of a Russia-China-India triangle (Political and Security overtones).

THE WAY AHEAD IN INDO-RUSSIAN TIES

Russia is one country that India cannot afford to sideline, as it is the only trusted partner with whom India has mutual compatibility and a close political, military and economic partnership for decades. Russia (and the Soviet Union) contributed to creating India's key strengths and capabilities in the nuclear, defence, space and heavy industry sectors when no other country was willing to support India's endeavours to modernise.

Even today, despite the hype surrounding the visits of other members of the P-5, India's relationship with Russia has brought it greater benefit than its ties with other major countries. With hopes high the questions now are: What has been achieved so far? What are the priorities? What we can expect from our trusted friend? What should we do to further consolidate this relationship?

The Path Covered

The Indo-Russian relationship has evolved over time. Russian foreign and security policy is based on the concept of a "multipolar" world, first formulated by former Foreign Minister and Prime Minister Yevgeni Primakov. It is in this context that Russia has its interest in the South Asian region where it gives primary importance to India.1 In October 2000 the "Declaration of Strategic Partnership between India and the Russian Federation" was signed in New Delhi since when there has been an all-round development in bilateral cooperation. In this declaration the system of Annual Summits was institutionalized. The previous or tenth summit was held in Moscow in December 2009 between Indian Prime Minister Manmohan Singh and Russian President Dmitry Medvedev. This year would be a very important stage in the development of bilateral relations, as it marks the tenth anniversary of the signing of the Declaration on Strategic Partnership between India and Russia.

During Prime Minister Putin's visit in March 2010, deals worth US $10 billion were signed to further strengthen defence and economic relations. In addition, five agreements were also signed. Prime Ministers Manmohan Singh and Putin held comprehensive and in-depth discussions on bilateral, regional and global issues. Cooperation in the area of atomic energy production for peaceful purposes and a roadmap for the construction of Russian designed nuclear power plants was agreed upon. A memorandum of understanding (MoU) for the production of satellite navigation equipment and services for civilian use and cooperation in the mineral fertilisers sector, 14 supplementary pacts on the Gorshkov aircraft carrier deal, and an additional agreement on military aviation ties were also signed. During Putin's visit, Information technology and telecommunications were also identified as focus areas for future economic cooperation between New Delhi and Moscow.

According to Indian Defence Minister Mr. A.K. Antony, Indo-Russian relationship has moved beyond buyer-seller to co-producer in the field of design development and scientific research. Almost 70 per cent of Indian military hardware is of Soviet/Russian origin. Russia is the only country with which India has established an institutionalized defence cooperation mechanism operating at the Defence Ministers level. In 2008 India and Russia agreed to extend the terms of the Indo-Russian Inter Governmental Commission for Military Technical Cooperation for another ten years till 2020. India and Russia are all set to sign their biggest ever defence deal pegged at $30 billion with the Cabinet Committee on Security giving a go ahead to a mega proposal for joint development and production of the fifth-generation fighter aircraft (FGFA).

In the field of Nuclear Energy, Russia is a long standing partner for India. Currently two nuclear power reactors are being supplied by Russia in Kudankulam and two more are planned. In 2009, India designated Haripur (West Bengal) as an additional site for the construction of nuclear power plants with Russian cooperation. An Inter-Governmental Agreement on broad based cooperation (cooperation in the field of use of atomic energy for peaceful purposes) and a Road Map for future cooperation was signed during the visit of Prime Minister Putin to India in March 2010.

Russia is the second most potent space power in the world. Russia's cooperation in India's Unmanned Space Flight project (Chandrayaan 2), the Human Space Flight Project and the development of Youthsat to be launched by India's GSLV are ongoing projects. In March 2010, a new area involving the joint manufacture of satellite navigation equipment for civilian users based on the Russian GLONASS system, commenced.

The sixteenth session of the India-Russia Inter-Governmental Commission on Trade, Economic, Scientific, Technological and Cultural Cooperation (IRIGC-TEC) held in

New Delhi on 18 November 2010 expressed satisfaction at the continuation of high level bilateral contacts. They welcomed the holding of the first-ever India-Russia Business Dialogue within the framework of the prestigious St. Petersburg International Economic Forum in June 2010 and expressed confidence that the MoU entered into by CII and SPIEF Foundation would pave the way for regular institutionalized B2B interactions and exchanges. The Working Group on Science and Technology (S&T) under the aegis of IRIGC-TEC, and the "Integrated Long Term Program (ILTP) are the two principal institutional mechanisms for S&T cooperation with Russia. The ILTP was recently extended for a further ten years beyond 2009 with a renewed mandate for "Innovation led technology growth". The 'Working Group' focuses on collaboration activities in mutually agreed priority areas. The ILTP programme focuses on collaborative research in basic sciences and in Inter-Academy exchange programmes.

There is great interest in Indian studies, dance, yoga and music in Russia. An India Cultural Festival will be held in Russia in 2011 and a Russian Cultural Festival will be held in India in 2012. The Russian side has also suggested timing the event with the 150th birth anniversary celebrations of Rabindranath Tagore which are scheduled for 2011.

The Priorities

With Chinese defence procurements on the decline following the creation of its strong defence industrial base, India constitutes a major portion of Russian defence exports. Russia is also ready to supply India strategic platforms and technology that no other country will - such as nuclear submarine on lease.

India and Russia have intensified their R & D collaboration and joint production. It is important that this spills over into other economic sectors in order to assist economic development and technological upgradation in both countries.

Trade and investment ties also need to be enhanced as these are very low. While India's imports from Russia in 2010 are US$ 1.642 billion, its exports are $0.399 billion (State Customs Committee of the Russian Federation: first quarter of 2010). There is a need to diversify the trade basket, both import and export. The business community in both countries is sceptical about its counterpart. The combination of Russian potential in high technology and availability of 30 per cent of world resources with India's standing in the fields of industry and engineering could result in major achievements. Economic cooperation is extremely important which if not strong would weaken the mutually beneficial ties.

Space exploration is another major priority area for India since it is a long term and ambitious endeavour and no state can embark upon it alone. The geopolitics of the 21st century dictate that there is a need to take Indo-Russian collaboration to greater heights and space collaboration could play a key role towards this end. Civil Nuclear Cooperation is another area of importance where there is vast scope for India-Russia cooperation.

Russia is not happy about India diversifying its sources of arms procurement. The issue of timely delivery of orders placed by India (for instance, aircraft carrier INS Vikramaditya or Gorshkov) is being addressed. Russia would have to resolve the internal issues that arise from its military industrial exports centring on Rosoboronexport. The two sides need to deepen their cooperation in this area and expand it to the more dynamic civilian sector.

India should participate in the Russian initiative to create a counterpart to Silicon Valley in Skolkovo, outside Moscow. The Russian IT and innovation sector is competitive and Russia enjoys enormous depth in scientific studies. India should enter into collaborative arrangements which would help the cause of innovation in both countries and their translation into concrete economic benefits.

India and Russia need to discuss how to enhance India's participation in Central Asia and benefit from the China-India-Russia initiative. Russia has reached out to Pakistan at the

Sochi Summit and strengthened its relations with China. India's participation in forums like SCO, RIC and BRIC needs to be strengthened, through which India and Russia can work to maintain regional security as well as enhance cooperation in the sector of environment and disaster management, in pharmaceuticals, metallurgy, biotechnology as well as in tourism.

India should promote a greater focus on Russia, and launch initiatives for the study of Russia in India. There should be greater effort in publicising the benefits of bilateral cooperation in both countries, for which there is very little visibility.

A RUSSIA–INDIA–CHINA TRIANGLE: 'PRIMAKOV'S TRIANGLE'?

Apart from the Indian and Pakistani nuclear tests, another major event made 1998 a watershed year: the Anglo-American bombing campaign on Iraq to punish Saddam Hussein for obstructing U.N. inspections of his alleged development of weapons of mass destruction elicited a much more dramatic response from Russia than international criticism of India's nuclear tests. Russian President Boris Yeltsin's Prime Minister Yevgeny Primakov called for the establishment of a *'strategic triangle'* among India, Russia and China to ensure peace and stability in the world. Primakov strongly criticized the air strikes by the United States and the United Kingdom on Iraq as being conducted without the mandate of the United Nations Security Council. Primakov's 'triangle' was variously described in US media as 'a coalition of the weak great powers pitted against its one superpower' or the *'Anti-NATO Axis'*.

China immediately rejected Primakov's call, saying that China pursues an independent and peaceful foreign policy, and furthermore kept a low profile. However, Russian diplomats said that China and Russia both feared that the US attacks against Iraq would become a model for unilateral action taken and carried out by Washington against the Democratic People's Republic of Korea and other countries. The Clinton administration had been close to attacking North Korea in 1993 and peace was saved only by the surprise self-styled mission of former US President Jimmy Carter.

Within one year of the bombing of Iraq, the Clinton presidency had set the trend for unilateral action in disregard of the United Nations with two large-scale aerial bombardment campaigns: first in Iraq; and then in Kosovo. Russia, and particularly Primakov himself, had strong links with Iraq, whereas China, having just entered into a 'Strategic Partnership' with the United States during Clinton's July 1998 visit to China, had no specific interest to defend there. However, Kosovo was to Serbia/Yugoslavia what Taiwan was to China and thus China went all the way in criticizing US and NATO policy in further dismembering the Yugoslav Federation. Russia had multiple interests in Kosovo, foremost in Huntingtonian terms as the core nation of Slavic-Orthodox civilization and secondly as the erstwhile leader of the Communist bloc to which Yugoslavia had once belonged. The weakened Russian military wanted to show that it still had some muscle and guts, and had taken a short cut to the airport of Pristina, Kosovo's capital, which stirred NATO Supreme Commander General Wesley Clark into ordering the British local commander, Lieutenant-General Michael Jackson, to evict the Russians with American air support. Jackson refused and the showdown between the American four-star and British three-star generals is recorded on dozens of websites. Jackson asked Clark: "What is your authority, Sir?". Clark smugly said: "Me, I am a four-star general, Michael". "I am a three-star general", Jackson thundered, "but I am not going to start World War III for you". Although a direct US–Russian confrontation was avoided, bilateral ties never recovered. After appointing five different Russian prime ministers in 1998 and 1999, and in failing health, Yeltsin abruptly resigned at the turn of the millennium. His chosen successor, Vladimir Putin, decided to await the outcome of the 2000 American presidential election before re-engaging with the United States.

The Chinese suffered even more dramatically from American transgressions in Serbia/Kosovo, when US B-2 bombers under

NATO's command 'erroneously' dropped five guided bombs on the Chinese Embassy in Belgrade, killing three Chinese and injuring twenty. US President Clinton telephoned China's President Jiang Zemin to make an instant apology, but Jiang refused to take the call. A spate of presidential, ministerial and ambassadorial apologies followed during the next few days, but no Chinese could believe that the bombing had been accidental. The whole episode is described in detail in a book by Susan Shirk, who as US Deputy Assistant Secretary of State for East Asian Affairs was then directly in charge of US–China relations. She writes that at the time of the bombing, the Chinese leadership was in a state of high alert because two weeks earlier, Zhongnanhai, the main compound of the ruling elite, had been surrounded by a surprise peaceful sit-in of Falun Gong, a Buddhist-inspired sect of yoga-type meditation and health exercises. Shirk quotes an insider source as saying that President Jiang stayed up on the night after the bombing to write a long memo, not on how to deal with the United States, but how to crush Falun Gong by means of ludicrous over-reaction. Media reporting about the bombing demonstrated how much control the Communist Party had lost over Chinese society since the proliferation of semi-independent commercial newspapers and the internet, which both sensationalized dramatic news events for higher circulation figures and profits, adding extra pressure on the government to adopt a hardline stance towards the United States. An investigation coordinated by Susan Shirk blamed the *'horrific blunder'* of the bombing, as she called it, on the CIA, using the wrong method to locate a targeted Yugoslav military agency and using outdated databases. Still, very, very few Chinese believed the Americans could make such a stupid mistake. In the minds of many, it must have been some lower-level anti-China conspiracy. Anyway, the Chinese domestic pandemonium had further complicated US–China relations: China no longer only perceived itself as an on-and-off adversary or 'enemy of the future' of the United States, but also the victim of today. In New Delhi, an academic security consultant with access to military intelligence also dismissed any American account of errors or blunders as a cover-up and is absolutely convinced that it was a premeditated attack on Chinese electronic devices and technicians, hidden in the embassy to help the Milosevic regime's air defences against American bombing:

Why did they, the Americans, bomb the embassy? Only those two rooms were targeted. I have very concrete information [about] what these two rooms were doing, what the people in those rooms were doing. The Yugoslavs brought down a B-117 stealth bomber and transferred it to the Chinese. The Chinese were developing a stealth bomber. Stealth technologies you get nowhere. Russians refuse to part with any of these technologies. There is no way they can get it from the EU because of the arms' embargo. So the only way to get it is through 'stealth!'

So, after eight years of volatility but with regular improvements, US–China relations under President Clinton ended on a sour note, and it would get worse. US President George W. Bush and his coterie of neo-con warriors were in no mood to continue the sweet-and-sour tactics that Clinton had played with the Chinese – and the Russians. Bush downgraded America's tentative 'strategic partnership' for the 21st century with China – agreed by Presidents Clinton and Jiang Zemin in 1998 – to one of *'competition'*, and talked of upgrading Taiwan and supplying it with any arms that it needed to defend itself.

Before '9-11' the Bush administration's policy towards China was one of 'congagement' – a blended strategy that transcends both containment and engagement and should embrace neither but should contain elements of both.

The Bush administration continued Clinton's policy of ending India's isolation by lifting the remaining sanctions for its 1998 nuclear tests. This conformed to the administration's de-emphasis of non-proliferation in favour of 'counter-proliferation' by means of the National Missile Defence. Interest in India had grown considerably in the US Congress against the backdrop of the 'rise of China', the spy-plane crisis and new escalating tensions over giant arms' sales to Taiwan. The Bush administration's public assertion that its new fervour for India had nothing to do with any anti-China strategy was dismissed by most observers as just diplomatic talk.

Nevertheless, Chinese Foreign Minister Tang Jiaxuan rejected the 'Primakov Triangle' and said that time had not yet come for a strategic alliance between the three countries: 'We are for discussion on issues of mutual interests, but it is premature to set up any mechanism at the government level'. By May 2001, China had just gone through its first crisis with the Bush administration over the EP 3 spy-plane incident near Hainan and the rearmament of Taiwan, but it chose to avoid confrontation with the new US president. A senior scholar, Sun Shihai, Deputy Director of the Institute of Asia-Pacific Studies under the Chinese Academy of Social Sciences, said that the trilateral partnership should not become a strategic triangle with military components that could be aimed at a third country, especially the United States. But he did emphasize the countries' convergence of interests on issues like the establishment of a multi-polar world, a just and equitable international political and economic order, as well as opposing neo-interventionism in the name of human rights.

The most important factor that kept the idea of an 'India–Russia–China triangle' alive was the broader *'Bush Doctrine'* – the embodiment of neo-conservative determination as divulged in their bible, the 'Statement of Principles' of the The Project of the New American Century. The manifesto advocated a

'Reaganite' foreign policy of military strength and moral clarity, more specifically a significant increase in defence spending and the need to strengthen ties with democratic allies and to challenge regimes that were hostile to American interests and values. Translated into action at the outset of the Bush administration, this meant a series of unilateralist priorities such as missile defence, withdrawal from the Anti-Ballistic Missile (ABM) Treaty, creation of a high-tech rapid-reaction military with overwhelming scope and power and a revitalization of the American nuclear weapons' industry. Bush first made his intentions firmly clear and then expressed willingness to talk, but as consultations, not as negotiations – in other words, you can express your opinion and we will listen but it will not affect our plans.

Renewed Russia–China Friendship Treaty

After US President Bush met with Russian President Putin in Slovenia on 16 June 2001, Russia and China signed a fully fledged bilateral friendship and cooperation treaty in July 2001, which stressed that its aim was not to recreate the old Cold War military alliance while also insisting that it was not directed against any country. Since the Mao–Stalin Pact of 1950, which had so scared the West, had quietly lapsed in 1979, it was the first time that Russia and China had concluded a major bilateral treaty. Yet analysts on both sides acknowledged that they saw the current relationship as a counterweight to the United States' status as the world's only superpower. Liliya F. Shevtsova, an analyst at the Carnegie Moscow Centre think tank, viewed Moscow's recent moves towards Beijing – at least in part – as a message to the Bush administration: 'The Kremlin is sending Washington a warning that if there is no change for the better in relations between Moscow and Washington – now at their coolest in years – Russia is quite ready to strike a closer alliance with Beijing', she said. India was not part of the project at that time because it had shown early enthusiasm for Bush's 'new concepts of deterrence, moving beyond the constraints of the 30-year-old ABM treaty and work[ing] toward deploying a ballistic-missile-defence system'.

According to one analysis, Putin mulled over China during his visit: whether to strike some kind of loose alliance with Beijing – and India? – to counter US supremacy. 'There was a month or two when it could have gone either way', one senior US official said during the negotiations about a new treaty to be signed by Putin and Bush on 24 May 2002, 'until Putin figured out that the Chinese didn't have a lot to offer'.

After the airborne assaults on the World Trade Centre and the Pentagon on '9/11', Putin was the first foreign leader to get through to Bush on the telephone. Condoleezza Rice, then National Security Adviser, conveyed to Washington Post columnist Jim Hoagland that there had been a steady evolution towards a strategic Russian choice that this crisis seems to have confirmed: 'That Russian choice is seen at the White House, as I understand it, to be one of pursuing alliance with and integration into the West rather than flirting with a Third Way strategy built on partnership with China and others who want to reduce American influence abroad'. The US design was clearly to bring Russia into a unidirectional – that is, subservient – partnership with the United States so as to lessen China's leverage on global questions, including missile defence. Sensing that Russia had a special role to play in Bush's 'war on terror', Putin seized the opportunity to recast US–Russia relations after ten years of decline and succeeded in reclaiming Russia's place at the big table. When Bush formally abrogated the ABM Treaty on 13 December 2001, Russia's response was to state pragmatically that it was no longer bound by the 1993 accord known as Start II, which outlawed multiple-warhead missiles and other especially destabilizing weapons in the two nations' strategic arsenals. Putin realized that it was better to accept grudgingly, rather than to resist NATO expansion as Yeltsin had done, and then later to back down.

Beijing responded in a very different way to Bush's ABM announcement. The Chinese considered it as targeted at them, not at the Russians. The Russians would under any subsequent missile agreement always retain enough warheads to overwhelm any future US National Missile Defence, whereas the Chinese only had a very small nuclear arsenal.

China said that the US plans to develop a multi-billion dollar defence system that would shoot down incoming missiles would undercut the deterrent value of its own small nuclear arsenal – about two dozen missiles capable of reaching the United States – and a successful missile umbrella could be stretched to protect arch-rival Taiwan.

The United States, however, has told China repeatedly that it is developing the missile shield to counter surprise attacks from 'rogue states' like North Korea and Iraq [sic!] and that the policy was not being pursued with China in mind. Beijing also feared that the Bush administration's action will mean that nations will no longer agree to any nuclear disarmament control treaties. This could push China into a regional arms race with India and Pakistan. "We have enough domestic concerns. An arms race is only a rich man's game. A poor man cannot play", said Professor Niu Jun, US foreign policy expert at Beijing University's Institute of International Studies. In the end, China's muted response showed that it had decided that there was nothing that it could do and that it was intent on maintaining stable relations with the United States.

While Russia's new Friendship and Cooperation Treaty with China, which was signed in July 2001, seemed to set both on a new strategic course, '9/11' had clearly turned Russia's priorities around. Despite Bush's initial ABM shock, Presidents Putin and Bush in May 2002 opened an entirely new relationship with the signing of a treaty that committed both countries to reducing their nuclear arsenals from about 6,000 warheads each to no more than 2,200 by the end of 2012. With the renewed Russo-American rapport, China appeared to be the loser, as reflected in Chinese President Jiang Zemin's reminder of the first anniversary of the new Sino-Russian strategic partnership, which should have paved the way towards a multi-polar world. China was the leading member in the newly founded Shanghai Cooperation Organization (SCO), and now in the wake of '9/11' US military bases were at China's doorstep in Uzbekistan and Kyrgyzstan, with Russia's approval.

'China–Russia Relations Remain Better than Russia–US Ties'

In December 2002 Russian President Vladimir Putin visited China to reassure the Chinese about the relevance and validity of the Russian-Chinese strategic partnership (first agreed in 1996 and consolidated by their Friendship Treaty in 2001). Despite recurrent frustrations about US hegemony, Putin wanted to maintain good relations with the United States while disagreeing with US President Bush's approach to terrorism. On the day of Putin's arrival in Beijing, the People's Daily published an article under the headline 'China–Russia Relations Remain Better than Russia–US Ties'. The Pravda newspaper explained that Putin himself had complained to Chinese journalists about NATO expansion, which under the current global situation of terrorism and nuclear issues was a negative development. Another new cloud above the US–Russia relationship was the imminent Anglo-American invasion of Iraq, which Russia energetically and China ephemerally tried to block.

After Beijing, Putin went to India where he again tried to sell the idea of a strategic partnership or 'strategic triangle' in Asia for Russia, China and India – with Moscow taking the lead. Putin tried to convince India of the compatibility of the triangle with good bilateral cross-relations between all involved, defining the triangle not as an anti-US coalition but just as a *'counterpoint'* to the US. Putin's aim, analysts say, is traditionally Russian – to centre Moscow solidly between East and West, Atlantic and Pacific, NATO and China.

Putin defined terrorism's main danger as secessionist movements that challenge state sovereignty. While Russia's main concern was Chechnya, China viewed the Muslim separatists in its western Xinjiang region as terrorists, and India maintained that the core problem of Kashmir was Pakistani-based terrorism. Putin supported the Indian view, but the United States viewed Pakistan as an indispensable ally in its wider 'war on terror' and China would also never renege on its key geostrategic alliance with Pakistan. From its defeat of India in the 1962 Border War, Pakistan was China's tool for keeping Soviet ally India off-balance and, more recently, China's back door to the Indian Ocean, Arabian Sea and the Persian Gulf.

The heart of Indo-Russian relations is defence cooperation and it embraces the joint production of Brahmos cruise missiles and the joint manufacture of advanced submarines. The SU-30 project is engaging almost all of the production capacities of Hindustan Aeronautics. Consequently, the aviation industries in both India and Russia have acquired the capacity to undertake the joint development, production and marketing of medium-range transport aircraft.

After the Anglo-American invasion of Iraq there were – not surprisingly – renewed calls for a 'Moscow–Beijing–New Delhi triangle', a potential alliance of three nuclear-armed countries of some 2.5 billion people that would theoretically be able to balance US power in coming years. Indian Prime Minister Atal Bihari Vajpayee had just concluded a successful visit to China and the two countries had expressed similar views on the American war on Iraq. All three countries were disturbed by the blatant disregard of the United Nations and protested against what they viewed as a rejection of the rules of the international game.

Russia, China and India still back the primacy of the United Nations Security Council in solving crises, and support the principle of non-intervention in the internal affairs of sovereign states. Apart from shared concerns over US dominance, the three have other common interests and mutually reinforcing needs. All three are weary of militant Islamic groups and want stability in Central Eurasia. The main weakness in the triangle, however, comes from China's and India's competitive relationship, with both holding conflicting visions of regional dominance, with China so far the winner. While Russia and China are opposed to US Theatre Missile Defence (TMD), which is in clear violation of the ABM Treaty, India offered its enthusiastic support to the United States. China, too, has a stake in Kashmir in the areas bordering Xinjiang and is a major arms' supplier to Pakistan. In short, Sino-Indian relations would continue to remain a stumbling block for materialization of the strategic triangle for which Russia had been canvassing.

But the arms' sale relationship between Russia and the two Asian countries was growing steadily. The trade provides Moscow with billions of much-needed dollars and important arms' export markets, while Beijing and New Delhi get sophisticated armaments ranging from combat aircraft to submarines. In 2003, Russia and India held their first joint naval exercises in the Indian Ocean, when a large task force of Russian surface ships and nuclear attack submarines simulated attacks on aircraft-carrier groups. The naval exercise was coordinated with a mission by long-range bombers. On 13 May 2003, several Russian strategic bombers – Tu-95 Bears and Tu-160 Blackjacks – flew from a base in Central Russia to the Indian Ocean to simulate an attack by long-range cruise missiles.

It has, however, been argued that the trilateral axis could hardly be feasible because the Indian nuclear and missile programme is not so much aimed at Pakistan, but is in fact deterrence against Chinese nuclear warheads. The would-be triangle is also seen as implausible because India and China also happen to be competing economies. Moreover, Russia and China have already solved their border disputes, while China and India are still divided by a chunk of barren terrain and the granting of asylum to the Dalai Lama and thousands of his followers. There have also been warnings that a well-armed and strong China may one day not just make Russia its junior partner, but even pose a threat to Russia's resource-rich Far East.

The 'Trialogues': No 'Equilateral' Triangle

On 3 September 2003 the first *'trialogue'* of the foreign ministers of Russia, China and India took place in New York. The three countries together represent the vast majority of the global population and theoretically could be able to balance US power in coming years. After the US invasion of Iraq, there was again more shared opposition to US policies than in previous years. India had new doubts about a closer relationship with the United States. As a counterweight to Islamic terrorism and at the behest of the United States, India had growing military ties with Israel, which were a very divisive issue in a country with the second largest Muslim population in the world after Indonesia. Bush had failed to condemn or even to mention terrorism in Kashmir in his UN speech earlier in the week. At the official level 'the dialogue between Moscow, Beijing and New Delhi will continue', said Russian Foreign Minister Igor Ivanov, adding that the three nations have a shared interest in a 'multipolar and just world'.

Russian President Vladimir Putin had been particularly insistent upon the triangle during his December 2004 visit to India. But China had so far resisted, and it is unlikely that India will be a party to overt anti-American actions in Central or South Asia, even though it will clearly collaborate more with China on trade and energy issues and for anti-terrorism purposes may even liaise with the Shanghai Cooperation Organization (SCO) now that China has offered it such an opportunity.

In April 2005, when China's major cities were shaken by violent anti-Japanese demonstrations, Chinese Premier Wen Jiabao was on an official visit to New Delhi. Wen used the occasion to pledge Chinese 'support for India's aspirations to play an active role in the UN and international affairs'. Part of the Indian media 'over-interpreted' this as Chinese support for Indian permanent membership of a reformed United Nations Security Council. Wen and his Indian counterpart Manmohan Singh signed a broad-based 'India-China Strategic and Cooperative Partnership for Peace and Prosperity', of which the main content was a five-year pact for cooperation in five high-tech sectors, in which these two fastest growing 'elephant economies' (that is, mammoth versions of 'tiger economies') have optimal synergy: India in software; China in hardware. The hope of China's Prime Minister Wen Jiabao was that an India–Russia–China axis will 'democratize international relations', a pointed indictment of US hegemonism. India, for its part, wanted improved cooperation with the dynamic economies of East Asia, a bigger regional role and a counterweight to Chinese and US sponsorship of Pakistan. Indian Prime Minister Manmohan Singh observed: 'India and China can together reshape the world order'.

The April 2005 Sino-Indian strategic partnership followed less than one decade after the establishment of the Sino-Russian strategic partnership, which was triggered by the United States dispatching two carrier-led task forces to the Taiwan Straits in

1996 in response to Chinese missile tests, and as a warning to the Taiwan electorate not to vote for independence. (Then) Chinese Premier Li Peng stated that the strategic partnership between the two countries would help to correct the 'balance of forces' in the world. This went in tandem with the 'Shanghai Declaration', to set up a security body of China, Russia and three former Central Asian Soviet republics, initially named the 'Shanghai Five', which aimed to counter further inroads by the US and NATO into the region and which in 2001 was renamed the Shanghai Cooperation Organization.

India and Russia had also concluded a strategic partnership in 2000. Under the accord, the two countries agreed to develop a common strategy in dealing with Afghanistan. Both New Delhi and Moscow were concerned that the radical Islamic agenda of the Taliban was having an impact on areas such as India's Kashmir and Chechnya in Russia. President Putin stressed Russia's unqualified support for India's bid for permanent membership of the UN Security Council, something that China was ambiguous about in 2005 and explicitly opposed in subsequent years as India moved closer to the United States. Nevertheless, China, India and Russia were now tied together by three bilateral strategic partnerships, of which two, Russia–China and Russia–India, had a robust arms' supply relationship as the strongest component, and the third, the Sino-Indian, had the least military–strategic content.

Vladivostok: Russia's Far Eastern Metropolis

Soon after this promising improvement in India–China relations, the new Russian Foreign Minister Sergei Lavrov met with his Chinese and Indian counterparts, Li Zhaoxing and Natwar Singh, in June 2005 in Vladivostok, their first meeting outside of a multilateral forum. They discussed security and this time also energy security and especially regional stability, considering the waves of instability that were engulfing Uzbekistan and Kyrgyzstan, which were allegedly instigated by Western-inspired *'orange revolutions'*. The symbolical event, the signing of a China–Russia border agreement that had been negotiated for four decades and that concerned two per cent of the 4,300-kilometre border, should set an example for China and India. China and Russia had fought a short border war on an island in the Ussuri River in 1969 but were reaching a final settlement now. Why couldn't China and India ? In terms of concrete results, the meeting produced a communiqué that did not mention the term 'strategic triangle' but stressed that it is in the interests of the three countries to strengthen their trilateral partnership, and that the mutually beneficial cooperation will contribute to the consolidation of peace and stability in Asia and the world at large. The selection of Vladivostok as the venue can be viewed as emphasizing Russia's status as an Asian power along with India and China.

A commentator in the Russian magazine Kommersant wrote that former Russian Prime Minister Yevgeny Primakov's dream had come true, as his 1998 'triangle' was designed to curb US influence, specifically the 2005 fight against 'colour revolutions' in former Soviet Republics:

In fact, yesterday's meeting in Vladivostok witnessed that Russia and China agree to create their own alliance to fight 'colour revolutions' in Central Asia. Lavrov stated that the uprising in Andijan was nothing else than 'the operation of Islamic extremists, Taliban leftovers and some Chechen terrorists'.

By putting responsibility for the Andijan events on international terrorists, Lavrov expressed solidarity with Beijing's official position. China is a most ardent supporter of Uzbek President Islam Karimov's 'fight with terrorism', including the slaughter in Andijan. This means that Russia is ready to share responsibility with China for everything that goes on in the region. This would be the first step to create a joint military bastion of Moscow and Beijing, which would be protecting Central Asian regimes from 'colour revolutions' and excessive American penetration into the region.

It would soon be clear, however, that Lavrov's and the commentator's rhetoric were too premature and way over the top. India was improving its relations with China, but far more substantially with the United States. The US is a huge trading partner for India and China, and Russia will not be able to compete at this point, at least not for the foreseeable future. Moreover, the Bush administration had in the meantime lifted restrictions on arms' deliveries to India, which was going to cause problems for Russian defence exports to India, and Washington did not have intentions of making such a concession to China. In addition, Sergei Karagonov, the Chairman of the Presidium of the Russian Council for Foreign Defence Policy, was convinced that Primakov's idea was not viable. He emphasized that none of the three countries would want to join a coalition in direct opposition to the United States.

Nevertheless, the 'Vladivostok Trio' had given some other substance to Primakov's triangle. The trio stressed the primacy of the United Nations, which the United States is sometimes inclined to bypass, and the need to reform it. The demand for 'consistent, sustained and comprehensive opposition to terrorism without any double standards' was a warning that India, Russia and China consider murderous secessionists in Kashmir, Chechnya or Xinjiang as dangerous as the US considers Osama Bin Laden and al-Qaeda. They also wanted the global oil economy to recognize Russia as one of the world's largest fuel producers, and India and China among the biggest consumers. To that end, India, which has put US$ 1 billion in Russia's Sakhalin-I project and might invest more, would host a meeting in October 2005 of Asia's principal oil producers and buyers. This would be another feather in the cap of India's Minister of Oil, Mani Shankar Aiyar.

In the energy sector, China and India for a long time seemed to become rivals that might get into armed conflict over oil and minerals. In January 2006, India and China put aside their energy rivalry. The two states' oil majors – CNPC and ONGC – signed a mega-pact for joint bidding in Central Asia, the Caspian Sea Region, Africa and Latin America. Indian Minister of Oil M.S. Aiyar explained that fierce Sino-Indian competition had driven prices up further: "Wherever the Indians have gone, the

Chinese are already there", wrote Madhu Nainan, chief editor of Petrowatch, a market intelligence newsletter in India. "Mostly, it is India that needs cooperation with China – and not the other way around." The biggest energy issue between the US and India is the construction of a 2,775 kilometres (or 1,725 miles), US$ 7.5 billion gas pipeline from Iran through Pakistan to India, which has already been under negotiation for fifteen years. India adamantly rejects any US pressure over its millennia-old relations with another ancient Asian empire: Persia, or Iran.

When Indian Prime Minister Manmohan Singh announced in March 2006, with the visiting US President George Bush at his side in New Delhi, that the two had reached agreement on a 'historic' civilian nuclear pact, China and Russia felt that their reluctant triangular partner was compromising its 'independent foreign policy' and that India felt that it had to reinforce its credentials that it was not a second Japan and would not subordinate its foreign policy autonomy to Washington. The countries' three leaders – Manmohan Singh, Hu Jintao and Vladimir Putin – met in a so-called 'outreach session' during the G8 summit in St. Petersburg in July 2006, which underlined that the latter two had now been accepted as crucial players in the world. But the three also held their first trilateral summit, the first of its kind among the three countries. The current G8 have 45 per cent of the world's GDP, whereas inclusion of China and India would move this to the 60 per cent level, thus enhancing the forum's ability to influence global political and economic relations. "Our approaches to key international problems are very close or, as the diplomats say, they practically coincide", Putin said in his opening remarks. Putin threw his support behind proposals to expand the G8 by including India, China and other outreach countries that Russia had invited to attend the summit: "Without such countries as India and China it is impossible to solve global economic and financial problems", he said. Putin outlined a new political agenda for the G8 to help mould a new multi-polar world. "Our world has not become safer after the collapse of the bipolar world", he said. "On the contrary, it has become less predictable. [...] We do not have the tools and instruments to address the challenges of today". An expanded G8 may become such a tool: "What mankind is concerned with today, what we are doing in G8 is to try and work out a new architecture of international relations", Putin concluded.

New Delhi

The foreign ministers of the three (re-)emerging giants met again in Delhi in February 2007 to further discuss ways to build a more democratic 'multi-polar world'. The three – Pranab Mukherjee, Li Zhaoxing and Sergei Lavrov – emphasized that 'they were not setting up an alliance against the United States, but on the contrary, intended to promote international harmony and understanding', a joint communiqué stated. The latter was a euphemism for blocking the launch of another US war against Iran. 'The key to building a multi-polar world order based on the principles of equality of nations – big or small – respect for sovereignty and territorial integrity of countries, international law and mutual respect', the communiqué routinely stated, required a 'democratization of international relations'. Thus the United Nations represented the 'appropriate instrument' for dealing with world problems. One Indian commentator, N.V. Subramaniam, compared the India–China–Russia triangle with the Six-Party Talks on North Korea: "Because the US wouldn't talk directly to North Korea, their bilateral [meeting] had to be upgraded by including four other parties, with China hosting it".

The 'Triangular Three' all had long agendas to discuss with the United States, but since they would not get far bilaterally, they conveyed their common demands trilaterally to Washington, foremost on Iran. Russia and China were vehemently opposed to Bush's war-mongering in the Gulf and so was India, but India was also negotiating a civilian nuclear deal with Washington. It did not want to anger Washington bilaterally, but through the triangle it could convey its opposition in a more circumspect way. Subramaniam referred to the Cold War game of the US, playing off China against the Soviet Union. At the 43rd Munich Conference on Security Policy from February

9-11, 2007, Russia's President Vladimir Putin attacked US unipolarity and NATO's eastward expansion with a clear intimation of the emerging importance of the India–China–Russia 'strategic triangle'. Putin found himself still too weak to take on the US alone, but splitting Europe and pushing the triangle with India and China might, according to his logic, have more chance of registering with Washington.

Harbin

In October 2007, the three foreign ministers of the triangle met once again – for the first time in China – in the northeastern (Manchurian) city of Harbin, built as a Russian railway hub on Chinese soil in the early twentieth century and acting as a sanctuary for White Russian émigrés after the Bolshevik revolution and for Jews during the Second World War. The Harbin Communiqué reiterated the principal elements of Delhi that: "the development of China, Russia and India is a major contribution to peace and development of the region and the world and is beneficial to the process of global multi-polarity". But the reality was that India had been increasingly veering away from Russia and China and closer to the United States and Japan. It was participating in a 'strategic dialogue' with a new 'military–political triangle' in the Asia-Pacific region involving the US, Japan and Australia. In September 2007 India held a large-scale naval exercise with them in the Bay of Bengal –its first-ever military exercise in a multilateral format – involving US aircraft carriers and submarines. It was named the *'Quadrilateral Initiative'* and described by analysts and commentators as a 'democratic coalition to contain China'. The exercise had been preceded by an appeal by former Japanese Prime Minister Shinzo Abe to the Indian Parliament during his August 2007 visit to create a 'broader Asia' or 'the arc of freedom and prosperity', based on common values of democracy, which would eventually incorporate the United States and Australia and specifically exclude China. Before Abe's departure, Japan's Defence Minister Yoriko Koike and the Commander of US Pacific Command, Admiral Timothy Keating, arrived in Delhi to finalize the details of defence cooperation and the Malabar 07-02 manoeuvres. Ironically, one day after the manoeuvres ended, Abe resigned as prime minister after just one year in office. Difficulty in passing the special bill – which allows Japan to refuel US and other allied ships in Afghanistan-bound operations – was the ostensible reason for Abe's surprise resignation, but the sudden resignation called into question the ability of Japanese leaders to pursue what Mr Abe called 'assertive diplomacy', a stance welcomed by Washington, which wants Japan to shoulder more of a global burden. Abe, a right-wing nationalist, was succeeded by Yasuo Fukuda, a moderate with a non-ideological and far more accommodating stance towards China.

Lavrov strongly criticized the emerging 'East Asian NATO' without any direct reference to India, although the import of his statements could not be lost on New Delhi. Never before, perhaps, in the saga of India–Russia relations had such a serious contradiction appeared in their respective perceptions over Asian security. In recent years, India had also been critical of US policy towards Iran, both on sanctions and a multi-billion dollar gas pipeline, linking Iran with India, but during late 2007, India had calculated that finalization of the long-stalled nuclear deal with the US was more advantageous to India. So, when the Bush administration announced a regime of unprecedented sanctions against Iran immediately after the Harbin meeting, branding Iranian security bodies as sponsors of international terrorism and virtually making Iran an enemy country under US law, Russia and China lost no time in criticizing Bush's move, but India kept mum. Later, at a joint press conference with his Russian and Indian counterparts, Chinese Foreign Minister Yang Jiechi criticized US plans for deployment of the missile defence system in Central Europe, saying that this would not only not ease global security concerns, but would undermine the global strategic balance. In contrast, Indian Foreign Minister Pranab Mukherjee simply maintained that India had no plans for cooperation with the US missile defence system. He stonewalled. He would not be drawn into any criticism of US plans.

China was obviously concerned about India's drift into the US camp, but the Chinese still liked to believe that 'India's DNA doesn't allow itself to become an ally subordinate to the US, like Japan or Britain'. And they were right. Left-wing opposition against the deal in India had reached a climax and many on the right accused the left of doing China's bidding. Then, in October 2007, Ai Ping, Director-General of the Chinese Communist Party's International Liaison Department, stated that China had nothing to do with this and that the nuclear deal was entirely India's internal matter. Ai said that China highly cherishes its sovereignty and independence, "so we must respect other people's sovereignty and independence". India's leftist parties oppose the deal because they see it as a way of bringing India into the US strategic orbit and of compromising sovereign decision-making on foreign policy, security and nuclear matters. Even the Hindu nationalist BJP, which has been traditionally pro-American and which negotiated a nascent alliance with the Bush administration in early 2004, says that the nuclear deal sacrifices national sovereignty. "A strategic partnership is not a synonym for strategic subservience, and that's why we are opposed to it", said Jaswant Singh, chief nuclear negotiator with the Clinton administration from 1998–2000, foreign minister in the last BJP administration and now a Member of Parliament.

Yekaterinburg

Interestingly, the 'Triangle's' foreign ministers held their most recent trilateral meeting on 15 May 2008 in the Russian city of Yekaterinburg (from 1924–1991 named Sverdlovsk) in the Urals, on the border of European Russia and Siberia, again emphasizing Russia's dual nature as a Eurasian country. The focus this time was on the need to fight terrorism and the drug threat. The three foreign ministers – Sergei Lavrov, Pranab Mukherjee and Yang Jiechi – 'supported the international community's efforts to improve the situation around Afghanistan and believe that in addition to these efforts, the establishment of drug security belts around the country would be useful'.

The ministers also focused on economic and military cooperation, touching on topical international matters, including the unilateral declaration of independence by Kosovo in February 2008. Lavrov said that Russia, India and China insist that talks between Serbia and its breakaway province, Kosovo, should be resumed. Unilateral secession is a common concern that the three share with Serbia, the common analogy being: China's Taiwan question; Russia's Chechnya; and India's Kashmir.

'Primakov's Arms' Sales Triangle'

Parallel to the triangular volleys of the Sino-Indian-Russian troika and the marathon dance around the Indo-US nuclear deal, another showdown was looming between the two biggest military export machines in the world: the battle between the 'Bear and Eagle' for the Indian arms' market. American arms' dealers made no secret of their desire to break Russia's domination of the Indian market, one of the most lucrative in the world, because India still imports much more of its hardware than China. Russia's Vladimir Putin working assiduously and methodically to rebuild Russia's position as a top player in the so-called

'Near Abroad' and the world at large during his final years in office as president. After the loss of so many rounds of arms' contract negotiations in East Europe, the Caucasus and Central Asia to the US and NATO, Putin and the Russian generals are in no mood to let India end up in the American orbit. William Cohen, former US Defence Secretary under President Clinton, who was leading a large delegation of American arms' dealers to India in February 2007, said that India was a US$ 30 billion opportunity over the next five years. American nuclear power companies hope that they will also get US$ 30 billion of a total market of US$ 100 billion, but there are many competitors.

The supreme prize for which all of the world's fighter aircraft manufacturers will contest is a replacement deal for 126 planes for the Indian Air Force. Will India buy Russian MiGs (or Sukhois) again as it has done for decades, or will it go for US, French or other European planes. Putin was the guest of honour on Indian National Day in January 2007 and he signed a deal for the Indo-Russian co-production of MiG engines and joint development of a transportation plane. Whether India in the end opts for US F-16s, F-18s or Russian MiG-35s or Sukhois is a step that will have long-term implications for the strategic orientation of India as a potential partner in the newly emerging regional economic–strategic triangle of Russia, India and China and the possible accession of India to the Shanghai Cooperation Organization.

Russia has a long history as the main arms' supplier of both India and China – to India from 1962 all the way through the Cold War and to China (re-)starting in the early 1990s. The two giant Asian nations bought 70 per cent of Russia's global arms' sales throughout the 1990s.

New Delhi has managed to purchase everything from tanks to fighter aircraft, to submarines. The biggest, but still incomplete, deal is the transfer of the Soviet-era aircraft carrier *'Admiral Gorshkov'* (launched in 1982) 'for free' (!) but on the condition of major refitting and additional aircraft deals. Under the deal, worth US$ 2 billion, the 'Gorshkov' is currently being refurbished by Russian shipbuilders. India would also take updated versions of 50 Mikoyan MiG-29K naval fighter aircraft, along with a training package for Indian sailors and aircrews. India would have to pay US$ 700 million for a refit of the vessel, plus it would have to purchase the MiG-29Ks and eight naval helicopters for another US$ 800 million. India was also offered options for upgrades to Indian port facilities in order to dock and service the 'Gorshkov' for a total of another US$ 1.5 billion.

In order to accommodate the upgraded MiG-29K, the 'Gorshkov' requires an extension to its flight deck, installation of an arrested landing system like that used on US and French carriers, plus a replacement of its maintenance-intensive steam propulsion system with a diesel power plant. All of this has proven to be too much to do for the originally agreed price. The Russian naval shipbuilder Rosoboronexport (ROE) is now demanding an additional US$ 1.2 billion to finish the job. The Indian naval command is appalled by this 'blackmail', but hardly has an acceptable alternative. This is where the United States came in.

America's 'Gift' for India: 48-year old 'Kitty'?

According to reports in the Indian and US media – apparently based on official leaks – US Secretary of Defence Robert Gates, on his visit to New Delhi in February 2008, carried with him a letter from US President George W. Bush offering a better deal for India than the one that it has now been struggling to get out of Moscow for four years. The Indian Navy will reportedly be offered the soon-to-be decommissioned USS *'Kitty Hawk'* aircraft carrier – also for free – provided that the Indian Navy will foot a big refitting bill and agree to purchase 65 of the newest model Boeing F/A-18E/F Super Hornets to be operated off the 48-year-old carrier, which is 22 years older but twice as big as the 'Gorshkov'. The 'Hawk' has made its last voyage and is waiting to be decommissioned, but the rumours that India is still interested in buying it persist on the internet.

The US is unlikely to win this 'dumping-contest' with the Russians. The Indian defence establishment has serious complaints over US equipment and unsatisfactory sales' methods. The Indian Navy recently bought the 36-year-old landing ship dock (LSD) 'Trenton' for US$ 50 million, the first-ever Indian naval ship purchase from the US. According to Indian navy standards, the service life of an aircraft carrier is 40 years and twenty for an LSD. A report to the Indian Parliament by the Comptroller and Auditor General (CAG) of the Indian Navy asserts that the USS 'Trenton', built in 1968 and rebaptized INS 'Jalasha', was purchased without undertaking a proper physical assessment, but with only a 'visual inspection' and an 'over-reliance' on – inadequate – information supplied by the US Navy. Furthermore, the ship was only delivered in a 'safe-to-steam' condition and would require upgrades and modifications, aspects that the Indian Navy kept hidden from competent financial authority. In February 2008, six Indian Navy sailors died aboard the 'Jalasha' following a toxic gas leak. In more alarming revelations, the CAG says that New Delhi had signed restrictive clauses assuring Washington that it would not deploy the INS 'Jalasha' for offensive purposes and would allow regular US inspections of the ship. Observers say that this is against established policy and bound to raise a political stink and accusations of New Delhi buckling under US pressure and possibly financial muscle.

While in New Delhi in February 2008 at the head of a large delegation of defence contractors, US Secretary of Defence Robert Gates welcomed the recent Indian decision to buy six Lockheed Hercules C-130J cargo aircraft, valued at US$ 1 billion. His main purpose was to help Lockheed Martin sell 126 F-16s and/or Boeing its F/A-18 Super Hornet, worth US$ 10 billion.

The importance of the deal is not only commercial, but that the new-generation aircraft will be in use with the Indian Air Force for the next 40 years, and clinching the deal therefore becomes absolutely vital for the US if it is to aim at 'inter-operability'. Gates knew that it is the sort of deal that will ensure that US–India military-to-military cooperation will become irreversible and will pin India down as the US's strategic ally in the region. Stung by the strong opposition against the US–India nuclear deal and the Jalasha scandal, Gates modestly said: "We're not looking for quick results or big leaps, but rather a steady expansion that leaves everybody comfortable".

Russia (and the United States) Favour India and 'Discriminate' against China

The US and Russia have been engaged in a cut-throat competitive bidding spree in India. This had already started with talks on the purchase of P-8i Poseidon long-range maritime reconnaissance patrol aircraft with anti-submarine war capabilities to replace Russian-made Tu-142M bombers. The deal could be worth US$ 2 billion, the biggest defence deal so far between Russia and the United States.

Some of the Russian transfers to India include weapons and technology that Moscow refuses to supply to China. Moscow and Delhi agreed to begin the joint development of a new, so-called fifth-generation fighter. This aircraft would be a potential rival in performance to the US F-22 Raptor, defence analysts in New

Delhi said. India also agreed in 2007 to buy another 40 Su-30MKI fighters from Russia for US$ 1.5 billion, in addition to an earlier order for 140 of these aircraft. Some military experts say that this versatile, twin-engined jet is probably the best fighter and strike aircraft in the world. But Russia has not offered it to China while Moscow is also offering to sell India its latest fighter: the MiG-35. In nuclear submarine technology, Russia has also been more generous with India than with China. The unspoken rationale behind this is obvious: Russia – not unlike the United States – considers China an emerging *'global peer rival'* and potential long-term threat, while India – at best – is deemed a secondary regional power.

China has become a top importer of Russian military equipment and systems, which is ironic given the historic antagonism between Beijing and Moscow from the late 1950s until the Soviet demise. Nevertheless, Russia, out of frustration with the United States' 'winner-takes-all triumphalism' and humiliation of the Yeltsin presidency by the Clinton administration, and for cash, during the 1990s agreed to sell China its sophisticated Sovremenny-class destroyers (now the flagships of the Chinese Navy), 'Sunburn' anti-ship missiles, and advanced Sukoi Su-30 MKK fighter aircraft.

Both nations have also agreed to cooperate on the joint development of new military technologies, including so-called 'asymmetrical' warfare (cyber-warfare) technology aimed at curbing US dominance in this area. During the 1980s, Israel was – dodging US objections –a 'covert' supplier of advanced military technology to China, estimated at US$ 4 billion. When Israel wanted to supply the Falcon, an airborne radar system equipped with advanced Israeli-made aeronautics on board a Russian-made plane, to China in 2000, the US Congress threatened sanctions against Israel. Only when Congress moved to cut the US$ 2 billion aid that it gives Israel annually did Israel buckle and had to pay US$ 350 million in compensation to China. The US did not, however, oppose Israel's supply of the Falcon to India.

Russia's arms industry is suffering a near collapse in exports to China as the Russian top brass agonizes over which technology can safely be sold to China, as well as Beijing's desire to receive licences to do the work itself, the independent newspaper Nezavisimaya Gazeta reported on 28 January 2008. The main issue is indecision: 'Russians feel genuinely concerned, in the medium to longer term, that Russian and Chinese interests may collide again', said Alexey Muraviev, a strategic analyst at Curtin University of Technology in Perth, Australia.

'There is this debate about whether we should arm the Chinese when they may eventually turn against us'. Nezavisimaya further reported that Moscow's willingness to deliver cutting-edge technology to India – another major importer of Russian weapons – had 'embittered the Chinese generals'. After orders peaked at more than US$ 2 billion a year earlier this decade, Chinese arms' deals with Russia shrank to almost nothing in 2006, and no major new contracts are in the pipeline, according to Russian, Chinese and US defence experts. Still, with the EU–US arms' embargo on China still in place, most analysts expect that Moscow and Beijing will eventually negotiate compromises that clear the way for future contracts: 'Russia still provides what the US and the EU will not supply'.

Russia 'Strong-Arming' India

As a logical next phase in its ambitions as a major power, India in 2002 undertook to establish its own military outpost in Tajikistan and spent over US$ 1 million to renovate a former Soviet airbase, Ayni, 10 kilometres from the Tajik capital Dushanbe. Ayni's value to India stems from Tajikistan's geographic location, as it shares borders with China, Afghanistan, Uzbekistan and Kyrgyzstan. A narrow strip of Afghan territory – the Wakhan corridor – separates Tajikistan from Pakistan. The Russians recently started to pressurize the Tajiks to deny India deployment and even access to Ayni, allegedly because of increasing Russian unease about India's new closeness to the United States. The Russian message was that if India wanted to have a strategic beachhead in Central

Asia, it has to keep its distance from the US. It also served as a warning to India to decide in Russia's favour in a host of big-ticket defence deals that are on the agenda:

'Don't buy too much American, or else!' There is another irritant in India–Russia relations, for which Russia itself is at fault: the endless delay in delivery of the aircraft carrier 'Admiral Gorshkov' and the steep hike in costs of the Sukhoi fighter aircraft.

On top of that, there is the China factor. What impact will the US and Russian arming of India have on Sino-Indian relations, while the United States maintains its arms' embargo on China and maintains pressure on the divided European Union to fall in line.

The US has in recent years rejected a policy of containment of China, at least publicly. Only the short-lived former Japanese Prime Minister Shinzo Abe openly advocated 'value-based diplomacy' (democracy and human rights) and containment, and appealed in a speech to the Indian Parliament in August 2007 for India to join, which India never did. Under its former inward-looking Prime Minister John Howard, however, Australia did, but the new Prime Minister Kevin Rudd, a Chinese-speaking former diplomat, cancelled Australia's participation in the 'Quadrilateral Dialogue', a coalition of democracies aimed at 'furtively' containing China, immediately after taking office. Indian Prime Minister Manmohan Singh, on his January 2008 visit to China, also reiterated the theme that India will not be part of any 'contain China scheme'.

Does the Triangle have a Future?

The 'Trio' of Russia, China and India was triggered by three events:

- The American sanctions against India over its May 1998 nuclear tests;
- The December 1998 Clinton–Blair bombing campaign against Iraq, a country with which Russia maintained close relations;

- The *'erroneous'* US bombing of the Chinese Embassy in Belgrade in May 1999.

The three countries had deeply shared grievances about – perceived – American/Western neo-colonialist arrogance, hypocrisy, double standards and deception, etc. US unilateralism provided a basis for continued – but just intermittent – solidarity, as the three of them had their own national bilateral agendas in pursuing better relations with each other and with the United States. While Russia and China shared opposition against the US-sponsored democratic 'colour revolutions' in former Soviet republics in 2005, India was more interested in expanding its relations with the United States. In 2006 the themes of their consensus were the democratization of international relations, multi-polarity, respect for the United Nations, which the United States often tended to bypass, and opposition to Bush's sabre-rattling against Iran. In 2007 the focus was on joint opposition against an emerging 'East Asian (!) NATO' – four democracies, including Australia and the United States – for the containment of China. After some confusion about its orientation, India dropped out this time, and in 2008 Australia as well. India would also not participate in the US-sponsored missile defence, at least not now, and the Indian communists succeeded in derailing the US–India nuclear deal. In 2008, the 'Triangle' also expressed opposition against the unilateral declaration of independence of Kosovo, but it remains to be seen whether they can hang on to this against the United States and the European Union. Opposition against further NATO expansion will probably be more effective, because the European Union itself is divided over this. China is neutral on the issue of Ukraine's and Georgia's accession to NATO and still resists Russia's request for closer military cooperation, such as in the Shanghai Cooperation Organization (SCO). Russia advocates collective security for SCO, but China advocates only cooperative security – anti-terrorism, anti-extremism and special dialogues on energy security.

The question is, will the Russia–China–India triangle survive as a viable grouping in Asian and global diplomacy, or will the inherent contradictions in the triangle render it marginal or irrelevant? There is a vast asymmetry in the countries' actual and potential power. The US design was to strengthen India against a much stronger China and to lock the fellow democracy into the position of an ally and military client state with restrictions on its sovereignty, similar to the formerly defeated Asian great power of Japan. It is now clear, however, that this is not going to work as Washington envisioned. India practises democracy, not based on crusading Bushist ideological zealotry but out of sheer pragmatism: it is the natural way to manage the internal dynamics of such a culturally diverse country. But India will never base its foreign policy on an agenda of spreading democracy or show prejudice against countries that are not Western/American-style democracies.

An accumulation of factors – foremost of which is the realization that negative relations with the United States during the Cold War have held India back, plus the recognition that China's normalization of relations with the United States in 1972, combined with Deng Xiaoping's reforms from 1978, have facilitated and accelerated China's rise – have convinced India that it must optimally expand its relations with the United States for reasons of geopolitics, economics, trade and investment, particularly high-technology integration. For reasons of history and internal divisions, however, it cannot do so on American terms. India needs stable relations with China and in recent years it has achieved significant improvement in its relationship with China, but this is not sustainable without a broader Asian 'balance of power' with outside participation of the United States and, perhaps in the longer term, the European Union/OSCE. At the same time, India wants to continue its close relationship with its Cold War ally Russia, perhaps in a diluted form but still substantial. As Sujit Dutta, a senior analyst with the Institute of Defence Studies and Analyses in New Delhi, puts it:

India is not going to be a junior partner of China. No question. If Russia accepts to be a junior partner of China because of this vast asymmetric power relationship and its contradictions with the West, then the only way that scenario will play out is

India becomes a junior partner with China or alternately that China accepts an equal status for India. Much will depend on whether China's nationalism becomes what it says: accepting multi-polarity as a basis for the new world order. Multi-polarity doesn't seem to be the essence of it, though, as we observe Chinese foreign policy.

In other words, India will need the United States and Japan to balance against China, and in the longer term something similar may apply to Russia. It is interesting to note what former US National Security Adviser Zbigniew Brzezinski said about this: 'In the longer run, I happen to think that Russia really has no choice but to become gradually more associated with the Euro-Atlantic community. Because if it isn't, then it's going to find itself essentially facing China all by itself'.

The 'trio' was not an alliance and will not be one, but just a *ménage à trois* of intermittent *'one-night stands'*, with the three countries taking common positions on selected, but not the most important, issues.

The endgame for the three countries in the mid-to long term may very well be that China will enter into a bipolar superpower relationship with the United States; India will become one pillar in an Asian and global multi-polar balance of power, underpinned by the United States; and Russia will return to Europe for the fourth time in its history, after three failed precedents since Peter the Great.

RUSSIA, CHINA, AND INDIA OVERCOME FRICTION IN THEIR RELATIONS

The Russia-China partnership has clearly helped to foster bilateral relations after more than two decades of tension and hostility. This partnership has also enhanced the international standing of both countries. At the same time, however, political trust is still rather weak. Moscow and particularly the Russian Far East are clearly worried that the further economic decline of that region will lead to its abandoning by Russians and even Chinese occupation.

China is not perceived by the majority of Russian experts as an immediate military threat, because it is not expected to close the gap with Russia in nuclear and conventional weapons anytime soon. However, more and more Russian commentators, including in the military, are worried about the consequences for Russia of arming China with sophisticated Russian weapons while the Russian army itself cannot afford to have them.

Russia's growing political, economic, and military dependence on China has provoked a certain alarm and anxiety in Russia's academic and political circles. Alexei Bogaturov believes that in spite of impressive rapprochement, Russia and China remain countries that have historically been in conflict and that the geopolitical source of the conflict has not been removed or reduced. Hence, he argues against attempts to pick China as an ally or key partner in the region. Such views are not rare in Russia, even among government officials, in spite of a general official euphoria and an informal taboo on anti-Chinese comments. Common views toward US politics and close military cooperation may not be enough to sustain and enhance the "strategic partnership" between Russia and China. To make it complete, the two countries will have to get rid of their traditional suspicion of each other and engage in a stable and long-term economic cooperation.

The relationship between India and China also has an important influence on the character of regional order and significant geopolitical implications. Friction in this bilateral relationship could have direct effects on China's relations with other neighbours. Stable and cooperative relations between India and China build trust and contribute to Beijing's own sense of security and confidence, providing a counterbalance should other important relationships deteriorate.

The near-rapprochement of relations (driven by the mutual consensus that economic development should have priority) between India and China diffuses, but does not dispel, three decades of friction. Four of the five primary causes of disquiet in India-China relations have been addressed by both powers: India's values-driven Tibet policy has ceased;

Chinese support for secessionist insurgents in Assam and the North East has been withdrawn; the collapse of the Soviet Union reduces Chinese fears of a containment-driven strategic nexus; and, most important, tensions stemming from border disputes between India and China are addressed, though not resolved, through the negotiation of confidence-building measures and agreements. The principal friction in contemporary relations between New Delhi and Beijing is India's belief (apparently well-founded) that China provides nuclear-related military technology and hardware to Pakistan. This abrasion is compartmentalized from India's overall bilateral relationship with Beijing. (New Delhi may be reassured by China's decision to join, and work constructively with, the Non-Proliferation Treaty Exporters Committee [or Zangger Committee].) New Delhi's preference for longer-term prudence in its relationship with China is one consequence of China's military nuclear exports to Pakistan.

India's approach to the management of tensions with China offers important lessons for other regional actors in how to manage relations (especially on sensitive issues) with China. New Delhi has handled Beijing more successfully than Washington has during the corresponding period. India and China have established and maintained regular reciprocal high-level personal visits between political leaders. Both states have improved trade relations and take care to compartmentalize intractable issues that continue to irritate long-standing tensions. Such a policy has perhaps returned dividends of its own with China in turn assuming a "position of `careful neutrality' on Kashmir." In contrast to recent US policy on China, India takes care to respect the principle of noninterference in the internal affairs of another state and eschews a values-driven foreign policy. These developments are especially significant given the depth of India's embedded longer-term strategic concerns with China and the record of mutual tension that has only eased in recent years. India's democratic status also may make it an attractive partner to those East Asian states condemned by the United States for abusing human rights or for falling short of democratic standards. The renewed Russian-Indian strategic partnership, fuelled by common concern regarding Islamic revivalism, has thwarted Moscow's initial intention to follow a more balanced policy in South Asia, improving in particular its relations with Pakistan. Instead, Moscow-Islamabad links have further deteriorated, especially because of the latter's pro-Taliban role in Afghanistan prior to recent events. Moscow's strategic interest in India motivates Moscow to promote India's inclusion into the leading forums and institutions of the Asia-Pacific. Having become a member of the Asia-Pacific Economic Cooperation (APEC) organization, Moscow is now backing New Delhi's bid for membership in this regional body. During consultations with the Indian Foreign Ministry in November 1998, Russian Deputy Foreign Minister Grigory Karasin noted that "Russia will try its best to help India develop ties with APEC and eventually to join the organization."

Although Russia and India have renounced an openly anti-Chinese policy, both countries continue to share suspicion and fear toward China. In spite of Moscow's public denunciation of India's nuclear tests in 1998, Russia appreciates India's concern about adequate military preparation in case of Chinese aggression. Moscow supports India not only morally, but also through the resumption of arms supplies, which, after a brief pause in the early 1990s, have been steadily increasing.

Challenges to US International Strategy

Some US officials admit that closer ties between Moscow and Beijing are cause for concern. They say, at the very least, debates are more complicated now on the UN Security Council, where Russia and China frequently make common cause against interventionist initiatives favoured by the United States and Britain. Deadlock on the UN Security Council reminiscent of the Cold War era is becoming a regular occurrence.

For instance, knowing that both Russia and China would probably veto military intervention in Kosovo, the Clinton Administration decided to work through NATO. Both Moscow and Beijing were concerned about external intervention on humanitarian grounds, which would be relevant to conflicts within Russia such as Chechnya, and within China such as its claims over Taiwan. Further, NATO was again conspiring to force the US value system on a Third World state.

Russia, China, and India watched the United States in conflicts throughout the 1990s and each learned the same lessons. Indian military and political sources were among the first to react to the Kosovo operation and to speculate on preliminary lessons to be learned. "We are studying what's going on there [in Kosovo] and drawing our lessons from it." A common theme in Indian, Russian, and Chinese thinking since Operation Desert Storm has been the importance of "force multipliers" provided by information technology, AWACs, mid-air refuelling, unmanned aerial vehicles, and electronic warfare capabilities. Analysts in all three countries believe their armed forces can succeed against a high-technology foe if they use these force multipliers in combination with clever low-technology tactics, urban guerilla warfare, financial terrorism, computer hacking, media warfare, diplomatic actions, and psychological warfare.

In light of the new "interventionist-oriented NATO doctrine" and the new capabilities of long-range precision conventional weapons, Indian military thinkers recommend upgrading its nuclear arms to deter Western intimidation and attack. This is a prime example of the drive toward nuclear weapons and its cascading effects predicted by

General Makmut Gareyev, President of the Russian Academy of Military Science. He believes that countries, including Russia, that are unable to match an opponent in high-technology conventional weapons will resort to nuclear weapons in order to deter conventional strikes. Until 1998, India held the principled position that nuclear deterrence was abhorrent to human sentiment, since it implies that if required to defend its own existence, a state will act with pitiless disregard for the consequences of its own and its adversary's people. But in remarks made on 15 March 1999, Prime Minister A. B. Vajpayee asserted: "The nuclear weapon is not an offensive weapon. It is a weapon of self-defence. It is the kind of weapon that helps in preserving peace. If in the days of the Cold War there was no use of force, it was because of the balance of terror." It is also true that India has begun revamping its conventional forces to push the nuclear threshold upward, creating more options with those conventional forces before resorting to nuclear weapon use.

In his article titled, "Nuclear Shadows on High Tech Warfare," Major General Wu Jianguo, former associate professor and dean of the Antichemical Warfare Academy, sums up the Chinese view of its nuclear capability: "When countries possessing nuclear weapons and high-tech conventional weapons are involved in a war in which the conflict is intensifying, the possible use of nuclear weapons cannot be ruled out. Nuclear weapons, therefore, are still a trump card in the hands of nuclear nations."

Many scenarios that would present a challenge to the United States could arise from the triangular strategic partnership. One possible conflict scenario is that of China and Taiwan. This is a possible conflict for several reasons. First, China is going through an economic modernization. This is good over the long run for encouraging political liberty. In the short run, however, as large state-owned enterprises are disestablished, the Chinese may have unemployment of millions to tens of millions and social and political disruption of one kind or another.

For thousands of years dictators have responded to domestic problems by playing the nationalism card and focusing attention on a foreign enemy or foreign problem. Taiwan will be front and centre because now it is a thriving, prosperous, free-enterprise democracy. Taiwan inescapably disproves those people in Southeast Asia and in the PRC who have said for years that Asians do not have an aptitude for democracy and need to be ruled with a firm hand. Taiwan is an affront to the leaders in Beijing the same way Poland's Solidarity movement in the summer of 1989 was an affront to the leaders in the Kremlin and the dictators in Eastern Europe. The Taiwan Strait is one of the most likely places over the next five to ten years where the United States might end up in a clear confrontation with another nuclear power.

How would such a conflict evolve? Top echelons of the PLA officer corps do not necessarily share a common point of view with regard to Taiwan, and the advice they give is not necessarily militaristic. However, a Western intelligence source surmises that high-ranking naval and air force officers support a militant stance in Taiwan. They, rather than the ground forces, have received the benefits of increases in the defence budget and are eager to test their new capabilities.

Beijing is not likely to haphazardly lob a few missiles over to Taiwan and see what happens. Beijing would have a plan and expect to win. The more probable scenario would be for the Chinese to effect simultaneous crises to distract the United States, forcing the Americans to choose between Taiwan and another ally. This quote from Chinese ultra-nationalist author He Xing lends credence to the "simultaneous crises" theory:

> China must pay close attention to those countries that are opposed to American interests, or are potential strategic enemies. It must be borne in mind that the enemies of enemies are one's own allies.... Know this: the more the United States encounters trouble in other places in the world, the more difficult it is for it to concentrate its power on dealing with China and the greater the opportunities for China's existence and development.

Hypothetically, Beijing might cooperate with Moscow on the timing of an attack on Taiwan. Moscow could simultaneously start a conflict with emerging democracies in the Baltics or the Caucasus. Or Beijing and New Delhi could cooperate on timing, with India engaging Pakistan, perhaps with the support of Moscow. Both Russia and China are arming other enemies of the United States such as Iran and Iraq. Iraq could be persuaded by Beijing or Moscow to simultaneously start a conflict with Kuwait, Saudi Arabia, or Israel. China could concurrently attack Taiwan and stop the food flow to North Korea, forcing millions of refugees into South Korea, and causing the United States to choose between helping Taiwan and assisting South Korea.

The possibility of a nuclear dimension to a conflict between China and Taiwan is all too real. On 2 December 1998, the Defence Intelligence Agency (DIA) reported that the PLA had conducted exercises that included simulated nuclear missile attacks on Taiwan and on US military forces in the region. DIA analysts determined that the missile units were conducting mock nuclear attacks on Taiwan and against US Army troops based in South Korea. US marines on the Japanese island of Okinawa and mainland Japan also were targeted.

The missile exercise directly threatened the 37,000 troops based in South Korea and the 47,000 troops in Japan, including about 25,000 marines on Okinawa. All of these China-Taiwan scenario options are conjecture, but they are not beyond the realm of possibility and are worth considering. That may be particularly so in the aftermath of the terrorist strikes on the United States on 11 September 2001 and the US response. The volatility of the current situation calls into question many of our previous assumptions about stability and the likely course of international and regional relations.

PREVENTING ANOTHER COLD WAR

A strategic partnership among China, Russia, and India is a blueprint for the next Cold War. What can we in the United States do to avert a return to the days of superpower tensions? This is a difficult question to answer, but the following concepts would seem to have promise:

Build a multinational missile defence network that would protect everyone involved against attacks or accidental launches.

Ensure that the US military is strong and that we have an effective national security posture in the Pacific. Explicitly and clearly support our friends who are engaged in fostering democracy and free markets in foreign countries.

Give depth to our relationships with other countries through diplomacy, foreign aid, and exchange programs, which in turn provides us early warning about developing situations.

Use our university system to continue educating foreign students. Increase intelligence gathering with regard to China, Russia, and India.

Continue to help Russia democratize, using US benefits as leverage to prevent a Russian alliance with Beijing.

Such measures will promote US interests, increase our awareness of developments in Asia, and help to ease tensions in what has suddenly become a more uncertain world. Even though our immediate focus may be on countering terrorism, other long-term aspects of international relations are also vital to US interests, and we must tend to them as well.

CHINA'S CONTINUING SALIENCE IN PAKISTANI FOREIGN POLICY

With India's recent rise as an economic and political power of global significance, Sino-Indian ties are now at a critical juncture as India tries to find the right policy mix to deal with its most important neighbour. Meanwhile, Chinese strategists remain concerned about U.S. attempts to encircle China and the profound effect on Chinese security of an eventual integration of India into a U.S. alliance.

China, according to this view, needs to remain vigilant against the growing network running "from Japan to India" that would suffocate China. As India struggles to emerge as a global power with an ambitious foreign policy agenda, China can effectively scuttle Indian ambitions by continuing with its diplomatic and military support to Pakistan. Much to India's chagrin, China has given ample indications in the recent past that it wants to follow that path. With the civilian government of President Asif Ali Zardari under intense pressure from the United States to do more to fight terrorism emanating from Pakistani soil, there are calls in Pakistan to adopt a foreign policy that considers China and not the United States to be Pakistan's strongest ally and most significant stakeholder. China's emergence as the leading global economic power coupled with recent attempts by India and the United States to forge a closer relationship has helped this suggestion gain further credibility.

Washington has historically been accused of using Pakistan in times of need and then deserting it for a policy that favours stronger relations with India to serve the larger U.S. strategic agenda. Pakistan remains angry about U.S. indifference after the United States used it to funnel aid to Afghan mujahideen and then turned its back on Pakistan after the Soviet withdrawal. Whereas only around nine percent of Pakistanis view the United States as a partner, around 80 percent of the Pakistani population considers China a friend.

The Obama administration's July 2011 decision to suspend a portion of U.S. aid to the Pakistani military has led many in Islamabad to become even more forceful in underlining Beijing's importance for Pakistan. Reacting to the U.S. move, Islamabad's ambassador to Beijing, Masood Khan, was quick to suggest that "China will stand by us in difficult times as it has been doing for the past years." Though Beijing cannot replace Washington as an aid-provider to Pakistan, the tension in U.S.—Pakistan ties provides an opportunity for Beijing to deepen its relationship with Islamabad. As it is, China is considered a more reliable ally that has always come to Pakistan's aid when India has been on the rise, even to an extent that China has conveniently turned a blind eye to Pakistan's strategy of using terror as an instrument of policy against India. Not surprisingly, Pakistan has given China a "blank cheque" to intervene in India—Pakistan peace talks. Pakistan also seems to have allowed Chinese engineers to examine the remains of the stealth helicopter destroyed during the raid that killed Osama bin Laden despite a direct request from the United States that China not be allowed to do so.

Forecast for the "All-Weather" Relationship

With India's ascent in the global hierarchy and U.S. attempts to carve out a strong partnership with India, China's need for Pakistan is only likely to grow. As tensions rose between India and Pakistan after the November 2008 terror attacks in Mumbai,

Pakistan's Chairman of the Joint Chiefs of Staff Committee went to China to seek that country's support, which was readily given. The visit resulted in the signing of a new agreement on military cooperation between the two nations, with Beijing agreeing to expedite the delivery of F-22 frigates to Pakistan's Navy.

Beijing has justified its arms sales to Pakistan on the grounds that India was buying similar weapon systems from the United States (it also is buying military hardware from the Russians). China has consistently defended Pakistan's desire for high capacity weapons systems as normal for an independent nation seeking to bolster its security. In the years preceding the attacks in Mumbai, China blocked UN sanctions against the dreaded Lashkar-e-Taiba (LeT) and Jamaat-ud-Dawa (JuD), the organizations that planned and executed the attacks, despite a broad global consensus favouring such a move. Only when tensions surfaced between Beijing and Islamabad on the issue of Chinese Uighur separatists receiving sanctuaries and training on Pakistani territory did China agree to a ban on JuD. More recently, China has refused to reconsider its objection in the United Nations to proscribing the Jaish-e-Mohammed's Maulana Masood Azhar and some prominent LeT operatives based in Pakistan, despite New Delhi's presenting detailed information on them to Beijing.

With the exception of China, other major global powers such as Britain, France, Germany, and Russia supported the U.S.—India nuclear deal as they were eager to sell nuclear fuel, reactors, and equipment to India. China, on its part, made its displeasure clear by asking India to sign the NPT and dismantle its nuclear weapons.

The official Xinhua news agency of China commented that the U.S.—India nuclear agreement "will set a bad example for other countries." Since the U.S.—India deal is in many ways a recognition of India's rising global profile, China was not very happy with the outcome and indicated that it would be willing to sell nuclear reactors to Pakistan. It was a not so subtle message to the United States that if Washington decides to play favourites, China retains the same right.

Not surprisingly, China's plans to supply two nuclear reactors to Pakistan in defiance of international rules have gathered momentum. Chinese authorities have confirmed that the China National Nuclear Cooperation has signed an agreement with Pakistan for two new nuclear reactors at the Chashma site Chashma III and Chashma IV in addition to the two that it is already working on in Pakistan.

This will be in clear violation of the Nuclear Suppliers Group (NSG) guidelines that forbid nuclear transfers to countries that are not signatories to the NPT or do not adhere to comprehensive international safeguards on their nuclear program. China has suggested that "there are compelling political reasons concerning the stability of South Asia to justify the exports," echoing Pakistan's oft-repeated compliant that the U.S.—India nuclear pact has upset stability in the region. The decision to supply reactors to Pakistan which has a record of dealing with North Korea, Iran, and Libya reflects China's growing diplomatic confidence and underscores its view of Pakistan as a prized South Asian strategic power.

Recent suggestions emanating from Beijing that China is likely to set up military bases overseas to counter U.S. influence and exert pressure on India have been interpreted in certain sections in New Delhi as a veiled reference to China's interest in having a permanent military presence in Pakistan.

Even though it might not be politically possible for the Pakistani government to follow through on such threats and openly allow China to set up a military base, New Delhi fears that Islamabad might allow Beijing use of Pakistani military facilities without any public announcement.

Indian concerns have also risen that China and Pakistan are coordinating their efforts in regard to border issues with India. The presence of the Chinese military in the Gilgit—Baltistan area of Pakistan Occupied Kashmir, purportedly to repair and upgrade the Karakoram Highway, has enormous implications for Indian security.

Overall, it has been rightly observed that China's policy toward Pakistan is "an object lesson in how to attain long-term national goals by calm calculation, forbearance, and diplomatic skill." Nevertheless, there are indeed limits to China—Pakistan ties. The relationship remains fundamentally asymmetrical: Pakistan wants more out of its ties with China than China is willing to offer. Today, while Pakistan's domestic problems are gargantuan, China will be very cautious in involving itself even more. In September 2011, China Kingho Group, one of China's largest private coal mining companies, pulled out of what was to be Pakistan's largest foreign-investment pact, citing concerns for the security of its personnel. Moreover, the closer China gets to Pakistan, the faster India would move into the U.S. orbit.

Amid worries about the potential destabilizing influence of Pakistani militants on China's Muslim minority in Xinjiang, Beijing has also taken a harder line against Pakistan. The flow of arms and terrorists from across the border in Pakistan remains a major headache for Chinese authorities, and Islamabad's inability and/or failure to curb extremism makes it difficult for the Chinese to trust Pakistan completely. If Pakistan wants to keep receiving support from China, then it needs to demonstrate progress on this issue.

As tensions rose between China and Pakistan in the aftermath of violence in the border town of Kashgar in Xinjiang in August 2011, President Zardari went to talk directly with local leaders and businessmen in Xinjiang, recognizing that if he was not able to mend fences with local leadership, Sino-Pakistani ties might be in real jeopardy.

China, at least publicly, has continued to emphasize that its relationship with Pakistan is far more important than isolated incidents of violence. To be clear, Chinese involvement in Pakistan is unlikely to match the U.S. profile in the country in the short to medium term, and it is not readily evident if China even wants to match the United States.

But flirtation with Pakistan gives China crucial space for diplomatic maneuvering vis-a'-vis India and the United States, and it will continue to utilize the relationship in pursuit of its larger strategic objectives. Pakistan is not going to be a common interest that binds China with either India or the United States any time soon. China was the only major power that openly voiced support for Pakistan after bin Laden's assassination, defending Islamabad and emphasizing that the Pakistani government may not have known about bin Laden's presence on its territory. During Prime Minister Gilani's visit, Chinese Premier Wen Jiabao affirmed that "Pakistan has made huge sacrifices and an important contribution to the international fight against terrorism, that its independence, sovereignty, and territorial integrity must be respected, and that the international community should understand and support Pakistan's efforts to maintain domestic stability and to realize economic and social development." Wen went on to state that China would like to be an "all-weather strategic partner," and would do its best to help the Pakistani government and people get through their difficulties. To underscore its commitment, China agreed to immediately provide Pakistan with 50 new JF-17 Thunder multi-role jets under a co-production agreement, even as negotiations continued for more fighter aircrafts including those with stealth technology. Despite this generosity, Pakistan wanted even more from China underscored by its expressed desire to have China take over the operation of Gwadar port in the Arabian Sea west of Karachi, in which Beijing has invested heavily in recent years and which serves an important role in the projection of China's naval prowess in the region. Pakistan has suggested that the port could be upgraded to a naval base for Chinese use. China, however, immediately rejected this offer, not wanting to antagonize the United States and India with the formal establishment of a base in Pakistan.

Bibliography

Ahmad, Ilyas : *Sovereignty, Islamic and Modern,* Allies Book Corporation, Karachi, 1965.

Alperovitz, Gar. *The Decision to Use the Atomic Bomb.* New York: Vintage Books, 1996.

Amitabh Sikdar: *India and China : Strategic Energy Management and Security*, Manas, Delhi, 2009.

Anil, K.C.: *Military and Democracy in South Asia : Challenges, Politics and Power*, Sumit Enterprises, Delhi, 2009.

Arend, A.: *International Law and the Use of Force in Afghanistan,* London, Routledge, 1993.

Averre, Derek: *'Russia and the European Union: Convergence or Divergence?'* 2005.

Bahedur, Kalim : *The Jamaat-i-Islami of Pakistan,* Progressive Books, Lahore, 1978.

Basrur, Rajesh M., and Hasan-Askari Rizvi, *Nuclear Terrorism and South Asia and Afghanistan*, Albuquerque, NM: Sandia National Laboratories, February 2003.

Benjamin, Joseph : *China-India Relations : Prospect and Retrospect*, Reference Press, Delhi, 2004.

Bhat, T.P. : *India and China : Trade Complementarities and Competitiveness*, Bookwell, Delhi, 2008.

Budge I: *The New Challenge of Direct Democracy*, Oxford, Polity Press, 1996.

Buzan, Barry : *Security: A New Framework for Analysis.* Boulder: Lynne-Rienner Publishers, 1998.

Coakley, J.: *The Territorial Management of Ethnic Conflict*, London: Frank Cass, 2003.

Debray, Regis. *Revolution in the Revolution.* New York: Grove Press, Inc., 1993.

Dhagamwar, Vasudha : *Law, Power and Justice : Protection of Personal Rights under Islam,* Popular Prakashan, Bombay, 2001.

Dixit, A.K. : *Military Wars and Rescue Techniques*, Cyber Tech Pub, Delhi, 2010.

Evelyn Goh, *Meeting the Afghanistan Challenge: The U.S. in Southeast Asian Regional Security Strategies*, DC: East-West Center, 2005.

Fletcher, Arnold: *Afghanistan, Highway of Conquest*, Ithaca, New York, Cornell University, 1965.

Ghosh, Ajoy : *China-Russia Conflict : Threat to South Asian Security*, Reference Press, Delhi, 2003.

Giustozzi, Antonio: *Koran, Kalashnikov, and Laptop: The Neo-Taliban Insurgency in Afghanistan,* New York: Columbia University Press, 2008.

Goldstein, Joshua S.: *Three-way Street: Strategic Reciprocity in World Politics.* Chicago: University of Chicago Press, 1990.

Gottlieb, Thomas M.: *Chinese Foreign Policy Factionalism and the Origins of the Strategic Triangle.* Santa Monica, CA: RAND Corporation, 1977.

Gupta, Asha: *Military Rule and Democratization : Changing Perspectives*, Deep & Deep, Delhi, 2003.

Habberton, William: *Anglo-Russian Relations Concerning Afghanistan 1837-1907*, Urbana, University of Illinois, 1937.

Haukkala, Hiski: *The EU-Russia Strategic Partnership: The limits of post-sovereignty in international relations*. Oxon: Routledge, 2010.

Hoffman, Bruce, *Inside Terrorism in Afghanistan*, New York: Columbia University Press, 1998.

Hurewitz, Jacob C.: *Diplomacy in the Near and Middle East: A Documentary Record 1535-1914*, Princeton, New Jersey, 1956.

Ikenberry, John G.: *After Victory: Institutions, Strategic Restraint, and the Rebuilding of Order after Major Wars*. Princeton, NJ: Princeton University Press, 2001.

Imtiaz, A.: *State and Foreign Policy: India's Role in South Asia*, New Delhi, Vikas, 1993.

Jagannath P. Panda: *China's Path to Power : Party, Military and the Politics of State Transition*, Pentagon, Delhi, 2010.

Kelly, John B.: *Indian Military and Pakistan War*, Oxford, Clarendon Press, 1968.

Kunju, N. : *Indo-Pak : Nuclear Cold War*, Reliance, Delhi, 2002.

Laquer, Walter, *The New Terrorism: Fanaticism and the Arms of Mass Destruction*, Oxford: Oxford University Press, 1999.

Moravcsik, Andrew: *The Choice for Europe: Social Purpose and State Power*. Ithaca, NY: Cornell University Press, 1998.

Nayyar, K K : *National Security : Military Aspects*, Rupa, Delhi, 2003.

Phuskele, Preeti : *India and China : Emerging Superpowers*, ICFAI University, Delhi, 2009.

Posen, B.R.: *The Sources of Indian Military Doctrine*, Ithaca, 1984, Cornell Univ. Press.

Prabla, Dixit: *Communalism: A Struggle for Power*, New Delhi, Orient Longman, 1981.

Rosen, P.: *Societies and Military Power: India and its Armies*, Ithaca, Cornell University Press, 1996.

Simon, D. : *Public Administration and Policy of Indian Military*, New York, Knopf, 1950.

Spector, Leonard S., *Going Nuclear*, Cambridge, MA: Ballinger Publishing Company, 1987.

Stein, Arthur A.: *Why Nations Cooperate: Circumstance and Choice in International Relations*. Ithaca, NY: Cornell University Press, 1990.

Thampi, Madhavi : *India and China in the Colonial World*, Social Science Press, Delhi, 2010.

Theodore, William : T*he Buddhist Tradition in India, China and Japan,* New York: Vintage Books, 1972.

Weber, Katja: *Hierarchy amidst Anarchy: Transaction Costs and Institutional Choice.* Albany, NY: State University of New York Press, 2000.

Wilborn, Thomas L.: *International Politics In Northeast Asia : The China-Japan-United States Strategic Triangle.* Carlisle Barracks, PA: Strategic Studies Institute, 1996.

Wishnick, Elizabeth: *Mending Fences: The Evolution of Moscow's China Policy from Brezhnev to Yeltsin*. Seattle: University of Washington Press, 2001.

Zhu, Zhiqun: *US-China In The 21st Century: Power Transition And Peace.* London and New York: Routledge, 2006.

Index

H

I

J

L

M

N

O

P

R

S

T

U

V

W

□□□